MONETARY MANAGEMENT

by

B. L. MATHUR
Faculty Member
Department of
Economic Administration & Financial Management
University of Rajasthan
Jaipur – 3020001

2001

DISCOVERY PUBLISHING HOUSE

New Delhi–110002

First Published–2001

ISBN 81-7141-591-1

Published by :
DISCOVERY PUBLISHING HOUSE
4831/24, Ansari Road, Prahlad Street,
Darya Ganj, New Delhi-110002 (INDIA)
☎ : 3279245 • Fax : 91-11-3253475
E-mail : dphtemp@indiatimes.com

Printed at : Tarun Offset

Preface

Monetary Management is the area of study getting currency importance in almost every nation of the world irrespective of their level of economic development. The ever rising challenges in the monetary sphere made it necessary in every nation, more specifically in the developing nations to accord fresh outlook to their monetary policies and management. The study of the subject becomes more important and relevant in the age of economic and financial sector reform.

The present book entitled 'Monetary Management ' is a humble effort for knowing Management and administration of monetary sectors presented in lucid style. Reference and example from Indian experience are given in plenty at various places of the book so that readers can get a fair idea of the subject matter. In the preparation of this book, I have liberally drawn upon the writing of a large number of eminent authorities on the subject as well as matter and data from publications of Government of India mentioning a few are *Economic Survey, India, Reserve Bank of India Report -Currency and Finance & Trend and Progress, Annual Report on Development Bankiing Industrial Development Bank of India, The Life Insurance Corporation of India, Unit Trust of India, etc.* The food-note indicate, though somewhat inadequately, I express my gratefulness for each one of them.

While no effort has been spared to remove printing and other mistakes, I sincerely hope and trust that readers will favour me by pointing out errors that might have crept in due to over-sight. I shall consider my efforts amply rewarded if those for whom the book is intended are benefited by it. Suggestions for improvement may be highly appreciated and gladly adhered to. I am also thankful to my Publisher for his active co-operation and fine get up of the book. Finally I must acknowledge the patience of my wife *Dr. Reeta Mathur* Assistant Professor in the Department, without which present book would not have been published at all.

B. L. Mathur

Contents

1

Introduction

CAPITAL FORMATION

Capital may be regarded as that part of the wealth of a country which is utilised for further creation of wealth. It includes all forms of reproducible wealth that are used directly or indirectly in the production of a larger volume of output. In the words of Colin Clark, "Capital goods are reproducible wealth used for the purpose of production." So far as the capital formation is concerned, it is merely the outcome of investment or the creation of investment goods. The growth of saving is a primary condition for capital formation. It includes the diversion of country's resources from the productin of consumer goods to the production of capital goods.

According to *Nurkse*, "the meaning of 'capital formation' is that society does not apply the whole of its current productive activity to the needs and desires of immediate consumption, but directs a part of it to the making of capital goods : tools and instruments, machines and transport facilities, plant and equipment - all the various forms of real capital that can so greatly increase the efficacy of productive effort.... The essence of the process then, is the diversion of a part of society's currently available resources to the purpose of increasing the stock of capital goods so as to make possible an expansion of consumable output in the future." Nurkse's definition merely implies the accumulation of material capital and neglects human capital. But economists like Singer and Simon Kuznets want to include both physical and human capital.

In the words of *Singer*, "Capital formation consists of both tangible goods like plants, tools and machinery and intangible goods like high standard of education health, scientific traditioin and research." Kuznets also observes, "Dometic capital formatin would include not only additions to constructions, equipment and inventories within the country, but also other expenditure, except those necessary to sustain output at existing levels. It would include outlays on education, recreation and material luxuries that contribute to the greater health and productivity of individuals and all expenditures by society that serve to raise the morale of employed population."

Significance of Capital Formation in Economic Development

Economists generally feel that capital formation plays a central role in the process of economic development. Most of the underdeveloped countries are found to be the victims of the vicious circles of poverty which can be broken in the words of Prof. Nurkse, through capital formation. The capital formation, as a matter of fact leads to the maximum utilisation of resources, accelerates the quantum of national output, income and employment, and as such solves the problems of inflation balance of payments and foreign debt. The following are some of the factors which make capital formation essential in the process of economic development.

(1) Building of Capital Equipment and Creation of Economic and Social Overhead Capital. The capital formation not only builds capital equipments and machines on a large scale to increase productivity in agriculture industry mining and plantations but also develops economic and social

overhead capital like construction of roads, canals, railways, airways, schools, hospitals, libraries and means of recreation. This will lead to increased economic development in the country.

(2) Raise the level of Output, Income and Employment. More savings followed by more investment are likely to increase the growth rate of capital formation that further raises the level of output income and employment. Lewis points here rightly that the central problem in the theory of economic development is the process of raising domestic saving and investment from 4-5 per cent to 12-15 per cent of national income.

(3) Technological Progress. The capital also leads to technological progress in the country which incorporates poor economies to attain large scale production through the implementation of specialisation and division of labour. The capital formation increases the efficiency of labourers as they are followed by machines tools and other equipments.

(4) Expansion of Market. The capital formation increase the horizon of market of different commodities both in the country and abroad. The capital formation removes all market imperfections through the creation of more economic and social overhead capital, and thus frees the poor countries from the vicious circles, both from the demand and the supply ends.

(5)Self-sufficiency of Economy. Most of the underdeveloped countries face a number of socio economic problems like unfavourable balance of payments, overburden of foreign debt, and inflationary conditions. The capital formation on the one hand increase the productivity in agriculture , industry and mining sectors and thus enhances exports of underdeveloped countries on the other. It also increases the per capita income of the people, the level of consumption and the domestic savings. More savings lead to rapid capital formation and that is the master key to solve all economic problems. Thus, the capital formation provides self-sufficiency to the economy and reduces the burden of foreign debt. The rate of inflation also comes down and the economy, thus, attains the objective of self-sufficiency and self-generation.

(6) Increase the Economic Welfare. As we know it very well the majority of nations in the world are economically poor. The underdeveloped economies have an objective of welfare state. The higher growth rate of capital formation may ensure economic welfare in these economies by fulfilling all the requirements of an increasing population in the developing economies. The capital formation leads to the proper utilisation of resources, establishes varius industries, increases the per capita income and satisfies the varied demands of the people. They enjoy a high standard of living and consume a variety of goods and hence their economic welfare increase.

Causes of Low Rate of Capital Formation

There is low rate of capital formation in underdeveloped countries for the interaction of varius economic social and cultural factors which have been operating there for the centuries together. The capital formation depends both on the savings and their investment in productive uses. The rate of capital formation in underdeveloped countries is as little as about 5 per cent, whereas in U.S.A. it is 15 per cent and in West Germany and Australia about 25 per cent. Some of the main reasons can be discussed under the following heads:

(1) Poverty and Low Level of Income. The main reason for the deficiency of capital in underdeveloped countries is the lack of savings. It is for the low level of productivity and income of the people. Masses of them live below the poverty line who are hardly able to get bare subsistence. The question of saving in such conditions does not arise. Ragnar Nurkse observes : "The low rate of capital formatin in these countries is a partial link in a vicious circle of poverty. The supply of capital is small because of the small capacity of the people to save which is the result of low level of real income. Low level of real income is the result of low productivity which in its turn is largely due to the lack of capital." It is generally believed that the savings in underdeveloped countries are very small because of widespread poverty that leads to low level of capital formation investment and poverty. Unless this vicious circle of poverty is broken the rate of capital formation cannot be raised substantially.

(2) Demographic Features. The demographic features also keep low level of the capital formation in underdeveloped countries. It is because there is low per capita income followed by a very high growth of population. Consequently, the growing labour force had to depend on obsolete equipment and techniques of production. Moreover in such economies people do not find themselves able to save for capital formation because of the big size of family liabilities. Lastly, a shorter life expectancy in such countries reduces the span of an available effective labour force. The low mortality rate among youths lads to leave additional liabilities to their children upon a few adults, and that ultimately reduces further the per capita income of the family. In this manner these demographic features also become very important for the low rate of capital formation in these poor economies.

(3) Lack of Economic and Social Overheads. In underdeveloped countries there is deficiency of economic and social overheads like transport communication power, water education health and so on. The existence of these infrastructural facilities determines largely the rate of savings and investment and the capital formatiion. Since there is deficiency of economic and social overheads in these economies we find low rate of capital formation.

(4) Lack of Enterprise. The entrepreeneurship is very essential in the process of economic development, while the entrepreneurial ability in underdeveloped economies is almost lacking, and that is another important factor responsible for the low rate of capital formation. The deficiency of capital poor infrastructure, low capital productivity, small size of markets, etc. lead to the deficiency of entrepreneurship and thus there is low rate of capital formation in these backward countries.

(5) Lack of Proper Financial Structure. The proper financial institutions are necessary for the mobilisation of savings and promotion of capital formation. The lack of financial institutions in such economies is another important burdle in the way of capital formation. A huge amount of capital is required for productive purposes and for raising low productivity in different sectors of the economy , but it is not easy to fulfil the growing demands of capital investments for the lack of proper capital markets and banking institutions. Consequently, the rates of savings and capital formation remain low for the poor mobilisation of savings in the society.

(6) International Demonstration Effect. The keenest desire of the masses to imitate the standard of living and patterns of advanced countries has been another important factor responsible for low level of domestic savings in underdeveloped countries. *Ragnar Nurkse* also feels that the demonstration effect tends to low rate of capital formation in these underdeveloped economies. This demonstration effects is generally caused by magazines, films, other publicity media and foreign tours. It results that the growing income is spent mainly on consumption items and thus savings become almost static which further reduce the rate of capital formation in these economies.

(7) Small Size of Markets. The small size of markets is another important cause of the low rate of capital formation in undeveloped countries. It discourages development of proper entrepreneurship and investment initiatives. The commodity markets are small for mainly two reasons. Firstly, the cost of products is comparatively very high, and secondly, the demand of products is generally limited because of the low level of income of the masses and their poverty.

(8) Poor Sources of Savings. Due to the poverty of masses, low level of income, and a very high propensity to consume the private savings are found tobe extrmly low in underdeveloped countries. However a few people receive very high incomes in the countries like India, Sri Lanka and Thailand. Among them are merchants, the big landlords, leaders and the speculators. these rich people rarely invest their savings into productive units. They generally utilise them for speculative purposes, for hoarding purposes and for short term loan purposes at a higher interest rate.

Besides the few rich, the middle class income group people and a number of cultivators are a good source of savings. But their savings are very small which they do spend on the education of their children, the building of houses and on the requirements of unforeseen circumstances. This expenditure of savings is unimportant in the context of productive investment.

So far as the business and corporate savings are very important sources of savings, they are also important sources of capital formation in the agricultural and industrial sectors. But the socialists leanings of the majority of underdeveloped countries sometimes weaken the confidence of investors for want of security for the long term investments.

Measures to Increase Capital Formation

Underdeveloped countries are poor because they are underdeveloped in resources. The most important problem of an undeveloped economy is, thus, to raise the rate of capital formation. Growing rate of capital formation is a primary conditions for rapid economic development. According to Alfred Bone, "The scope of capital available for new investment determines to a large extent the scope for economic progress. The mobilising of real capital has, thus, become one of the vital prerequisites of economic development are rather clear. It will essentially be possible if there is a curtailment of consumption of the people and that may therefore, be much painful.

The source of capital formation may be divided into two parts : (i) domestic resources, and (ii) International resources. The process of capital formation includes three steps : (i) measurers to increase real savings; (ii) mobilisation of savings through financial institutions; and (iii) investment of savings. Now we discuss here these domestic and external resources of capital formation.

Domestic Resources

The problem of capital formations in undeveloped economies is two-fold- to increase the propensity to save among people and secondly, to utilise current savings for capital formation. The domestic sources of savings for capital formation may include a number of measures like increase in national income, savings drive, establishment of financial and credit institutions, mobilisation of gold-hoards, increasing profits, fiscal and monetary mesures, and so on.

(1) Increase in Nationa Income. Towards the end of increasing the volume of savings, it is very important to increase the national income and per capita income of the people. The growing per capita income will lead to enhancement in the domestic savings in the country. But the national income can be increased by raising the level of productivity which can be done through specialisatioin and division of labour, rationalisation, use of latest techniques of production and optimum resource utilisation.

(2) Establishment of Financial and Credit Institutions. In underdeveloped economies the majority of people keep their surplus part of income in the form of cash, jewellery and gold. In these economies there has been a shortage of banking and other financial institutions. It is, therefore, quite essential to set up banking and other financial institutions. It is, therefore, quite essential to set up banking and other such institutionsin unbanking areas and nongrowth centres which are likely to deposit small savings of the people on the one hand and to provide credit to the needy people for improving productivity in agriculture and other allied occupations and industry on the other. A well developed capital market is essential for capital formation. "Such agencies will not only permit small amounts of savings to be handled and invested conveniently but will allow the owners of savings to retain liquidity individually and finance long-term investment collectively."

(3) Mobilisation of Domestic Savings. The mobilisation of domestic savings is the central idea for solving the problem of increasing savings which are primarily essential for capital formation. The savings can be raised through proper publicity and social education that can inculcate saving habits amongst people. Besides, the promotion of small savings is possible through several schemes - life insurance compulsory provident fund, provident fund cum pension cum life insurance etc. expansion of bank offices, particularly in rural areas and also through cooperative societies including apex institutions like the central and the state cooperative banks.

Domestic savings in an economy can be increased either by increased production or reduced consumption or by both. Concludingly, it can be said that the process of increased savings is the creation of a surplus over the consumption which can be mobilised for capital formation. In poor countries the amount of this surplus is negligible because. The volume of this surplus can be increased by the following measures : (a) raising the productivity of the people, (b) curtailing the consumption of the rich, (c) increasing profits, and (d) fiscal measures.

(a) Raising the Productivity of People. Due to the low per capita availability of capital the chances of increasing the investible surplus by means an enhanced productivity of the people are very meagre in underdeveloped countries. In these countries the production per capita can be increased by the maximum utilisation of the existing resources which are in most of the cases underutilised. The maximum utilisation of capital - plant, machinery and manpower - is possible through multiple shifts, greater application of trained and skilled labour and adoption of new methods or techniques of production. The production technique may be westernised that may be regarded essential to increase per capita productivity of the people.

(b) Curtailing the Consumption of the Rich. The process of capital formation includes essentially the curtailing of consumpton of the rich class. It is generally believed that the curtailment of consumption does not provide comfortable savings in underdeveloped countries due to the low level of consumption of the masses. In this connection , Prof. Myrdal observes : There is no other road to economic development than a compulsory rise in the share of that national income which is withheld from consumption and devoted to consumption." Thus, two things need to be emphasised : Firstly, the rate of savings can be increased by curtailing the consumption of the rich and secondly, it can also be increased by diverting an increasing percentage of the increments in national income to capital formation.

(c) Increasing Profits. In his analysis Lewis believes that the ratio of savings to national income is a function of the ratio of profits to national income and not just of inequality of income. He maintains that the voluntary savings constitute a larger share of national income where the inequalities of income are low and the income distribution is fair. In case there is unequal distribution of income, the availability of voluntary savings to investments will be meagre. Despite that the total incomes from profits, interest and rent, as Lewis says, constitute a small share in national income in an under developed country, the savings can be raised from 5 to 12 per cent by increasing the rate of profit. The share of profits in the national income can be raised through legal protection, use of imported technique, control over inflation, provision of investment opportunities, and the expansion of capitalist sector in the economy.

(d) Fiscal Measures. The chances of voluntary savings are generally found to be meagre for capital formation in underdeveloped economies. The State can mobilise them easily through fiscal and monetary measures. These measures may include the policy of taxation, reduction in public expenditures or non-planned expenditures, expansion of exports, raising revenue by public loans, foreign aid and deficit financing. The State can also increase its savings for capital formation by running public sector undertakings more efficiently with larger profits. Moreover, the State should follow such a growth oriented long term savings policy that could have put the economy towards a self-generating and self sustained growth.

International Resources

The domestic resources may not be sufficient for capital formation in an underdeveloped economy. Also they should be supported by the following international resources: (i) Foreign aid, (ii) Export promotion and restriction on imports, and (iii) Favourable terms of trade.

(i) Foreign Aid. Since domestic resources are found to be insufficient in an underdeveloped country for capital formation, it is essential to import foreign capital, both loans and grants from advanced countries and international financing institutions. Another important way of importing foreign capital is to set up joint ventures whereby foreign investors' technical knowhow along with capital and other means of production like scientific management, enterprise, etc. must be utilised.

(ii) Export Promotion and Restriction on Imports. The foreign reserves and foreign capital can also be increased through a well planned programme of export promotion. This is a very significant policy of capital accumulation because our exports pay for imports. Similarly, the restriction on consumer goods imports is also an important external source of capital formation. In this respect there should be a policy to restrict all luxury imports and this saved foreign currency would be utilised in importing capital goods essential for export promotion. It will, thus, further increase the foreign currency reserves for capital formation through increasing exports.

This measure can best be fruitful if the domestic resources as saved by imposing restrictions upon imported consumer goods are not utilised on luxury or semi luxury goods manufactured at home. In case consumers spend more on domestic consumer goods, it will lead to increase in the imported capital goods and will, hence, reduce, domestic investment in capital goods units because the resources will be diverted from domestic capital goods sector to consumer goods sector. Therefore, it is also essential to increase unvoluntary domestic savings if the restriction of luxury imports is to lead to an increase in capital formation.

(iii) Favourable Terms of Trade. Majority of underdeveloped countries are poor. To them, the favourable terms of trade may be more helpful in economic development, as the essential capital goods will be largely available. To take more benefit out of favourable terms of trade it is necessary that the increased domestic income due to larger exports should be saved and utilised in production. Since the favourable terms of trade are not a natural way of capital formation. Nurkse rightly suggests that such savings should be obtained unvoluntarily by taxation to "give the country a command over additional imports of investment goods."

In conclusion, it can be said that capital formation is an important phenomenon in economic development. It is, however, essential to state that there are also other important political social cultural, technological and entrepreneurial factors which determine widely the rate of capital formation in an underdeveloped economy.

The process of capital formation involves three inter-dependent activities. The first activity is the formation of saving. But all the people in an economy do not save for production. Thus their savings have to the mobilised for productive purposes. This is the second activity. The third activity is to use the saving for investment. Thus investment is the third activity which leads to increase in productivity.

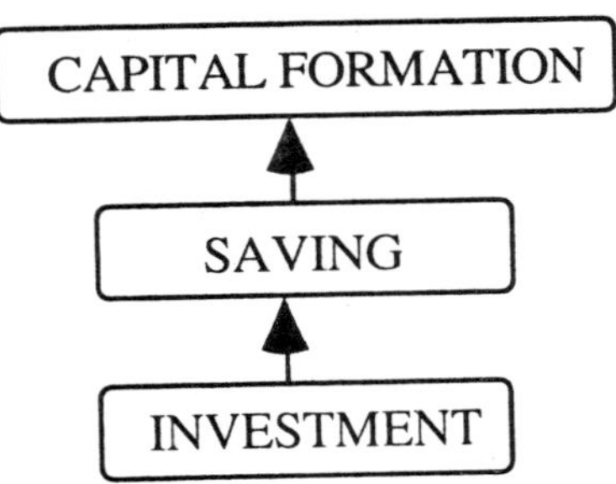

Investment, which is effected by the level of saving is an essential ingredient in the economic growth of an economy. Investment (or capital formation) is the very core of economic growth. No economic development is possible without the construction of irrigation works, production of tools and implements, factories, building of dams, bridges, roads, railways, ships etc. In the view of many economists investment occupies strategic position in the process of economic development. In underdeveloped countries like India where process of economic development, is in quite progress it is quite necessary to step up the rate of investment (i.e. capital formation) so that the country accumulates a large capital stock to accelerate production. It must be remembered that the term investment does not include the investment in physical stock of capital alone, it also includes investment in human stock of capital. Human skill and abilities also play an important role in the process of economic development. This part of investment is more important in under developed economies to raise the level of productivity.

Saving.

Saving is the excess of income over current consumption i.e., S = Y — C Where S = Saving; Y = Income; and C = Consumption. Thus something out of current consumption is set aside to become available for production purposes. Saving depends upon many factors like power to save, will to save, opportunities for collecting saving i.e., provision of banks, insurance companies etc. In countries where the above factors are favourable there is more saving. There are three sources for domestic saving viz., (i) Public Sector, (ii) Private Corporate Sector, and (iii) Household Sector.

Investment.

Investment refers to the additions made to the nation's physical stock of capital such as machines, plants factories transport equipment material etc. Investment is a flow and it refers to the additions to capital stock in a period of time while capital refers to stock capital goods at a particular time.

The Concept

The concept of wealth from the investment standpoint is perhaps the simplest and may therefore be used as starting point. By wealth is meant, any economic good or service which satisfies a human need, and has, consequently, the power of commanding other goods or services in exchange. The exchange value resulting from the fact that a given object or service is desired must, however, be measured in terms of some unit, and the rate of exchange between goods is their price. One such good is money, which marks money a form of wealth devised for the special purpose of acting as a means of promoting exchange and of measuring the value of commodities in exchange. We thus include money under the head of wealth, but of course, can not regard wealth in any sense as money except that it is indirectly a means of commanding money.

Production is the process of ringing wealth into existence-that is to say, of changing the character or form of goods and services so as to adopt them for use. Consumption, on the other hand, is the application of these goods and services to their specific objects. That is, to the satisfaction of human needs or desires. Capital comprises forms of wealth especially adopted for further production as tools and machines, which themselves do not satisfy any consumption desires. Ordinarily, savings are defined as that part of the periodic production of wealth which is devoted to the creation of capital.

Investment is the process of applying such savings to the creation of specific forms of capital. There has been a long controversy about the question whether savings are or are not, in fact, practically equivalent to investments. The use made of the term, however, differentiates the two concepts and regards saving as he mere decision not to consume produce goods, whereas investment is the actual use of the savings thus made to some specified purpose.[1]

Theory

The theory of investment can be considered from the social point of view. The social point of view which regards the flow of the annual income into investment, the influence of speculation upon the community, etc., is important in connection with the control of investment as well as the forecasting of changes in investment conditions. For the individual investment and investor, a corresponding series of problems arises, involving the shaping of policies that best conform to these broad social changes. As the more fundamental set of consideration, those which relate to the social theory of investment should receive first attention. Viewing investment as a process which goes on in every society, we may ask exactly what that process consists of, and what limits or conditions it. By investment in the border sense of the term is meant what is usually referred to by economists under the name of savings, but including the further thought that money savings are actually applied to the creation of what are called capital goods.

By capital in the economic sense is meant the forms of wealth whose service is found in the production of consumable goods, either directly or indirectly. They do not themselves yield any satisfaction, but they make it possible to obtain such satisfactions by the use of the product which they turn out. For example, if a person having a deposit of Rs. One Crore in his bank account, devotes himself to the construction of a power house, and thereafter sells the power so generated, he has used his one crore rupees in the creation of capital, and that capital yields a service in the form of "power", which can be sold and so reconverted into "money". This process may be described as "investment'.

The outcome of investment is the establishment of a flow of income from the capital in question, corresponding to a continuous stream of resulting economic goods or services. Thus, it is clear that investment is a process of converting funds into capital, using the capital for the production of goods and services which are sold for funds that can be expended as may be desired. This last process of reconversion is the earning or receipt of income, such income being the flow of values which comes from the use of capital in the way indicated. It is clear that the process has no necessary connection with money, although it is usually described in terms of money, so that we can say that "investing money" or getting money income out of investment.[2]

The application of money to a purpose which does not involve immediate use on the part of the owner is investment. Therefore, the investment of money involves the use of current funds for a purpose other than to satisfy the immediate consumption needs of the owner. This is known as investing of money. It is an operation which involves, as a rule, the transfer of titles to money, they being passed into the hands of others who agree to return them with a payment for their use which is known as "interest or dividend". Thus others who obtain the use of such funds can not pay interest or dividend, however, unless they succeed in earning it. They must therefore use what they thus borrow not for consumption but for the purpose of producing more goods or services which are disposed of to others, and which consequently bring back a larger amount of goods or, in current phrase, money, than what was parted with. If we eliminate these intermediaries, and look simply at the basic character of the operation, we shall see that it consists of using current funds to the production of more and more wealth.

Every use of wealth involves risk element. The investor may succeed in transferring his responsibility to others. Investor may put his money into saving banks, life insurance corporation or investment trust, but such a transfer of responsibility does not eliminate the risk element. It merely places the duty of making the decision upon the shoulders of the investment institutions. Their decision may be correct or may be incorrect. The typical investor wishes to find enterprises for the use of his capital in which the risk element is minimum, but he can never find such a enterprises, in which risk element is eliminated. Therefore, risk is a regular element in investment, and any theory of investment must recognize the function of risk bearing as a part of the process by which capital is placed at the service of the society, and is made to yield an income.

The investment theory in a government controlled or managed economy or planned economy says that through governmental action, it is asserted that far wiser and better use could be made of the savings of the society than is made under the capitalistic economy. Here is an assumption that the government can use the savings of the society better and with greater foresight than can the individual at the present time or the corporate organisation working for him. To this is sometimes added the thought that the Central Bank or investment institutions can direct these investment and serves as abridge for determining when and how they shall be made.

Investment must be regarded as either positive or negative. It may result in rendering existing capital forms obsolete and thus result in loss, though the effect may be the turning out of a much greater supply of goods than was previously available. On the other hand, it may simply result in marginal gains or profits, or, in rare cases, it may produce practically no effect whatever from the earnings point of view. In the analysis of the investment process from the money point of view, it is desirable to consider to factor entering into demand for, and supply of, investment funds. Looking to the demand for investment funds, we can recognize some factors which determine its intensity. They are the rate of economic development, the financial market and the business cycles. The activity of demand for investment resources, other things being equal, will be greater or less as the business cycle passes through one or the other of its various phases.

The demand for capital for domestic investment reaches a peak when industrial development attains its full growth. In a country which is practically fully exploited and in which industry is sufficiently equipped, the need for new investment funds is likely to be less; and even if savings are more, it is difficult to find an outlet for them in the domestic market. It is for this reason that some developed countries are exporters of capital, and that in many cases they have found it necessary to seek outlets in so many developing countries of Asia and Africa. In such countries, the volume of savings is greater than the opportunities for investment, with the result that funds must be invested in other countries. In the reverse case, in which a country has reached a phase of active economic development, and has more opportunities opened to it wherein new capital can be employed to advantage in increasing industrial production, every effort will be made to attract savings; and when their supply is less from the internal resources, the attempt will be made to arrange them from external resources.

The supply of investment resources is always largely affected by the amount of risk which is involved in their use. In a country like India where political unsuitability and weak central government exist or where road, rail and communication network is insufficient, the risk of investment is fairly high. Where risk is limited, the return on investment is lower, and the result is a study, reliable flow of funds into investment channels at reasonable cost.

Along with above mentioned factors which tend to control the supply of capital available for investment, it is desirable to consider also the character of the investment set-up that can be used by the investors. Thus, for instance, the existence of satisfactory arrangements for banking and security distribution invariably tends to stimulate the growth of savings. Postal savings systems have been found in many countries to be great stimulators of savings, and the same thing is true for the investment banks, popularly known as life insurance corporation of India, Unit Trust of India etc. The presence of stock exchanges tend to create an interest in securities, and a more receptive attitude on the part of the investors at large with respect to the investment of funds in companies which involve some risk. The satisfactory institution of banking largely influences the ability of businessmen to obtain the funds needed for the development of their operations. Thus it may be fairly said that both the supply and the use of capital are greatly affected by the character of the organizational set-up which is available for savings, distributing and using the capital.

Income on investment is a payment to the owner of the funds for their use. It must be sufficient in amount to induce the investor to prefer the application of these resources to investment rather than to immediate purchase of commodities. If an absolutely safe investment could be conceived, the interest on that investment would be merely the minimum amount necessary to induce owners of funds to save and part with them. No such investments, however, can be found; and accordingly, income on investments must be regarded as consisting of at least two elements. *First* is interest on capital and *second* is payment for risk. In addition to these above elements, a *third* is usually to be recognized as payment for management to cover the time and expense involved in dealing with the funds, transferring them, rendering them available, keeping them idle for the average time between investment changes, and the like.

The amount of the funds available for capital investment at any time may be increased or decreased by the policy decisions of the central bank or the commercial banks. Bank deposits represent the liquid funds of the country which can be directed to anyone of the several channels. Any unit of it may be employed for consumption of devoted to investment, according to the decision of its owner. The rate charged for bank funds, or the rate of interest for short term loans, is ordinarily more sensitive and readily changed than is the rate on long term investment, on the other hand, the policies of the central bank may depress artificially rates of interest on long term capital advances, through creating a plethora of short term funds available for investment.

Objectives of Investment

Investment is the sacrifice of certain present value for the uncertain future reward. It entails arriving at numerous decisions such as type, mix, amount, timing, grade etc. of investment and disinvestment. Further, such decision making has not only to be continuous but rational too. Broadly speaking, an investment decision is a trade off between risk and return. All investment choices are made at points of time in accordance with the personal investment ends and in contemplation of an uncertain future. Since investments in securities are revocable, investment ends are transient and investment environment is fluid, the reliable bases for reasoned expectations become more and more vague as one conceives of the distant future. Investors in securities will, therefore, from time to time, reappraise and re-evaluate their various investment commitments in the light of new information, changed expectations and ends.

Investment decisions are found to be the outcome of three different but related classes of factors. The *first* may be described as factual or informational premises. The factual premises of investment decisions are provided by many streams of data which are taken together, represent to an investor the observable environment and general as well as particular features of the securities and firms in which he may invest. The *second* class of factors entering into investment decisions may be described as expectational premises. Expectations relating to the outcomes of alternative investments are subjective and hypothetical in any case but their foundations are necessarily provided by the environmental and financial facts available to investors. These limit not only the range of investments which may be undertaken but also the expectations of outcomes which may legitimately be entertained. The *third* and final class of factors may be described as valuational premises. For investors generally these comprise the structure of subjective preferences for the size and regularity of the income to be received from and for the safety and negotiability of specific investments or combinations of investments as these are appraised from time to time.[3]

"Investment" or "Investing", like "value" is a word of many interpretations. There are basically three concepts of investment:

1. Economic investment-that is, an economist's definition of investment;

2. Investment in a more general or extended sense, which is used by "the man on the street";

3. The sense in which we are going to be very much interested namely, financial investment.

In the following explanation each type of aforesaid investment is reviewed to point out characteristics each possess.

The term *economic investment* has a rather precise meaning in the literature of economic theory. Typically it includes net additions to the capital stock of society. By "capital stock of society" is meant those goods which are used in the production of others goods. This is a gross societal, or aggregate point of view. In society there are a number of goods (such as building and equipment) which are used to produce other goods, and that these means of production are considered part of the capital stock of society. For a number of reasons, economists also include inventories (that is, the goods produced and still in the manufacturer's hands) as part of that capital stock. Thus, a net addition to the capital stock-an investment means an increase in buildings, equipments or inventories over the amount of equivalent goods that existed, say, one yea ago at the same time.

The every day usage of the term investment can mean a variety of things, but to the man on the street it usually refers to a money commitment of some sort. For example, a commitment of money to buy a new car is certainly an "investment" from an individual's point of view. But these are so in very general and in very extended sense of the word since no rate of return is involved, nor is a financial return or capital growth expected.

Financial investment is a form of this general or extended sense of the term. It means an exchange of financial claims-stocks and bonds (collectively termed securities), real estate mortgages, etc. The term financial investments is often used by investors to differentiate between the pseudo-investment concept of the consumer and the real investment of the businessman. Semantics aside, there is still a difference between an "investment" in a ticket on a horse and a construction of a new plant; between the pawning of a watch and the planting of afield of corn. Some investments are simply transactions among people, other involve nature. The latter are "real" investments; the former are "financial" investments. In this study investment would imply the employment of funds with the objective of realising additional income or growth in value f investment at a future date.

In the foregoing numerous academic definitions of investment speculation and gambling, it can be observed that most of them are framed around the following three differentiating factors:

1. What is the motive of the buyer? The investor presumably buys to procure an annual return under conditions of safety, whereas others buy for appreciation.

2. What type of security is bought-high grade or low grade? The investor presumably buys high-grade securities, the others low-grade.

3. How long is the security held? The investor presumably holds for the long-term, the speculator for the short-term.[4]

Features of Investment

In choosing specific investments, investors will need definite ideas regarding features which their portfolios should possess. These features should be consistent with the investors' general objectives and, in addition, should afford them all the incidental conveniences and advantages which are possible under the circumstances. The following are the suggested features as the ingredients from which many successful investors compound their selection policies.

1. Safety Principal— The safety sought in investment is not absolute or complete; it rather implies protection against loss under reasonably likely conditions or variations. It calls for careful review of economic and industry trends before deciding types and/or timing of investments. Thus, it recognizes that errors are unavoidable for which extensive diversification is suggested an antidote.

Adequate diversification means assortment of investment commitments in different ways. Those who are not familiar with the aggressive-defensive approach nevertheless often carry out the theory of hedging against inflation-deflation. Diversification may be geographical, wherever possible, because regional or local storms, floods, droughts, etc. can cause extensive real estate damage. Vertical and horizontal diversification can also be opted for the same. Vertical diversification occurs when securities of various companies engaged in different phases of production from raw material to finished goods are held in the portfolio. On the other hand, horizontal diversification is the holding by an investor in various companies all of which carry on activity in the same stage of production.

Another way to diversify securities is to classify them according to bonds and shares and reclassify according to types of bonds and types of shares. Again, they can also be classified according to the issuers, according to the dividend or interest income date, according to the product which are made by the firms represented by the securities. But over-diversification is undesirable. By limiting investment to a few issues, the investor has an excellent opportunity to maintain a knowledge of circumstances surrounding each issue. Probably the simplest and most effective diversification is accomplished by holding different media at the same time having reasonable concentration in each.

2. *Adequate Liquidity and Collateral Value*— A n investment is a liquid asset if it can be converted into cash without delay at full market value in any quantity. For an investment to be liquid it must be (1) reversible or (2) marketable. The different between reversibility and marketability is that reversibility is the process whereby the transaction is reverse or terminated while marketability involves the sale of the investment in the market for cash. To meet emergencies, every investor must have a sound portfolio to be sure of the additional funds which may be needed for the business opportunities". Whether money raising is to be done by sale or by borrowing it will be easier if the portfolio contains at planned proportion of high-grade and readily salable investment.

3. *Stability of Income*— Stability of income must be looked at in different ways just as was security of principal. An investor must consider stability of monetary income and stability of purchasing power of income. However, emphasis upon income stability may not always be consistent with other investment principles. If monetary income stability is stressed, capital growth and diversification will be limited.

From the study of the table -1 given above it is clear that

(i) The domestic saving and investment are increasing at a very low rate;

(ii) The rate of domestic saving has been continously less than the rate of domestic investment up to 1975-76. For the first time in 1976-77 the rate of domestic saving was more more than the rate of domestic investment. Also in 1977-78 and 1978-79 the rate of saving was more than the rate of investment. But in 1979-80 again the rate of saving has been less than the rate of investment but since 1988-89 the rate of domestic saving was more than the rate of domestic investment.

(4) Capital Growth— Capital appreciation has today become an important principle. Recognising the connection between corporation and industry growth and very large capital appreciation, investors and their advisers constantly are seeking "growth stocks". It is exceedingly difficult t make a successful choice. The ideal "growth stock" is the right issue in the right industry, bought at the right time.

(5) Tax Benefits— To plan an investment programme without regard to one's status may be costly to the investor. There are really two problems involved here, one concerned with the amount of income paid by the investment and the other with the burden of income taxes upon that income. When investors' incomes are small, they are anxious to have maximum cash returns on their investments, and are prone to take excessive risks. On the other hand, investors who are not pressed for cash income often find that income taxes deplete certain types of investment incomes less than others, thus affecting their choices.

(6.) Purchasing Power Stability— Since an investment early always involves the commitment of current funds with the objective of receiving greater amounts of future funds, the purchasing power of the future fund should be considered by the investor. For maintaining purchasing power stability, investors should carefully study;

Table -1

Growth of Saving and Investment in India

Year	*At per cent of gross domestic product at market price.*		*At per cent of net domestic product at market price.*	
	Gross Domestic Saving	*Gross Domestic Capital formation (Gross Investment)*	*Net Domestic Saving*	*Net Domestic Capital formation (Net Investment)*
1960-61	13.7	16.9	9.3	12.7
1965-66	15.7	18.2	11.2	13.8
1968-69	14.1	15.4	9.5	10.8
1973-74	19.3	20.0	15.0	15.7
1974-75	18.2	19.1	13.8	14.8
1975-76	20.0	19.9	15.4	15.3
1976-77	22.0	20.4	17.4	15.7
1977-78	21.3	19.7	16.7	15.0
1978-79	24.4	24.6	19.7	19.8
1979-80	22.5	22.9	17.1	17.6
1987-88	20.2	21.3	19.6	20.7
1988-89	22.0	21.6	20.1	20.0
1989-90	24.0	22.5	21.2	21.1
1990-91	24.0	22.8	22.8	22.0
1991-92	23.1	22.0	22.2	21.9
1992-93	22.3	21.3	21.7	21.6
1993-94	21.4	21.3	20.8	20.3
1994-95	24.4	23.2	23.1	22.9

(1) the degree of price level inflation they expect,

(2) the possibilities of gain and loss in the investment available to them, and

(3) the limitations imposed by personal and family considerations.

(7.)Concealability— To be safe from social disorders, government confiscation or unacceptable levels of taxation, property must be concealable and leave no record of income received from its use or sale. Gold and precious stones have long been esteemed for these purposes because they combine high value with small bulk and are readily transferable.[5]

However, when compared to other countries, the rate of saving and investment in India are extremely low.

Saving and investment are the two interdependent activities. With the increase in one the other is also increased.

Following are causes of low saving and investment in India;.

Cause of Low Saving. The following are the causes of low rate of saving in India.

1. Failure of the Five Year Plans- Because of the failure of our five year plans, many shortfalls occurred in different sectors of the economy — in agriculture, industry and services the production had been far behind the targets. As a result of it there was a very low increase in the national income. Since saving depends on the level of income. It was natural that the rate of investment was also low.

2. Rapid Increase in Population- Since 1951 the population of India has been rising at a rapid rate and consequently the larger portion of income is spent on consumption and there is very little left for saving. So rate of saving is low.

Causes of Low Investment- The following are the cause of low rate of investment in India.

1. **Low saving-** It has been already explained that saving is the only means of investment and the two are interdependent. With the increase in one the other is also increased. Thus when the rate of saving in India is low, the rate of investment is bound to be low. For accelerating the economic development of the country, during the period of planning the rate of investment has been kept higher than the rate of saving in India, and this gap between saving and investment has been filled up with the help of foreign aid.

2. **Failure of Public Sector.** Since the commencement of planning (1951) the government of India has greatly increased the role of public sector. For instance the number of public sector industries in India in 1951-52 was 5 and the investment was of Rs. 29 crores. But in the number of public sector enterprises rose to 246 and the investment to Rs. 1,72,438 crores as on April 1st 1995.

Measures to raise the rate of saving in India

To increase the rate of saving, the following methods are suggested.

1. **Promotion of voluntary savings and mobilisation of saving in the household sector-** Saving in the Household sector should be encouraged through promotion of small saving scheme, including thrift habits among people etc. Savings can also be increased through the formation of cooperative credit societies in rural areas. Banking habit among the rural population should be developed. For this work commercial banks have to introduce flexibility in their working. This will encourage the households with relatively small earning to save.

2. Raising the rate of saving in the public sector- There is ample scope for raising the rate of saving in the public sector. In order to increase saving in the public sector, the following steps are suggested :

(i) The government should impose tax on agricultural income of the rich and wealthy farmers. Such taxation will increase the resources of the public sector and thereby increase savings.

(ii) Luxury items should be taxed heavily. By doing so, the government will collect more revenue and as a result of it the saving in the public sector will increase.

(iii) The government must plug all loopholes in the tax collection system so that there should be least or no tax evasion. This will increase the revenue of the government and thereby incrase saving in the public sector.

(iv) All types of wasteful expenditure in the public sector must be stopped. Again all type of inefficiency and routine work must be avoided to increase production in the public sector. Increased efficiency in the public sector would increase the profits of the public sector which will also increase saving in the public sector.

(v) There should be full utilisation of productive capacities of industrial units in the public sector. This would increase the production and revenue in the public sector and increas saving also.

3. Suitable fiscal and monetary measures- The government can raise the rate of saving in India by adoptng suitable fiscal and monetary policies. Fiscal policy refers to the government policies concerning taxation, public income, public expenditure, public debt, compulsory saving etc. Similarly, with the help of suitable monetary policies which concern with establishment and expansion of financial institutions suitable interest rate, control of inflation maintenance of equilibrium in balance of payments, the government can raise the rate of saving in the country.

Measures to increase the Rate of Investment in India

The following measures are suggested to raise the rate of investment in India.

1. **Provision of Cheap Credit-** Credit is very costly in India since the rate of interest is very high. The high rate of interest reduces the margin of profit of the enterprises and lowers the inducement to invest. Thus investment in India remains low. So in order to encourage investment the rate of interest must not be kept high. Moreover, there is need to create an investment climate which will increase the level of investment in the country.

2. **Reduction in Taxes-** High taxes on the producing sector also lower the inducement to invest and keep the level of investment low. This is so because high taxes reduce the margin of profit of the enterprises to the minimum and so they are discouraged from making more investment. Thus to raise the level of investment in India, it is necessary that the government reduce taxes on the producing sector. Rather it should give incentives like tax exemptins, cheap supply of power etc. to promote investment in the country.

3. **Improving the supply of power and other inputs-** Power is one of the most important inputs in the modern industrial world. Unfortunately in India there is shortage of power . Industries do not get sufficient power to work to their full capacities. As a result of it output is reduced and consequently the income of the enterprises also falls. This reduces the incentive to investment. Thus more power should be generated to raise the level of investment in India.

4. **Role of government in raising the level of investment in India-**The government can do a lot in increasing the rate of investment in India. The governent can help in improving the relations between labourers and employers by taking suitable measures. This would create an investment

climate . Further the government can help in stepping up the rate of investment through deficit financing. Through deficit financing the government can build up infrastructures for industrial development in the country. The government can also increase the level of investment in India by importing direct foreign investment in the country or obtain loan from other countries. But the government should use foreign capital with caution.

REFERENCES

1. Dolley, James C., *Principles of Investment*, Harper & Brothers, New York, 1940. P. 243.
2. Clendenin, John C., *Introduction to Investment*, Mc-Graw-Hill, Inc., New York, 1950, PP. 253-255.
3. Bhalla, V. K., *Investment Management*, S. Chanda & Co. Ltd., New Delhi, 1996, P. 3.
4. Alexander Godon J., & William F. Sharpe., *Fundamentals of Investments*, Englewood Cliffs, N. J., Prentice Hall, 1989, P. 5.
5. Amling, Federick., *Investment: An Introduction to Analysis and Management*, Englewood Cliffs, N. J. Prentice-Hall, 1984, P. 7.

❑

2

Money

EVOLUTION OF MONEY – BARTER SYSTEM

In the early times before the advent of the money people used to exchange the commodites of their need with one other without bothering about their exact value. One individual desirous of getting goods produced by others used to exchange his goods with that person who possessed that goods. For example : If person X produced A goods and Mr. Y. produced B goods. If X wanted B goods which was produced by Y then they exchanged it with Y by giving him some of his A goods. Similarly Y got A goods by exchanging his B goods with Mr. X .In Economics, this system of exchanging a commodity on the basis of other is termed as barter. Hence barter economy is the economy in which goods are exchanged but not sold or bought.

Barter beyond all doubts , is the simplest form of exchange. According to *S.E. Thomes,* "... direct exchange of one commodity for another is termed barter." This system prevailed for a long time because people were still ignorant to the activities of buying and selling. Moreover in the village independent economies nothing was produced for the market but for self-consumption. Economic consciousness was still silent and people were still to know the value and implications of selling and buying.

Exchange of commodities was the sole method to get those commodites produced by others. They satisfied their every want with this system of exchange. As the time passed human contact started increasing and that gave momentum to the machinery of exchange which occurred rapidly.

The individuals had not solved the problem of getting others commodities but with adoption of exchange media they had some what postponed the burden. Unware of the complexities which grew afterwards when exchange process became so complicated as to put everything in disorder and dissatisfaction. It became also equally impossible for the people to get the commodities of their desire. It became also equally impossible for everything to be acquired through exchange . It was also not certain that every one will agree to excharge his commodities. The greatest difficulty was to measure the value of a particular commodity.

Thus barter failed to secure the benefits for which it was created. It presented so many difficulties which consequently paved the way for the emergence of money as the medium of exchange.

Under Barter System of system of exchange prevailed in the following manner

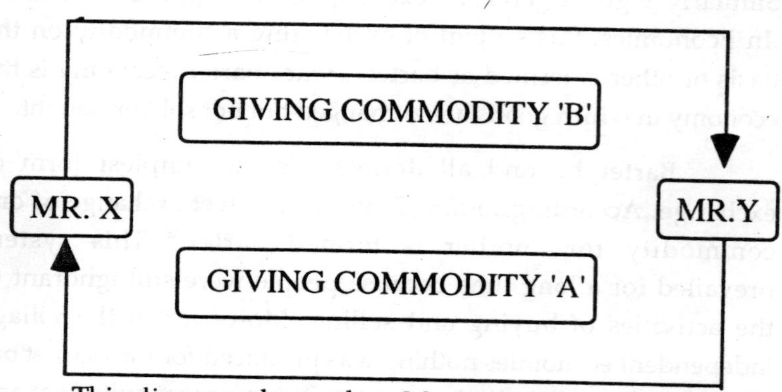

This diagram shows that Mr. X gave commodity 'A' to Mr. Y and in return Mr. Y gave commodity 'B' to Mr. X. Hence Mr. X came to possess commodity A and B . Similar Mr. Y also

came to possess commodity A and B. This barter enabled both and individuals to use the commodities produced or kept by each other.

Advantages of Barter

The barter system has following advantages :

(1) *Simplicity* - It is the simplest form of exchange. The whole system is very simple and is devoid of any complications of modern day exchange.

It is suggested as the best form of exchange in the field of international trade. In case every country exchanges in terms of barter, there would be no problem related to foreign exchange.

(2) *Harnonions*-In its social aspect the barter plays a valuable role in maintaining harmoney among the members of the community. It ensures personal contracts which is essential for healthy social life.

(3) *No mal-adjustments in Production*-The chances of *overproduction* or *underproduction* are very remote in the barter because no one produces for the purposes of marketing or earning profit. So, there are no problems of rise of of prices (inflation) or decreasing prices (deflation) or in other words the acute '*dearness*' or '*cheapness*'.

(4) *Production for Social Needs* -Barter ensures need based production. Only those goods are produced that are acquired by the community because the goods are perishable and are difficult to store.

(5) *No Question of Concentration of Wealth* - In the absence of proper store of value, wealth collection is not possible and therefore there is no chance for wealth being concentrated in a few hands and consequently there will exist no extreme inequalities of income and wealth in the society.

Limitations and Defects of Barter

The barter system was full of advantages yet it was not without certain limitations. Following are some of the important limitations of barter system

(1) *No Common Measure of Value* - When an in individual produces certain commodity he wants some price to sacrifice his commodity and unless there is some unit of measurement and that unit of measurement is correct he may not be interested in exchange. In the barter system there was no common factor to measure the value of different commodites.

(2) *Indivisibility of the Goods* -Barter system is based on the exchange of the commodites with each other so as to satisfy the need of all those who want certain commodity which is not produced by them. But sometimes it becomes difficult to measure the part of the commodity while exchanging with some other and a comparatively small commodity.

(3) *Lack of Desire for Mutual Exchange or Lack of Coincidence of Want* - To make the exchange complete, both the parties should agree to exchange the commodities offered by one other. But it is impossible to find those two individuals who will always have same wants to be satisfied. Certainly not. One may not give the required commodity to other in exchange of latter's commodity.

(4) *Difficulty in Storing the Value* -Under the barter system the production was in the form of goods and services. Every one possessed some kinds of goods. For example some possessed cows, others cloths, someone milk; other one food-grains etc.

(5) *Difficulty in Making Deferred Payments* - Under the barter one commodity was exchanged with or other commodity. Payment was done in the form of commodity. The cases of mistrust or undue payment or unjust payment were promiment in this system.

In the absence of money, goods and services were exchanged with goods and services. This system was known as Barter System. But it was full of difficulties. Soon it was felt that there should be some commodities to act as a medium of exchange. At different times different commodities were used as medium of exchange and whenever any commodity was used for this purpose it was known as money. In this way we learn from history that different commodities, *viz.*, 'Cowries', skins, cattle, etc., served as money in different periods of times. By and by difficulties regarding the storing of the commodities began to be felt. Such commodities perish on storing. So coins began to be made from metals like iron and copper. Later on gold and silver coins replaced iron and copper coins. These coins were full-weighted coins. To economise the use of these precious metals paper money was invented. In the beginning paper money was convertible into gold or silver. It was possible because paper money was backed by cent per cent gold or silver reserves. But in our times the need of money has increased to enormously that cent per cent metallic reserves cannot be kept against the issue of paper money and hence we have inconvertible paper money.

The Word Money, what we see it today in different shapes, colours, face value and design and which determines the direction of trade in modern age' has been desired form the Latin Word' Moneta".According Asia" *Prof. Willion F. Spaling* 'Moneta' denoted the Roman Goddess of prosperity 'JUNO' in whose temple, forgotton portions of of human activities whose accurate time of birth is not with in the records. Lord *J.M. Keynes* has expressed in this regard that "Money , like certain other essential elements in civilisatin is far more ancient institution than we were taught to believe some few years ago. Its origin are lost in the mists when the ice was melting; and may well stretch back into the paradisial intervals in the human history of the integlacial periods, when the wealther was delightful and the mind free to be fertile of new dideas in the Island of the Hesperides or Atlantis some Eden of Central Asia."

As pointed in the foregoing explanation of Barter System that before the origin of money, its all work were performed by the barter. Barter though with full of inconvinence. Under the Barter System there was a binding on people to get other's goods exchanged it with some goods of theireown, according to the consent of both the parties. They calculated the value of the commodity in the form of units which were absolutely based on Just their thought and opinion. No body was obliged to follow others scale of measurement in exchanging his commodity.

Different Units in Different Communities

In the absence of money the units used as the base of exchange were not identical to other. Not only this, but it was entirely different. The difference was because of the difference in religious, cultural and evolutionary background of the commodities. Further, it was much affected by geographical conditions e.g. climate, weather, location and surroundings. In the presence of aforesaid amibibuity cattle was the most undisputed unit in the regions comprised of Europe, Asia and Africa which were based on agriculture. On the basis of record available historians hold the view that during the regim of king Dionysius; Taxation policy was based on cows. In Roman kingdoms and Persia the cow was also used as the medium of exchange.

Situation in Few Areas

In cold Countries, skins, furs were the most common unit of exchange . These things were in very great demand in these countries and had become the standard unit of exchange.

In Tropical areas plume of birds tiger, Jaws, Lion, Jaws etc. used as the unit of money and medium of exchange.

In the countries living by Sea-Shore adopted the common things to be found in such areas lke coweries, shells, Sharkteech etc.

The Leather Money'

Evidences are available that leather money was discovered and widely used in USSR in the regime of *Peter* , the Great the then Russia's emperor and also in ancient Rome

Thus, "Through the centuries man has used many things as money; stones shells, iron, fish-hooks ; wampum, gold and silver, were used as basic money, or "money of ultimate redeumption ". Invention of money is the most fundamental invention in this field of Economics. Such view has been expressed by *Prof. Crowther*, "Money is one of the most fundamental of all man's inventions. Every branch of knowledge has its fundamental discovery. In mechanics it is the wheel , in science fire in politics the vote similarly in economics in the whole commercial side of Man's social existence, money is the essential invention on which all the rest is based. "

Paul Finzing in his book ' Primitive Money' gives a list of the materials which were used by the different countries as the medium of exchange; some of them are as follows :

Material	*Country*
Whale Teeth	Figi Island
Stone disc	Yap Island
Beads	Pelew Island
Feather	Santa Cruz Island
Buffalloes	Combodia
Coweries	Uganda
Shells	Angola
Cattle and Cloth	Sweden
Calves	Hungary
Gold-Dust	Japan
Tobacco	Bermudas

The Difficulty

The use of animal and wild things as money had created number of problems mainly because of the immobility of the animal as well as its indivisibility. Animals were oftenly made prey to the natural calemities causing a great loss to the owners. They were also subject to death and decay and lacked a clear cut measuring standard. Efforts were made by men to find a way which could be more safer in this regard.

Origin of Metallic Money

The development of man's economic activities taken him out from pastorage stage. In this way animal money was replaced to *'metallic money'*. It is evilent from the view held by Mercentalists more gold more power." Reference is also found in *Rigveda* for use of gold and silver as the metals for the mettalic money. Peopole started gold and silver, storing because they possesses the store of value. This pattern spread in the shape of coins and become common in China in the 11th century and in 4th century B.C. in India accoring to *Sir G. Mac Donald*..

With the increasing use of metallic money, discovery of more gold required and accordingly some gold mines were discovered in california in U.S.A. and also in Australia, which Swept, (though partially.) the coinage of early days. Soon it became to be commonly recognised as the real money and medium of exchange.

A resurrection arised in the smooth functioning of gold coinage as money with the fall of Roman Empire. Due to emergence of certain uncommon situation, gold became the first target of hoarding, which restricted its supply bringing on adverse effect on the coinage system. It not only became scarce i n supply but also made transactions rigid. These incidence motivated people indulged people in mal-practices of hoarding which harmed the gold coinage. Thus, because of lack of lomogenity it became difficult for the people.

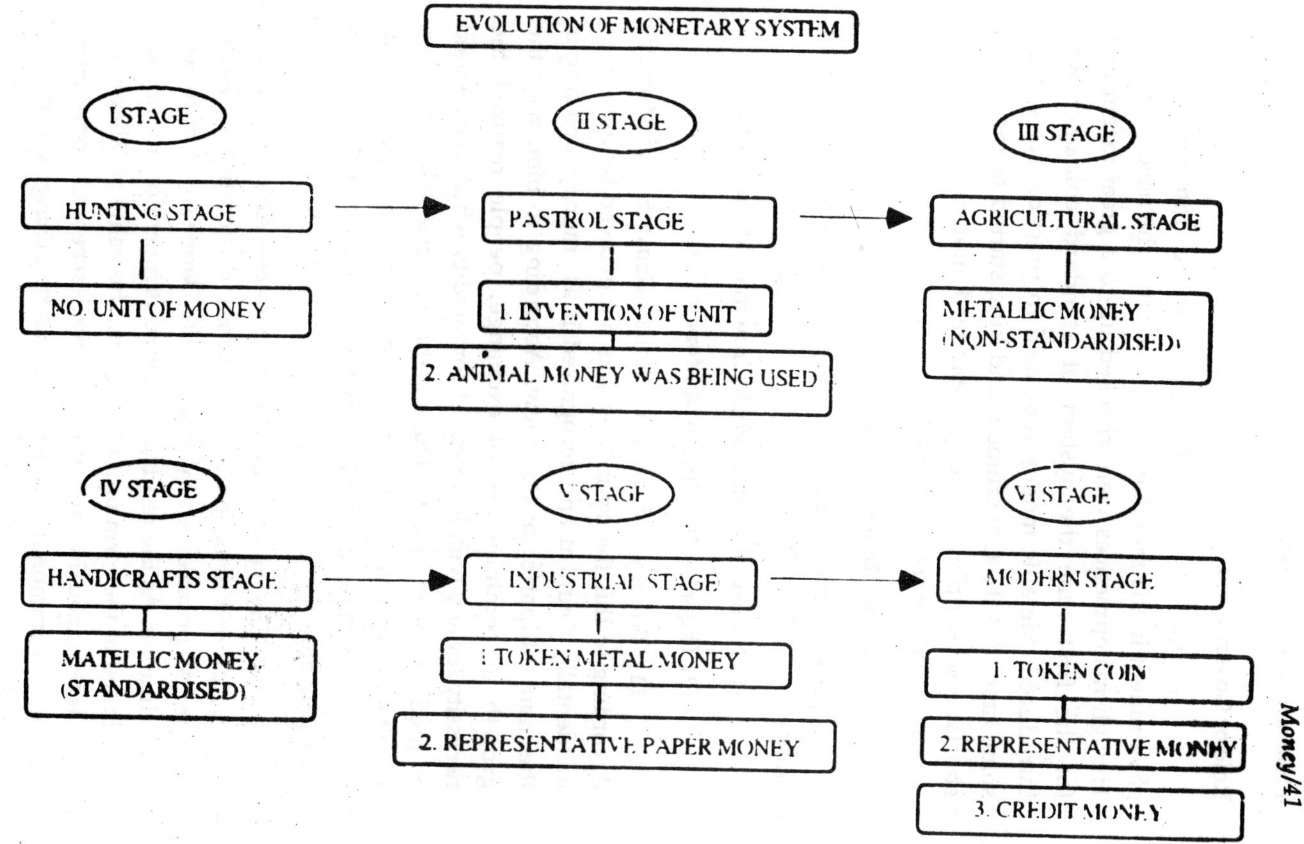
EVOLUTION OF MONETARY SYSTEM
I STAGE
HUNTING STAGE
NO. UNIT OF MONEY
II STAGE
PASTROL STAGE
1. INVENTION OF UNIT
2. ANIMAL MONEY WAS BEING USED
III STAGE
AGRICULTURAL STAGE
METALLIC MONEY (NON-STANDARDISED)
IV STAGE
HANDICRAFTS STAGE
MATELLIC MONEY. (STANDARDISED)
V STAGE
INDUSTRIAL STAGE
1. TOKEN METAL MONEY
2. REPRESENTATIVE PAPER MONEY
VI STAGE
MODERN STAGE
1. TOKEN COIN
2. REPRESENTATIVE MONEY
3. CREDIT MONEY

Role of Government

In the face of difficulties arised interference of government in the monetary system became the need of hours. Though malepractices were checked up-to a great extent and for the first time the system of standard coinage was introduced. Metallic money remained in practice for a quite some time. But the Government and king started facing accute shortage of supply of enough standard money to meet the market needs for transactions.

Principles of Evolution of Money

There are two principles with regards to evolution of money:

(1) Theory of Spontaneous Growth of Money; and

(2) Theory of Evolution of Money.

(1) Theory of Spontaneous Growth of Money– According to this theory money was not evolved by men. Men incidentally found it and recognised it as money. Spading is the main supporter of this view. According to him, with the growth of common use of exchange, people realised the necessity for any widely accepted commodity which can be used as medium of exchange. During this exercise whatever men found suitable was recognised as money. Hence according to this theory money was not evolved by men but it was spontaneously found by him.

(2) Theory of Evolution of Money– According to this theory, money was evolved to avoid difficulties of barter system. As pointed out by *Adam Smith,* Money was born with specialisation. As the result of continuous invention, money was developed in the form unit of account. The value of other goods was determined in the ratio of a well accepted commodity. Gradually common measure of value started using as medium of exchange.

There are sufficient arguments in favour and against above two theories. *W.A.L. Coulbor* has expressed the view that it will be a matter of imagination if we observe something about the evolution of money. It will be sufficient for people just to know that men started use of money in whatever form may be and were engaged in changing its shape with the change in requirements.

DEFINITION OF MONEY

Money is one of the most intelligent creations of man. Every person does all things with a view to earn money. Why do people need money? What is money? Everyone earns money, spend money and holds money. It plays a dominant role in all the fields of economic activities viz., consumption production, exchange, distribution and public finance. Thus money is something which everybody uses and understand what it is but it is rather difficult to precisely define money or at least to give a standard definition which may be acceptable to all. Consequently the term has been defined differently by different writers. Looking to the complexity and controversies, let us study some of the standard definitions of money.

Money has been defined differently by different anothorities on the subject. In a narrow sense money means the metallic coins only but in the widest sense it includes each and every form of medium of exchange *viz.*, gold , silver, copper, paper notes etc. From what has been mentioned above , we conclude that anything is money which can serve as the medium of exchange. The definitions of money can, thus, be grouped in two broad categories and sub-categories as shown in the Figures-1.

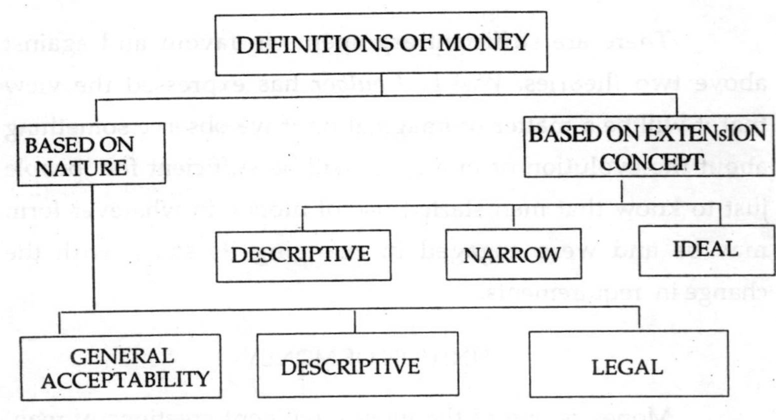

FIG-1

I. DEFINITIONS BASED ON NATURE OF MONEY

On the basis of the nature, the definitions of money can be classified into three groups:

(1) General Acceptability Definitions

(2) Descriptive Definitions

(3) Legal Deficitions

1. General Acceptability definitions

Some authorities have attempted to define money on the basis of its general acceptability. According to them anything which is generally accepted by the public in discharging their business obligations and for the payment of goods and services may be termed as money. Under this category we include definitions given by *Marshal, Keynes, Robertson. Ely* etc.

(i) *Marshall* defines as "Money includes all those things which are (at any given time or place) generally current without doubt or special enquiry as a means of purchasing commodities or services and of defraying expenses."

(ii) According to *Robertson*, "Anything which is widely accepted in payment for goods or in discharge of other kinds of business obligations."

(iii) *Ely* defines as, "Money consists of those things which, within a society, are of general acceptability."

(iv) *Pigou* defines it, "In order of anything to be called as money, it must be accepted fairly widely as an instrument of exchange, which means that a good number of people are ready to accept it in payment for goods and services provided by them."

(v) *Seligman* defines, "Money is one thing that possesses general acceptability."

The essence of above definitions is that any thing which is generally accepted for payment may be termed as money. Thus anything which is accepted without hesitation for routine transactions and payment of debts is money. The scope of definitions given under this category is too wide. In these defiaitions money also includes cheques, drafts and bills of exchange as these are also widely accepted for payment in developed countries.

2. Descriptive or Functional Definitions

Definitions of money included under this category are those which explain basic functions of money. These definitions are also termed as functional definitions. The following are the important descriptive definitions:

(i) According to *Crowther*, "Money can be defined as anything that is generally acceptable as a means of exchange (i.e., as a means of setting debts) and that at the same time acts as measure and as a store of value."

(ii) According to *Coulborn*, "Money may be defined as the means of valuation and of payment."

(iii)According to *Nogaro*, "Money is a commodity which serves as an intermediary in exchange and as a common measure of value."

The above definitions are very simple and practical and also logically sound. These definitions do not define money but describe what money does. These definitions describe micro characterstics of money (such as power of creation of faith, wide acceptability or utility). There is a great difference between definitions and description. One cannot be substitute to each other.

The basis weakness of general acceptability and functional definition is that these definitions have not given importance to legal acceptability of money. Though peoples have utmost faith in it but legal acceptability is a must for anything what we term it as money.

3. Legal Defiaitions

Money has also been defined in legal terms. In legal terms money is what the law has proclaimed as money. Legal definitions of money are based on the state theory of money. These definitions present lawyer's view of money but fails to give a satisfactory defination of money. However efforts have been made to define money in legal terms.

(i) According to Prof *Knapp*, " Anything which is declared by the state as money is money.

(ii) *Hawtrey* defines money as "the means exhibited by the law (or by the custom havng in force) for the payment of debt."

II. DEFINITIONS BASED ON EXTENTION OF THE CONCEPT OF MONEY

On this basis efforts have been made to define money keeping in view three approaches :

Wider approach-If we look money in wider sence then it includes all the form of medium of exchange *e.g.*, gold, silver, copper, metallic coins, paper notes, cheque, bill of exchange etc. On this ideology some economists defines money in wider sense :

Prof. Hartley Withers defines, "Money is what money does."

If we accept this definition as the definition of money then the scope of money becomes wider as from this point of view cheques, draft, hundi, may also be recognised as money. In under-dveloped areas even coconut has also been termed as money. This point of view regarding definition of money may not be accepted widely as cheques, draft, bill etc. and other are thought appropriate means of payment but their hoarding is not possible.

Narrow approach- *Sir Robertson* and his followers are of the view that "money is anything which is widely accepted in payment for goods; or in discharge of other kinds of business obligations. If we recognise any thing as money then gold is the metal which can be accepted in lieu of payment by all the nation. In this circumstance only unit of money made of gold or silver will only be included in the definition of money. Thus only to accept metallic money as money (not paper money as money) is the example of narrow approach.

IDEAL APPROACH

It can be safety concludes after going through all the afore- said definitions of money that these definitions give importance to the simple aspect of money. No definition gives importance to the overall character of money. If we want to know the overall character of money through its definition then the following definition seems to be ideal :

"Money is a commodity which is used by the public without any hesitation for present and future payments and it is also recognised by state."

In this definition element of acceptability and state recognition both have been given due importance.

Milton Friedman, prominent U.S. economist and his followers are of the view that even bank deposits, readily available for payment should also be accepted as money. Hence, he recognises cheques and other letters of credit as money too. No doubt, it is a liberal attitude with regard to definition of money. In developed countries cheques and other letters of credit are widely used in business transactions and payment of goods and servics and where money transactions are not preferred.

The above definitions make it clear what money is, the only qualification for a commodity to be called as money is its general acceptability—a commodity may it be gold, silver, copper or any-thing else is money if it possesses quality of general acceptance as a medium of exchange and passes from hand to hand in the discharge of debts. But it must be remember that credit instruments and securities which usually do not possess general acceptability are excluded from our conception of money. Modern money has no relation between its intrinsic value and face value. But it must have purchasing power or general acceptability.

CHARACTERISTICS OF MONEY

The study of economic history reveals that all sorts of commodities like cattle, skins, tobacco, shells, cowries etc. were used as money at one time or the other. The following are the important characteristics of money:

1. Money is not Consumer Goods– Money is not an ordinary consumer goods. Money is quite different from consume goods, As observed by *Stonier and Hague,* "In normal circumstances, however money has its seperate and distinct functions. It is not an ordinary consume good. It will be a piece of metal or paper, a mark in ledger, data in a computer, and so on."

2. Money is not Capital Goods– Capital goods transform the factors of production in to certain useful things either for consumption or to be further used in production. Hence function of capital goods is to create utility or satisfying power in the hitherto unused or 'useless' or crude resources i.e., it is the physical transformation of reseources. But money can not perform any physical transformation.It performs an essentially different operation from that perform by capital goods. Capital goods can be useful and of the same utility but the token money is only of valuable help in exchange economy where the sale and purchase depends upon exchange.

3. Money has General Acceptability– Money does not create any hesitation in the mind of acceptor as it possesses the quality of general acceptability.

4. Money has its Face Value– Money as the medium of exchange always bears value. Every coin, promissory notes or credit money always bears written value on its face.

5. Money Bears Seal– To avoid any kind of hesitation or suspicion a recognised seal is always stamped on money. For example Indian promissory notes bear "Ashoka". In the case of credit money, name of the bank is always printed on it .

THE USES OF MONEY

The uses of money are best understood when we consider the alternative system in which money was not present. This was barter system. It was full of difficulties.Following are the important difficulties noticed in the Barter System.

1. Lack of Coincidence– To begin with there was lack of coincidence between the buyers and sellers. It was very difficult to find two persons whose exchangeable goods suited to each other's wants, *e.g.*, weaver of cotton might want shoes in exchange for his cloth. But it was not easy to find a shoe-maker who required cotton cloth. Thus barter resulted in waste of time and energy.

2. Indivisibility–Difficulty arose from the fact that commodities meant for exchange were indivisible. The exchange of goods of unequal value was not possible *e.g.*, a man had a horse and he wanted a few commodities. Now he could not cut the horse into pieces. For want to sub-division exchange could not be possible.

3. Lack of Common Measure of Value– There was no common measure of value. There were different articles and each article was assigned different values. Then how to exchange goods of different value? The transaction was possible only if the two parties agreed on an acceptable rate of exchange. But in the absence of a common denominator by which the exchange rate could be expressed exchange was difficult.

4. Lack of Storing Value– The difficulty was felt in storing value. Many goods could not be stored for a long time *e.g.*, goods like fish, eggs, fruit, vegetables, etc., lose value and wholly perish after some time.

Necesscity is the mother of invention :At last money came into being. The emergence of money removed all these difficulties of the Barter economy. Now double coincidence of wants is no more necessary. Money serves as a medium of exchange. Now anything can be bought directly with money. It provides a common means of value and possesses a general purchasing power.

Money is also capable of subdivision. Transactions of the smallest value are conducted through money. By virtue of the fact that money can be stored for long periods without losing its value, the huge superstructure of the modern banking and credit system has become possible. Banks can build large credit and so borrowing and lending has become possible. Large sums of money borrowed and advanced increase production and trade and provide us with a variety of goods.

Price mechanism which is the essential feature of modern system of production owes its origin because of money. Money gives a general purchasing power to its possessor. He can purchase from any one and at a time most convenient to him.

The use of money for settlement of obligation represents a great step forward from the old Barter economy.

Money, in fact, is the central point of all economic activity. It has completely revolutionized the primitive economy. The great poet **Horance** once observed "all things human and divine renown honour and work: at money's strive go down." Even in socialistic countries , the importance of money cannot be undermined.

FUNCTIOINS OF MONEY

The functional purpose of money is to serve as a medium of exchange. It also serves as a unit of account which we generally call as measure of value. These are fundamental or primary functions of money. In the secondary capacity it serves as a standard of deferred payment and as a store of value. Money is put to different uses in an economy. Thus it also perform several other functions in a modern economy. The functions of money are best understood when we divide them in to following categories *viz*,..

(i) Primary or Basic Functions.

(ii) Secondary Functions.

(iii) Contingent Functions

(iv) Other Functions.

Primary Functions

The primary functions of money are two-fold. The most important functions which the money performs as primary functions are discussed as below:

(1) Medium of Exchange — The first function of money is that it serves as a medijm of exchange. It is the most important function of money. It is the only function which led to the discovery of money in its use as the medium of exchange. Money has put an end to the difficulties of Barter economy. There is no need of exchange commodities for commodities. On the basis of its general acceptability, goods and services are bought and sold on the basis of money. *Benham* says, "A person will accept money in payment not because he wants money for its own sake, but, because he knows that other people in turn will accept it from him in return for the goods and services which he himself requires." People hold money because it helps them to get what they require for themselves in their everyday life. We can purchase any thing directly with money. A person may or may not accept rice or wheat but he will happily accept money in exchange for his own commodities.Money gives a general purchasing power to its possessor who is free to buy commodities of any quality and in any quantity at any time and place and from any person he likes. Thus the medium of exchange is evidently the most important function of money. On the basis of its general acceptability people need not worries for its rejection.

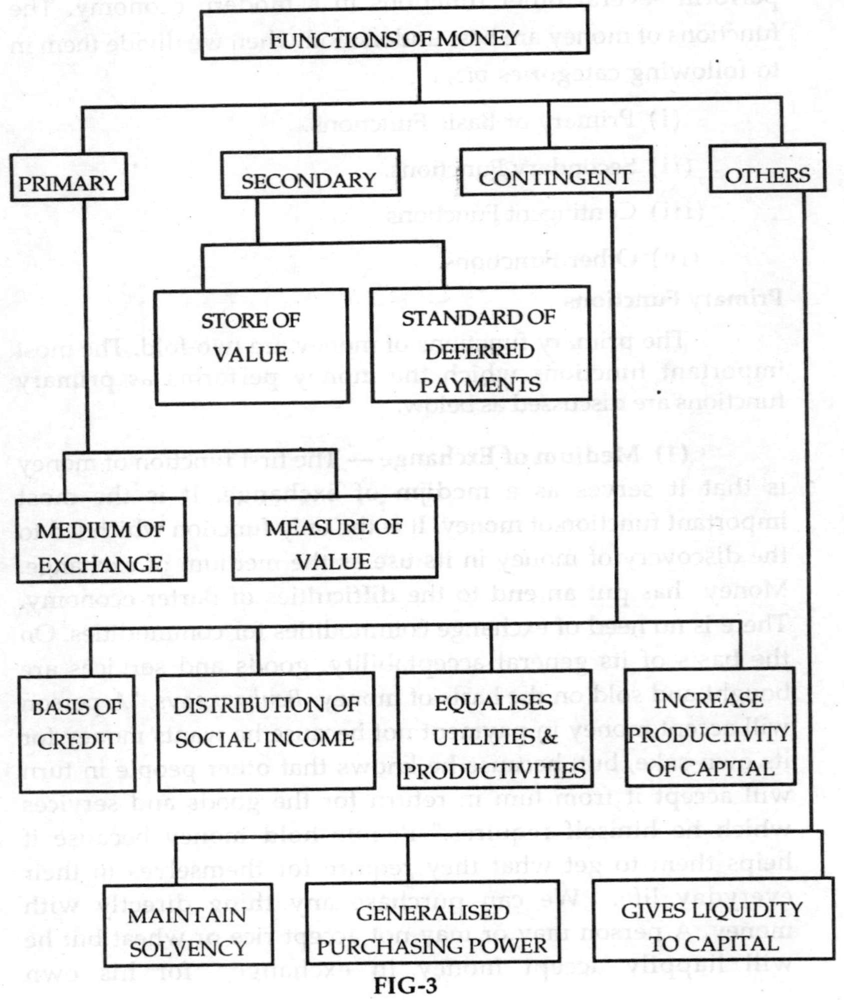

FIG-3

(2) Common Measure of Value—The another important function of money is that it measures the value of all goods and services *i.e.*, it is used as a common measure of value. Money is described as measuring rod.. In doing so, money has been able to remove the most of the inconveniences of barter under which people could not find as to how much could be exchanged for how much. Before the advent of money, there was no common measure of value. Under barter economy there was no common measure of value and there was great difficulty of expressing value of commodities and keeping account. But this difficulty has been removed by money which expresses the value of any other commodity with this mechanism. We are able to express the value of goods and services with the help of money. Price fixation is done only on the basis of this function of money. As observed by *Monlton*, "The development of monetary unit as a measure of value gave the necessary commensurability to pound, quarts and bushels–and to wheat, cattle and cloth and was thus one of the most significant developments in history. It was the final step in the evolution of means of communicating ideas. It made language and numbers intelligible for the purpose of business."

Secondary Functions

The following are the secondary functions of money:

(1) Store of Value—Money possesses the quality of purchasing power. As such goods and services can be purchased with the help of money at any time in present or in future, because it can be stored without much loss in value. Money is not a perishable commodity but a durable media by which saving of individual, profit in the form of money can be preserved. We want to store our wealth and money serves the purpose best means to do the same. In the words of *Stoneir* and *Hague* "It is a form in which wealth can be kept intact from one year to next. Money is a bridge from the present to future. It is therefore essential that the money commodity should always be one which can be easily and safely stored."

(2) Standard of Deferred Payment -This was not possible but difficult in barter system to store in the form of commodities. Most of the transactions in modern business are made on credit basis. The payment is not made in cash but kept reserve to be paid in future. Money is used for deferred payments i.e. payments are due today but have to be made at a later stage. In the barter system credit transaction were not possible. But under the system of money exchange, such types of transactions are made frequently.Buying or selling on credit or giving of debts for future dates is possible only it the value of the standard in which such future payments are to be made is fairly stable. Money provides basis for deferred payments because of certain reasons. *First,* it possesses stable value as compared to other commodities. *Second,* it is more durable as compared to other commodities and *Third,* it has quality of general acceptability and accordingly is always needed by all.

(3) Transfer of value—Money serves the purpose of transfer of value from one place to the other. The economic development widened the field of exchange. The markets have extended from local to national or even international. The purchase and sale of goods are not confined to a particular area but extended to distant lands. Money enables to sell goods and services at one place and to purchase the other necessary goods and services at other place. A person doing business in Delhi with his account in Bangalore can get his amount transferred through Bank to Bangalore without any complication. It has become possible only with the help of money that any one can transfer his assets from one place to another. The purchasing power can easily be transferred from one person to another or from one place no another with the help of money which has the quality of general acceptability. This was not possible under barter system.

Contingent Functions

Money performs some more functions. These functions have been well described by *Prof. Kinlay* and are popularly known as contingent functions. According to *Prof. Kinlay,* the following are four contingent functions of money.

(1) Money is the Basis of Credit—The modern business activities are based on credit. The importance of credit has increased manifold in all the countries of the world. It is general assumption that business activities can develop rapidly on the basis of credit. Money provides basis to credit. Cheques, bills of exchange, hundies and other credit instruments are now widely used in business.

(2) Distribution of Social Income—Production is the result of joint efforts of various factors of production. The share of each factor in the total production is determined in terms of money. It was difficult task in the barter system to determine the share of each factor of production in total production. Money helps in distribution of social income among various factors of production.

(3) Liquidity and Uniformity of Wealth—Money is the most liquid form of capital. It can be put to any use. Every asset can be exchanged in money as it provides liquidity to all kinds of assets. Money can easily be converted into any type of asset according to the need of the holder. Likewise any asset at any time can be converted into money. Because of this quality that money possesses, capital is transferred from less productive to more productive areas. The quality of liquidity of money has increased the mobility of capital.

(4) Equalisation of Marginal Utility of Wealth—In order to get the maximum satisfaction out of his income, every consumer wants to equalisation of marginal utilities of commodities purchased. Out of his limited financial resources consumer wants to spent a particular amount of money in such a way so as to equalise marginal utilities.

Other Functions

In modern business activities, money performs certain other functions as discussed below:

(1) Helps to Maintain Solvency—A business firm is presumed to be insolvent if it fails to discharge his liabilities in terms of money. Thus, the repayment capacity of a firm is measured in terms of liquid money.

(2) Represent Generalised Purchasing Power– Purchasing power stored in term of money can easily be put in any use as per the requirements of the use. There is no binding to utilise the money for the purpose it is saved. The user may use it for any other purpose in order of urgency.

(3) Liquidity to Capital– Modern economic thinkers lay stress on liquidity aspect of money. Since money is the most generally and widely accepted commodity, persons and firms always like to hold a certain amount in the form of liquidity. The most liquid form of capital is money. As such it is that form of capital which can be put to any productive use. There are variety of motives for which it is required to keep the capital in liquid form. These motives are– income, transactions, precationary and speculative.

Before the advent of money, there was nothing to be used as a medium of exchange. But in whatever form of as medium of exchange, money is an old institution like other elements of human life. It is true that in the absence of any universal recognised medium of exchange as we see today it in the form of money, society was passing through difficulties and inconveniences, but creation of money has proved one of the most intelligent creation of man.

IMPORTANCE OF MONEY

Money plays a very important role in the modern economic organisation. It is hard to think for the economic development in the absence of money. We cannot think of a society without money. In the modern world money is the guiding star of all economic activities. Money plays a significant role in all the branches of economics–production, consumption, distribution, exchange and public finance. Money serves as the basis of the pricing process by means of which the economy in guided.As observed by *Marshall* "Money is the pivot around which the economic science clusters." The importance of money can be explained as follows:

1. Advantages to Consumer– In modern time the place of money is equally valuable to the consumer. If the money is taken away from the consumer, he will under the complication of what to do. The invention of money has most benefited to the consumer mainly in the following ways:

(a) *Storage*-It facilitates the consumer to store the purchasing power in term of money.

(b) *Postponement*-It has become easy for the consumer to postpone his demand today if he so desires.It guides their way in the market.

(c) *Equalise Utility*-Every consumer wants to satisfy his maximum wants with less sacrifice of money. He will not never be ready to spend more than the utility of the commodity. It facilitates the consumer to equalise the marginal utilities obtainable from different commodities. Money helps the consumer in measuring the marginal utilities of the commodities.

(d) *Credit*-Money has also extended credit facilities to consumer

2. Advantages to Producers– Money helps the producers in the following ways:

(a) Helps in Production– We can not think to perform production function without the help of money.

(b) Division of Labour– Money plays an important role in modern production system. Division of labour and specialisation could be possible only after the intervention money.

(c) Mobility of Capital– Money is the most scarce factor of production now-a-days. Money increases the mobility of capital as it is the most liquid form of capital. Capital formation is only possible when there is an exact unit of measure the amount of the capital in the country.

(d) Savings and Investment– People earn income for their work in the productive process, which is divided into the saving and investment. The amount of savings are mobilised in a single channel of investment which moves the economic machinery upward and down ward. A person saves in the form of money and deposit in various institutions to earn interest which in turn invest it. Thus money has made saving and investment possible.

(e) Calculations in Production– Every producer is interested to know certain facts before starting the production. Money plays very significant role in knowing these facts based on certain calculations.

3. Money Facilitates Trade– Money facilitate trade because it serves as a medium of exchange–

(a) It has made possible rapid exchange of goods and services. Now, not only in the region of the same country but even outside the national frontiers one can undertake an exchange with the help of money.

(b) The invention of money has made future transaction possible.

4. Eliminates the Drawbacks of Barter System– The various difficulties and inconveniences of cumbersome barter system have been removed by money. Barter's difficulties have been replaced by fast growing use of money in every field of exchange. The exchange mechanism has undergone an instantaneous transformation with the introduction of monetary system.

5. Importance in Distribution– The share of individual factor of production in total production can be easily determined in terms of money.Money has enabled the employers to pay the various works undertaken by the different factors of production. It has become easier for the organiser to evaluate the value of the services rendered by various factors of production to enable that factor to work again.

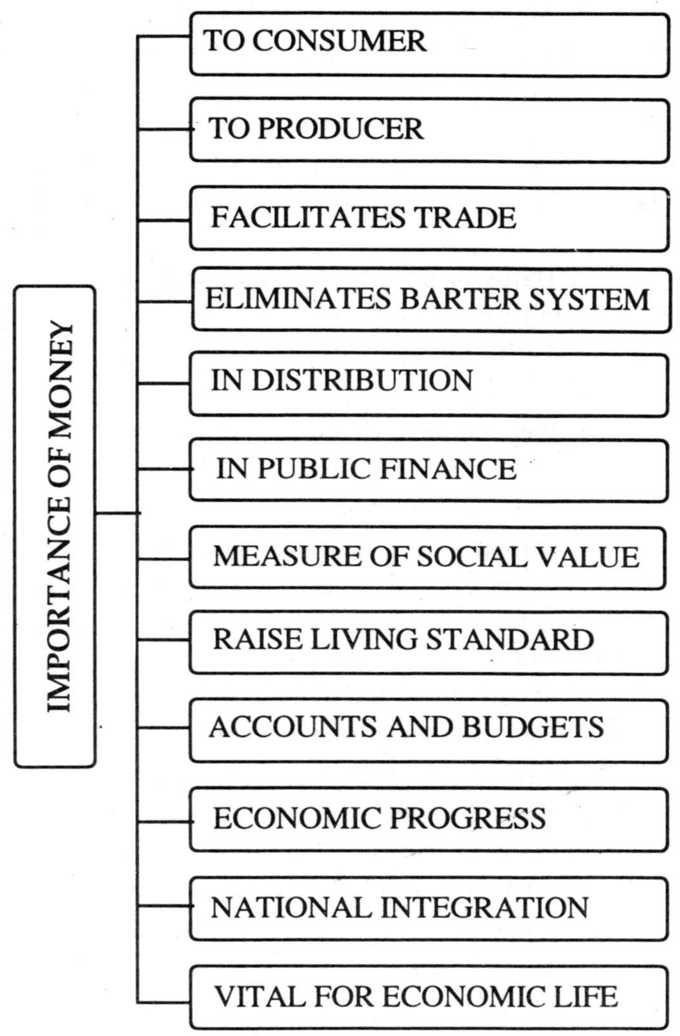

FIG-1

6. Significance in Public Finance– It has become easy for the government to collects taxes, fees, penalty, interest etc. in term of money. Planning for development is undertaken on the basis of money. Unless an exact measurement of the requirements are done in the form of money, it is difficult to plan for public revenue and expenditure.

7. Measure of Social Value– The utility of social welfare schemes can be easily measured in term of money. This responsibility has fallen on the shoulder of the modern governments to create certain public utilities like road, transportation, courts, defence, health facilities etc., for the welfare of the people. Government needs money to fulfil these wants.

8. Helps to raise Living Standards– Money helps in raising overall production which in turn creates demand for new products. It ultimately lead to raising living standards of the society.

9. Preparation of Accounts and Budgets– Money serves as a unit of accounting and thus makes possible efficient accounting and budgeting system.

10. Barometer of Economic Progress– Economic progress of a country can be easily measured in terms of money.The spead of development is realised on the basis of the value of money. It is the signal and measuring rod of the economic development of the country. It determines the trend of the development, rate of the development and spread of development.

11. Strengthen National Integration– Money has expanded the market which, in turn, extended the industrial and commercial activities. In this way money help strengthening national and international relations.

12. Money is vital for Our Economic Life- Money plays sifnificant role in determining the economic life of the people all over the world. Our position in the society depends upon the amount of money we possess. Money has transferred the pattern of economic life with the passage of the time.

The above mentioned importance of money now-a-days for which a few pages will not be sufficient to explain. The class war between the capitalists and Labourers has been in the past and is still going on merely for the sake of money. In the political field; it is rightly said, "who holds the purse holds the power." It is true in the social and other walks of life also. Money has improved and disrupted the sweet relations between the individuals, businessmen and countries.

It can be safely concluded that money is an indispensable organ of modern economy and society. It is hard to think smooth functioning of economy in the absence of money. It is only money that has affected the motto of the life of an individual, a society or a nation. No one in this universe remains unaffected by the use of money. Money has been recognised as the root cause of overall progress of the society.

DEFECTS OF MONEY

Though money is a source of many blessings to mankind in a modern society, it is wrong to conclude that money is an unmixed blessing. It is true that money is essential for modern industrial society and it plays a dominant role in all the fields of economic activity, viz., consumption, production , exchange , distribution, public finance etc. But it must not be forgotton than money is also a source of peril and confusion. Some writers, more particularly Marxian writers, are of the opinion that money is not necessary , rather it is the source os all evils in the present society. It is said that money is only an instrument which helps in economic progress but it is not the controlling authority.

We discuss below some of the more serious defects of money.

1. *Economic Instability* - One great defect in money is that its value often changes giving rise to serious fluctuations in prices and affects the society adversely . Different classes of people in a society are affected differently. Instability in prices increases risks of production and trade and shakes business confidence. As a matter of fact both the periods, rising prices (inflation) and falling prices (deflation), are harmful. Periods of rising prices (falling value of money) are always accompanied by distress and social unrest. Strikes and all

kinds of industrial disputes take place. Ultimately the entire productive machinery is put out of gear. Deflation (rising value of money) hurts employers. Depression follows and general unemployment ensues. During the first war and post-war period (1914-18) , the world suffered from galloping or hyper inflation when money lost all its value and during 1929-33, the world experienced the general depression and there was unimaginable unemployment. Thus these economic fluctuations are due to the use of money and so there is a reason to say that modern world is afraid of money.

2. *Over Capitalisation and Over Production* - With the invention of money, borrowing and lending operation in business have come within the reach of common man. It has become easy in the business to utilise more capital then requirement. It gives rise to the problem of over-capitalisation. Over-Capitalisation in turn results in over-production. Over-production creates varities of problems in the economy e.g., steep fall in prices, un-employment, recession etc.

3. *Money Strengthen Capitalism* - Capitalism is regarded as child of money. Money is the main source of credit. Credit facilitate businessmen to obtained borrowed funds for the expansion of their activities. It concentrated capital in the hands of a few rich people or so called industrialists. In this process money multiplied and helps rich to become richer.

4. *'Money' and 'Purchasing Power' are not be Synonymous* - Normally 'money and purchasing power' are regarded as synonymous. But in fact they may not be synonymous in certain circumstances. It is possible for a person to have money but not the purchasing power. This is what happened in Germany after the First World War as a consequence of which the value of Mark (Currency of Germany) had fallen to zero due to great inflation and the price of commodities touched to sky-high . It was a situation under which though the German people had money but they had no purchasing power.

5. *Money Gives Birth to Trade Cycle* - Operation of Trade Cycle is a routine phenomenon in capitalistic economy. In the process of trade cycle boom period follows slumps and slump follow boom. Operation of trade cycle generate instability in economy results of which different section of community faces varities of difficulties and inconveniences. Money is only responsible for the operation of trade cycle.

6. *Inequality of Income* - Another defect of money is that it has created gross inequality of income in the society. During the periods of changes in the value of money there is redistribution of income. Money helps in the accumulation of wealth in the hands of the few and in this way creates inequalities in the distribution of income. Money has made the rich still richer and the poor still poorer. Thus money is responsible in dividing the modern society into the rich (Haves) and the poor (Have-notes).

7. *Money tends to become Master* - Money serves the mankind so long as it is kept under control and it functions as Man's servant. When it goes out of control, it proves total to the economy. Whenever the money supply exceeds its demand, its consequences proves horrible. In such circumstances money not becommes only Man's master , but it also shatters the economy. It is therefore, correct to say that money is a good servant but a bad master. Therefore, it will be on safer side to keep money within the manageable limit.

8. *Money makes the Society Corrupt* - Another defect of money is that leads the society to corruption and immorality. Love of money is the root of all evil. Money is regarded as a devil which prompts a man for any kind of crime. According to one German economist, *Von Mises,* "Money is regarded as the cause of theft and murder, of deception and betrayal . Money is blamed when the prostitute sells her body and when the bribed judge perverts the law. It is money

against which moralist declaims when he wishes to oppose excessive materialism. Significantly enough , avarice is called the love of money and all evil is attributed to it. "

Conclusions - The defects of money as explanied above are not for the sake of money but for the love of things it can purchase in its exchange . In fact, without money, the modern economic system which is so complex cannot function properly. Money has, therefore, becomes an internal part of the present society. The only thing is that great change in the value of money must be avoided. If money is kept under control, it will certainly be a source of blessings to mankind in modern society.

ROLE OF MONEY IN VARIOUS ECONOMIC SYSTEM

The money plays a significant role in all types of economy whether it is a capitalist, or a socialist or a planned economy. We cannot imagine any type of economy in the absence of money. Some argue that money is not necessary in socialism but they are wrong in their conception. Money is as important in socialist countries as it is in capitalistic countries . It performs all functions of money *i.e.* , medium of exchange, measurement of value, store of purchasing power etc. in a socialist country. We shall discuss here under the importance of money in different economies.

Importance of Money in Capitalistic Economy

The capitalistic economy recognise the right of individual property . It is free from all government control. All factors of production are owned , controlled and operated by private entrepreneurs. The owner of the property in a capitalistic economy can use his property, according to his own choice. Naturally the choice is guided by the price mechanism i.e., before taking up any economic activity, a businessman or an industrialist considers the costs, prices and the rate of profit. He therefore, engages the various factors of production in such activities which may produce good return. Thus, profit motive is the prime factor in capitalistic economy.

As we know , the capitalistic economy cannot function without price mechanism and price mechanism cannot function without money. Thus, money is the life blood of capitalistic economy, which cannot function without its price mechanism is expressed in terms of money. The following points should noted in this regard. -

1. *Consumer can make a rational choice of goods* - As we know, every consumer wishes to derive maximum satisfaction out of his limited resources of expenditure . Price mechanism helps him to achieve this objective . Before purchasing the goods, the consumer compares the price of the commodity with the utility surrendered (in terms of money) and the utility of goods purchased.

2. *Production Decisions are Based on Money* - Price mechanism or profit motive helps the producer in making production decisions. He always keeps his eyes fixed on the price-mechanism that guides to him in his productive activities. What is to be produced , and how much to be produced is decided by the producer in accordance with the market conditions or dictates of the price mechanics. A producer will not decide to produce anything which may yield loss or may not be profitable to him. These decisions cannot be taken if price mechanism is not expressed in terms of money.

3. *Money Simplifies the Distribution System* - The production processes complex in capitalistic economy. All factors of production are engaged simultaneously in the production process and the output is the result of their combined efforts. Prices mechanism also determines the share of remunerations of the factors of production. The reward of factors of production (*i.e.*, wages, rent , salary , interest etc.) is determined in advance and the monetary terms according to the demand for and supply of them.

4. *Decision regarding Saving and Spending* - The price mechanism again helps the individual in arriving at the correct decision regarding saving and spending. Interest rate is the value of money. If interest rate is higher savings can be attracted and mony can be borrowed and invested in the business. Thus, it becomes a source of capital formation . If interest rate is lower, savings will be discouraged and spending will be encouraged . Thus , the price of money decides whether to save or spend.

5. *Price Mechanism regulates the Fow of Investment* - The price mechanism (in the form of profit) regulates the flow of investment into different channels. The producer will prefer to invest funds (money) in projects which are more profitable . Higher the rate of profit in a particular use on industry, the greater will be the flow of investment in that use or industry. The producer keeps on substituting funds from less profitable to more profitable uses. If a particular industry or use is expected not to earn a reasonable profit, it may likely to be closed.

6. *Money is the basis of Credit* - Money provides basis of capitalist economy through credit. Further transactions or speculative transactions are possible only in capitalist economy and only due to the presence of money. Without money, such types of transaction are not possible. This function of money has expanded the limits of markets from local to national or international.

Thus, price mechanism (profit motive) is the should of capitalist economy . Without it, capitalism will breakdown.

Importance of Money in a Socialistic Economy

A socialist economy is one in which all economic activities are planned, controlled and guided by the government or its agencies. There is no free market and no right of property is given to individuals. Now, the question is whether money has any role to play in such a completely controlled and guided economy. *Marx, Lenin* and other socialists were against the use of money. Marx even believed that money is the root cause of exploitation of labour by the capitalists as they get surplus only due to money. Socialist, believe that socialist economy can work even without money. Marx visualised an ideal communist state where money would be abolished land goods would be exchanged for goods.

When Bolshevik (communist) Party came to power in Russia after Russia Revolution of 1917 , currency notes and coins were replaced by a system of cards in selected areas. It was also endevoured to avoid the use of money through extensive use of direct controls and free distribution of goods. But soon it was realised that it was impossible to introduce communism without money and money circulation. In 1921 . *Leon Trotsky* realised the necessity of money in the economy. He clearly stated " *The blueprints produced by the offices must demonstrate their economic expediency through commercial circulation, Without a firm monetary unit, commercial accounting only increase the choos".* The Russian economy is a good example of socialist planning and control, but production and income transaction are carried on through money. All commercial transactions are carried on in money though money occupies an inferior and subordinate position in the economy. Thus, it is very clear that even socialist economy cannot work without money. The fact are _

1. *Guide to Economic Activities* - Money guides economic activities even in a socialistic economy. Price system, according to Oscar lange, serves as a guide to economic activity. But the price system has no meaning unless prices are expressed in terms of money. So, money in a socialist economy serves as a medium of exchange and as a standard of value. No economic transaction can take place or the commercial efficiency cannot be measured without money.

2. *Allocation of Resources* - Money is also needed for the allocation of resources. The planning authority in a socialist country has the responsibility to allocate the economic resources of the country in different lines of production on the basis of social needs. The resources cannot be fairly allocated unless they are expressed in terms of money as they are based on the pricing system. George *Halm* and *Von Mises* Wrote - " *Even if the aims of production should be determined by the dictator, the allocation of resources according to these aims would have to be the result of the working of a pricing process by means of which it is possible to compare the usefulness of the available resources in different fields of employment.*

3. *Distribution of Income* - Money, in a socialist economy, is also needed for distribution of income because distribution of goods on an equitable manner, among millions of consumers is difficult without monetary mechanism. Marx ideal solution of "to each according to his need" proved quite impracticable because there is not objective criterion for judging the needs of the people. Any type of distribution on any basis is bound of prove quite irrational and arbitrary . Thus distribution of income even in a socialistic economy is guided by the price system based on money.

The socialist economy also use money even though the economy is fully planned, directed and controlled by the state. The money , however, plays a minor role in influencing economic activities as the pricing system is given a minor role.

Importance of Money in a Planned Economy

Money has, also an important role to play in a developing planned economy. A planned economy is generally followed in under-developed countries where there is no shortage of real/natural resourcdes. The need is only to tap those resources in a planned manner. The state undertakes the responsibility for the development of these dormant natural resources either through state agencies or through private enterprises but under the guidance of the government. The development of economy or tapping of natural or real sources needs monetary resources which are in plenty in these countries and the governments has to provide monetary resources to activate the real resources.

❑

3

Paper Money Standard

The paper money is the accepted currency system managed by the government. The system is also known as managed currency standard. Managed money is also known as paper standard. The regulation and control of paper money standard lies in the hands of government.

The paper money standard came into being due to the failure of the gold standard and other metallic standards. In modern time the paper currency standard performs the function of money. Under this system, paper currency circulates in the market, at the same time coins are also circulates to make the fractional payments. Currency is issued by the Central Bank of the country, but its control lies in the hands of government.

Merits of Managed Money or Paper Standard

Paper money has several advantages over the Metallic money. Following are its merits :

1. Portability : Paper Money is easy to carry in comparison to the Metallic Money. Paper Currency in huge amount can be taken away from one place to another without any difficulty. It can be kept without any difficulty and there is also easiness in the transactions.

2. Economical : To issue paper Money is not a costly affair for the issuing government. It involves less expenditure in the printing of currency notes. It also leaves the government to the use the precious metals in more important matters. Thus vast amount of precious metals are saved. Per-unit issuing cost is low in the case of paper standard.

3. Flexible and Elastic : The issue of paper currency is quite flexible for the economy. Government can issue new currency notes without any difficulty. More currency can be printed in less time. It can be adjusted according to the demand of currency in the market. It is elastic currency system which keeps the capacity to adjust itself with the requirements of the economy.

4. Helpful during Emergency : In the time of financial emergency governments can issue notes to meet the economic difficulty. During war huge amount of money is required which can be easily met by this system of issuing currency.

5. No Problem of Scarcity : There is no scarcity problem before the government regarding the shortage of material. Such situation may come in the case of Metallic currency system due to the scarcity of gold or the Standard Metal but in the case of Managed Money it is never expected.

6. Helpful in the Formation of Policies : Through the paper currency government are absolutely away from any restraint. They can adopt any suitable policy to stablise prices and business to bring the conditions fit for full employment. Free movement policies become difficult in the case of Metallic Standard due to various reasons.

7. Easy to Fight Deflation : Deflation occurs when less supply of money exists in the market. In the case of paper standard, currency can be circulated without any difficulty. Supply can be increased to check the deflationary process.

8. No loss due to Debasing : In case of precious metals circulating as currency great loss is incurred due to wear and tear of the coins. But in the case of paper currency no such fear *originates*. A currency can be changed into new one. The question of the loss of precious metals, in the system of paper currency does not arise.

Demerits :

Paper Currency Standard posesses several merits but it is not out of demerits. Following are the demerits of Paper Money Standard:

1. Inflation : It is not difficult for the government to issue paper currency. There is no restriction , like that of the scarcity of metals etc. Finding it easy, government may issue such an amount of currency which may be more than market demand. It may adversely affect the economy.

The government , when fail to control its expenditure takes the shelter under the deficit financing which means circulating more new printed money without any further increase in the production. The inflation has always kept its link with the Managed Money or paper standard.

2. Non-Monetization : Paper Money does not possess any standard value. It is accepted in the market because it keeps legality behind it. In the case of inflationary situation , government can create a very difficult situation before the people by non-monetizing or demonetizing paper currency. The holders beome sad and gloomy as their hard earned money becomes valueless-by only a declaration of government.

3. Limited Area of Function : Paper money is national in its operation. It operates only in the national territory without any international recognition. In case of gold standard the situation is not so. But in case of paper standard every government issues its own currency which operates in its own territory.

4. Instability in Exchange Rates : Under paper standard every country issues paper currency according to the requirements of its own country. Hardly any attention is paid to the exchanges rates in the face of national monetary difficulties. An exact relationship between the currencies of the two countries is always in moving position. It some times creates a kind of confusion among the exporters and importers . To quote *Paul Einzing* :

"The adoption of paper currency provided additional temptation and opportunity for departures from the policy of stability on higher to unknown scale." Unstable rate of excahange depresses the volume of production of goods and services in the world.

5. Increasing Demoralisation : Paper Money (like Fiat Money) also induces demoralising atmosphere in the economy. Its fluctuations affects the price level, and further unstable price level affect the moral standard of the thinkers.

Prof. David Kinely has expressed his fear in following words:-

"Fiat paper has well called the alcohol of commerce whose fumes entering the brains of individuals and of the government officers seem to make them incapable of sober judgement or self-restraint in the matter of further issue, and further demoralisation takes place, even the monor lapses in the management and control of paper currency may bring disastrous effects that cannot be conceived of under any other form of monetary standard."[1]

Looking into all these merits and demerits it appears that the paper standard may prove dangerous and harmful only when its management is not done properly. The fear of non-monetization, deflation etc, are only the works of improper or unintelligent government. If the paper Money is managed properly its demerits can be removed.

Supporting the case of paper standard *Prof. Agnas* has expresed the legitimacy of happenings under incapable government:-

"If an irresponsible and reckless government does even happen to get into power, and run into debt, it never hesitates, even under the gold standard to abandon gold and print paper money. History supplies a long series of instances when even gold has not been a effective check at all. "[2]

Types of Paper Money

The paper money may be classified into four category as mentioned below:

(1) Representative Paper Money.

(2) Convertible Paper Money.

(3) Inconvertible Paper Money.

(4) Fiat Paper Money.

These have been discussed in detail in *chapter* 2.

PRINCIPLES OF NOTE ISSUe

There are two main principles of note issue:

(I) The Currency Principle– Under this principle security is the first consideration and hence the note-issuing authority is required statutorily to keep cent-percent metallic cover. In order to ensure public confidence in currency and stability in price level this principle exercises some check on the note issuing authority. Due to this binding, the government is not free to issue paper currency to an unlimited extent. No doubt the principle serve the purpose to ensure confidence in the currency but there should be sufficient flexibility. The rigidity of the principle restricts government to issue more currency even in the times of crisis. Flexibility is the main characteristic of a sound monetary system.

There are some inherent qualities and weaknesses of this principle as mentioned below:

Qualities– The main qualities of the principle are:

(1) In order to hold cent per cent metallic cover, the issuing authority is not free for any kind of arbitration.

(2) Public have full confidence in the system.

(3) Savings in depreciation of metal.

Disadvantage– In practice the principle suffers from the following disadvantages:

(1)Lack of Flexibility– The principle avoids the currency requirements of trade and industry in the country. Due to lack of flexibility, it is not possible under the system to expand note issue without proportionate increase in metallic cover.

(2)Lack of Economy– As the precious metals used as metallic cover remain without any use. Thus the principle suffer by the weakness of lack of economy.

(3)Not Suitable for Poor Countries– The principle is not practical for poor countries already having lack of precious metals-likegold or silver.

(II) The Banking Principle– The banking principle of note issue provides elasticity and ignores security. The monetary authority is not under an obligation to maintain cent per cent metallic reserve for the note issue under this principle. The authority is free to expand the quantity of paper currency looking to the need of trade and industry in the country.

There are two advantages of banking principle (1) elasticity and (2) dual saving of precious metals. The principle on the other hand also suffer from two weaknesses (1) in the lack of security, there is always fear of inflation, and (2) lack of people's confidence.

VARIOUS SYSTEMS OF ISSUING MANAGED MONEY

In the light of the above two principles, following are the eight systems of issuing paper currency:

1. Minimum Reserve System.
2. Proportional Reserve System.
3. Fixed Fiduciary System.
4. Fixed Maximum Fiduciary System.
5. Simple Deposit Scheme.
6. Percentage Deposit System.
7. Bond Deposit System.
8. Original Assets System.

1. Minimum Reserve System– In this system a minimum gold Reserve is kept by the central bank according to the provisions of the law. There is no upper limit to the issue of currency.

This system is considered to be one of the easiest, economical, and elastic methods of issuing currency. This system has been adopted in India which requires the Reserve Bank of India to keep a minimum Reserve of 200 crores. (Rs. 115 crores in the form of gold and Rs. 85 crores in the form of foreign exchange.)

According to an amendment (1957) the R.B.I. has been empowered not to keep foreign exchange provided bank is able to get approval of the central government for the purpose.

Merits of Minimum Reserve System—

The following are merits of Minimum Reserve System:

(i) Economical– The note issue under this system need not to be backed by cent-per cent metallic reserve. Thus there is no need to keep idle gold or silver in the form of metallic reserve.

(ii) Flexible– This system is more flexible as the monetary authorities are free to issue as much currency as required after keeping a minimum amount of gold and foreign securities.

(iii) Wider Suitability– The system is suitable for almost all the countries irrespective of their level of economic development. The relatively poor countries may also adopt this system of note issue.

Demerits of Minimum Reserve System.

There are merits of the Minimum Reserve System but the system is not free from demerits as give below:

(i) Fear of Inflation– Under this system the authorities are free to issue any quantity of currency just backed by keeping minimum reserve. As such there are always possibilities of excess money supply

(ii) Non-convertible– The system does not permit for the convertibility of paper currency into gold or silver as these metals are not backed before issuing the currency.

(iii) Lack of Public Confidence– Because of the disqualification of non-convertibility, the public has less faith in the currency issued under this system.

2. Proportional Reserve System– In this system the Central Bank is required to keep a proportionate reserve of the currency issued by it. It is not fixed as to what should be the amount of reserve but it depends upon the amount of paper currency. The general proportion is kept between 25% and 40% of the total currency.

This system is less flexible than the Minimum Reserve System. But if due to any reason the Gold Reserve falls it will curtail the total supply of currency. It is flexible but not without evil consequences.

Merits of Proportional Reserve System–

As under the system paper currency issued is backed by certain proportion of metal–gold or silver, the system possesses the following merits:

(i) Flexible– The method is flexible because by keeping small percentage of metallic reserve the quantity of money issued can be increased.

(ii) Convertibility– Since certain percentage of reserve are kept against paper currency issued, the system ensure convertibility.

(iii) No Fear of Inflation– The system restricts the inflation as the issue of paper currency under the system is controlled by keeping certain percentage of gold or silver reserve.

(iv) Public Confidence– As the issue of paper currency under the system is backed by metallic reserve and provides convertibility the public has full faith in the system.

(v) Economical– The system is also economical since the note issue is backed by only a certain proportion of metallic reserve.

Demerits– The following are the demerits of this system–

(i) Costly– The metallic reserve in the form of gold or silver remain idle which can be put into more profitable uses otherwise.

(ii) Inflexibility– Though under the system it is easy to raise the quantity of money but it is difficult to reduce the quantity in circulation.

(iii) Impracticable Convertibility– Theoretically the paper currency issued under the system possesses the quality of convertibility but in practice it looks only imaginary.

3. Fixed Fiduciary System– Under this system the law of the nation provides for the issue of unbacked, unsupported money by the government. If the government wants to issue more currency beyond this limit then it has to back such currency by 100% gold reserve.

The system provides a check over the temptation to issue non-convertible currency in the economy. It also keeps the greed of the government under control. But at the same time this system is not flexible at all. Money circulation can only be increased when enough quantity of gold is available. It does not suit to a developing economy where monetary expansion is required.

This system was adopted first of all by England through to Bank of England Act, passed in 1884.

Merits of Fixed Fiduciary System–

The following are the merits of Fixed Fiduciary System:

(i)Public Confidence– The system inspires full confidence as it ensure the convertibility of the entire issue.

(ii)Safety– The method also possesses the quality of safety as the issue is backed by cent per cent metallic reserve after a certain limit.

(iii)Avoids Fear of Over-Issue– In this method of note issue, it is essential to keep cent-percent gold reserves beyond the fiduciary limit. Hence the system avoid any possibility of over issue of paper currency.

Demerits of Fixed Fiduciary System–

The following are the demerits of Fixed Fiduciary system:

(i)Difficult to Measure Fiduciary Limit– It is difficult to measure as to what should be fiduciary limit in the issue of paper currency. The limit once determined can be extended or contracted as per the need of the economy.

(ii)Lack of Flexibility– The system is lacking flexibility. In this system it is difficult for the government to increase the money supply unless arrangement of metallic reserves is made.

(iii)Expensive– The issue of paper currency after the fiduciary limit requires metallic cover of the precious metal which remains unutilised and make it as an expensive system of note issue.

(iv)Impracticable– The system is impracticable particularly for those nations where there is shortage of metallic reserves.

The system is not suitable for developing countries like India. In these countries demand for currency may .vary from tme to time. This system was in operation in India till 1920s and afterwards replaced by the Proportional Reserve System.

4..Fixed Maximum Fiduciary System– It is an improvement over the Fixed Fiduciary System. In this system a maximum fiduciary limit is decided by the central government beyond which the central bank has no power to increase the issue of currency.

The fixation of maximum limit depends upon the quantum of trade, commerce and other factors which determine the demand money. Generally, as a precaution the limit is placed at a higher amount than the requirement. The alteration in the change of the fixed maximum amount is rests with of the government.

The Metallic currency system, however, can be adopted by the central bank according to tthe needs of the country. This method was adopted by Japan in 1941, and by England in 1939.

Lord. J. M. Keynes has felt that if the economy wants to avoid irresponsive increase in the circulation of money, this system is the most suitable.

To quote *Lord Keynes:-* "If the volume of note issue is to be regulated by law this is perhaps the best system."

Merits of Maximum Fiduciary System– The system has following merits :

(i) Saving of Precious Metal– The system is flexible enough as it does not unnecessary block gold or silver reserve. These metal can be put to use elsewhere in the economy.

(ii) Flexible– The maximum fiduciary limit of issue is determined keeping in view industrial and business requirement of the country. The limit can also be raised from time to time hence the system is more flexible.

(iii) No Danger of Inflation– In this system the government is not free to issue paper currency beyond the prescribed maximum limit. Hence, the system is free from the danger of inflation.

Demerits– This system has the following demerits:

(i) Misuse of Power– There are all possibilities under the system that government may fix the fiduciary limit keeping in view political interest. It may inspire government to raise the limit with a view to serve political interest. Hence, there is danger of misuse of the system by the Government.

(ii) Limited Flexibility– Although the system has a quality of flexibility but in practice the limit is confined to only certain extent. Beyond the maximum fiduciary limit the government can not issue paper currency.

(iii) Wrong Determination– Determined maximum limit can prove some times wrong. In such a circumstances the problem of inflation or deflation can arise.

5. Simple Deposit Scheme– This is the simplest method to issue paper currency in any economy. The paper money which is issued is called 'Representative Paper Money' since it represents the gold reserve kept at its back.

In this system 100% of the currency is backed by gold reserve hence 100% gold reserve is required. It is one of the safest ways to issue paper currency but it is too costly and rigid system. In the absence of gold, currency can be not issued inspite of the urgent requirements in the economy.

Merits of Simple Deposit System–

The following are the merits of Simple Deposit System:

(i) Public Confidence– The public have more faith in this system as the system is backed fully by gold or silver or both the reserve.

(ii) Simple– This system is also simple as compared to other system. The system is simple because currency equivalent to gold or silver reserve can only be issued by the authorities.

(iii) Convertibility– The paper currency issued under this method is fully convertible. The reason is that cent per cent gold or silver reserves are backed against the issue of currency.

(iv) Control of Inflation– Due to the condition of keeping of cent per cent metallic reserve the paper currency cannot be over issued under this system. Therefore it restricts the pressure of inflation on the economy.

Demerits of Simple Deposit System–

There are also some demerits of the system as described below:

(i) Lack of Flexibility– Due to the requirements of keeping metallic reserves it is always not possible to issue paper currency in sufficiency. Hence it is not possible for the authorities to increase the supply in case of emergency.

(ii) Costly– The gold and silver reserves remain idle against the issue of paper currency. Therefore the system proves costly.

6. Percentage Deposit Scheme– This is nothing but a modification of the Proportional Reserve System. This system provides for keeping an amount of Reserve which determines percentage of the total currency issued. This system facilities that the Reserve can be kept in a fixed percentage in the gold and foreign exchange. For example prior to the adoption of Minimum Reserve system in (1956), Reserve Bank of India kept 40% Reserve. Sixty percent of this Reserve was kept in the form of foreign exchange (hard currency): which implies that out of 40% of Reserve; its sixty percent *i.e.* 24 percent was kept in foreign exchange (*i.e.* £ sterling) and 16% (*i.e.* 40% of the total Reserve) was kept in gold.

7. Bond Deposit Scheme– This system provides for issuing of paper money without keeping gold or any Metallic Reserve. The currency is backed by government bonds and securities. USA adopted it in 1913. The greatest fear under this system is that in the absence of metalic reserve requirement inflationary tendency may emerge.

Merits of Bond Deposit System–

The following are the merits of Bond Deposit System:

(i) Economical– The paper currency issued under this system need not to be backed by metallic cover in the form of either gold or silver. Hence the system is economical.

(ii) Avoids Fear of Over-issue– The entire paper currency issued under the system is backed by government bonds/treasury bills. Therefore the system is free from any danger of over-issue of paper currency.

Demerits–

The following are the demerits of this system:

(i) Fear of Inflation– The issue of paper currency under this system is not backed by metallic reserves. Hence the fear of inflation always persist under the system due to over-issue of paper currency.

(ii) Lack of Elasticity The system is lacking of elasticity. The entire issue needs to be backed by government bonds and securities. This creates lack of elasticity in the system.

(iii) Lack of Public confidence– The system does not have public confidence due to lack of convertibility of paper currency issued under this system.

8. Original Assets System– This is a peculiar system of issuing currency notes. Under this system bank can issue the currency with the full backing of its own assets. No other Reserve than the assets of the bank is required. This system, because of its far-reaching evil consequences has not been adopted by any country.

Which one is Better?

The adoption of a particular type of system depends upon the financial conditions of the country, the level of development etc. For under-developed countries Proportional Reserve system is considered to be a desirable system.

It is generally held that Minimum Reserve system is better than all the systems of issuing Managed Money.

REFERENCES

1. David Kinely-Money,P.32

2 Agnas: The Problem of Foreign Exchange, P. 155.

4

Types of Money

Money is anything that is generally accepted as a medium of exchange. The only qualification for a commodity to be called money is its general acceptability. Difficulties of Barter economy was the main reason for evolution of money. There are various kinds of money as classified by different economists. They have emphasised on different aspects of money. The following are the main classifications of money.

I. On the basis of Nature

Money on this basis has been classified by professor *J.M. Keynes* in two categories.

1. Actual Money
2. Money of Account

1. Actual Money-Actual money is that which actually circulates within the country and which is generally accepted as a medium of exchange and through which all payments are made and received. It is the money in the real sense which flow in the economy and on the basis of which contracts of various kinds are discharged. It is the actual money in terms of which purchasing power is stored *e.g.,* in Indian rupee coin, rupee notes, fifty paisa coin, 25 paisa coin, 10 paisa coin etc. are actual money.

2. Money of Account-Money of account is that in terms of which debts, prices and other transactions are expressed and accounts are maintained. The theory was expounded by Lord *J.M. Keynes*. According to keynes money of account is the money in which debt and prices and general purchasing power is expressed. For example, in India accounts are kept in rupees and paisa and all debts and contracts are also expressed in these terms and so they are money of account in India.

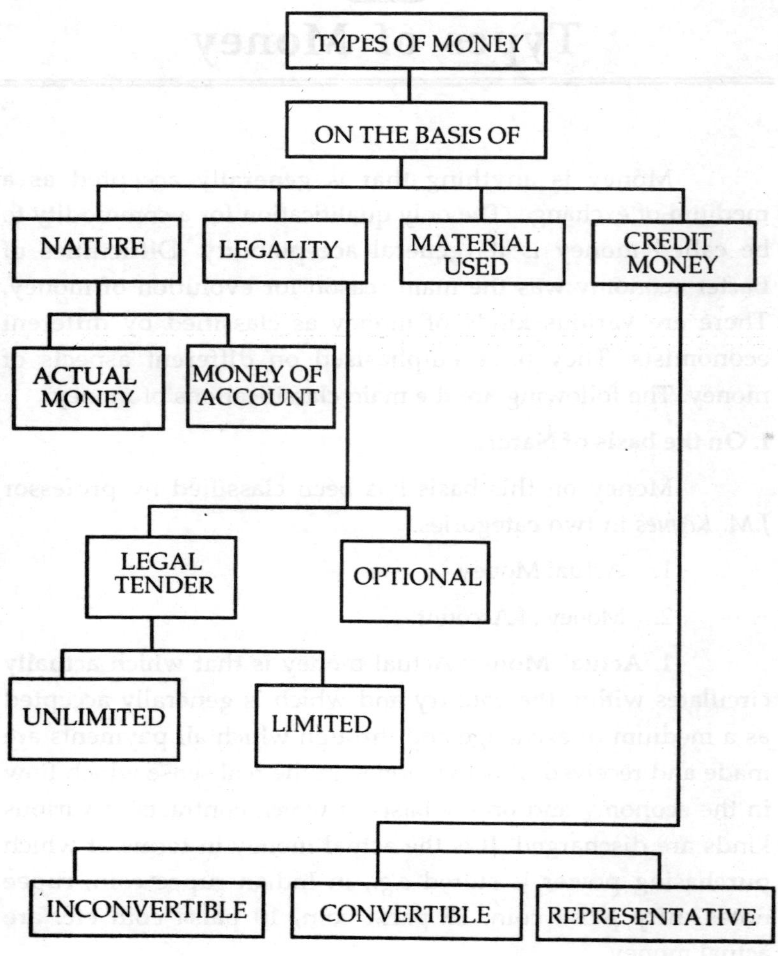

Professor Keynes has further classified **money proper** into two category:

(i) Commodity Money, and

(ii) Representative Money

(iii) Managed Money

(i) Commodity Money-Commodity money is composed of money metals and its intrinsic value is equal to the face value. It is the full bodied money or standard money. It serves both as a medium of exchange and store of value.

(ii) Representative Money- It is the kind of money which is made to cheap metal and works as the medium of exchange. Mostly it is in circulation in form of paper money. It has also been held as fiat money because it is a kind of token or representative money. The notes issued by the governments or issued by the banks in the shape of bank notes are examples of representative money. This kind of money circulates freely as medium of exchange but does not serve as 'store of value'. They represent store of value *i.e.* they are convertible into commodity money.

Representative money is further classified into convertible money and inconvertible money. The former is actually convertible into coins on demand at a fixed rate, while the latter is not convertible.

(iii) Managed Money : It is the kind of money resembling to Fiat Money but it is related to an objective standard of value. It is a hybrid between commodity money and fiat money."

II. On the Basis of Legality

On the basis of legal point of view money may be again classified in *two* categories.

(1) Legal Tender Money

(i) Unlimited legal tender money

(ii) Limited legal tender money

(2) Optional Money

(1) Legal Tender Money– It is that money which is accepted as payment for debt or any other transactions. It has the force of law at its back. Legal Tender Money is the kind of money to which every individual is legally under obligation to receive it as a mode payment. No body can refuse to accept any amount of this money on any ground if it is genuine. In India one rupee note and half rupee any ground if it is genuine. In India one rupee note and half rupee coin are legal tender money but the coins less than it are limited Legal Tender Money.

Legal tender money is further divided into (i) unlimited legal tender money and (ii) limited legal tender money.

(i) Unlimited legal tender money is one which has to be accepted as a medium of payment up to any amount. The rupee in India is an example of unlimited legal tender money.

(ii) Limited legal tender money, on the other hand, is one which has to be accepted only upto a certain limited amount. For example, in India smaller coins of 25 paisa, 20 paisa, 10 paisa, 5 paisa etc. are limited legal tender money. One can refuse to accept these beyond a certain prescribed limit.

2. Optional Money– It is the kind of money just opposite to Legal Tender Money. It is not the legal obligation of any one to accept this kind of money. It will be at liberty of the acceptor to accept this kind of money and payment or price of the big liquidation or debt. Optional Money is not a legal tender money but it is generally accepted in discharge of debt and in other payments. Bank notes, cheques, bills of exchange etc. are examples of optional money.

Diagramatic Description of Money
(According to Keynes)

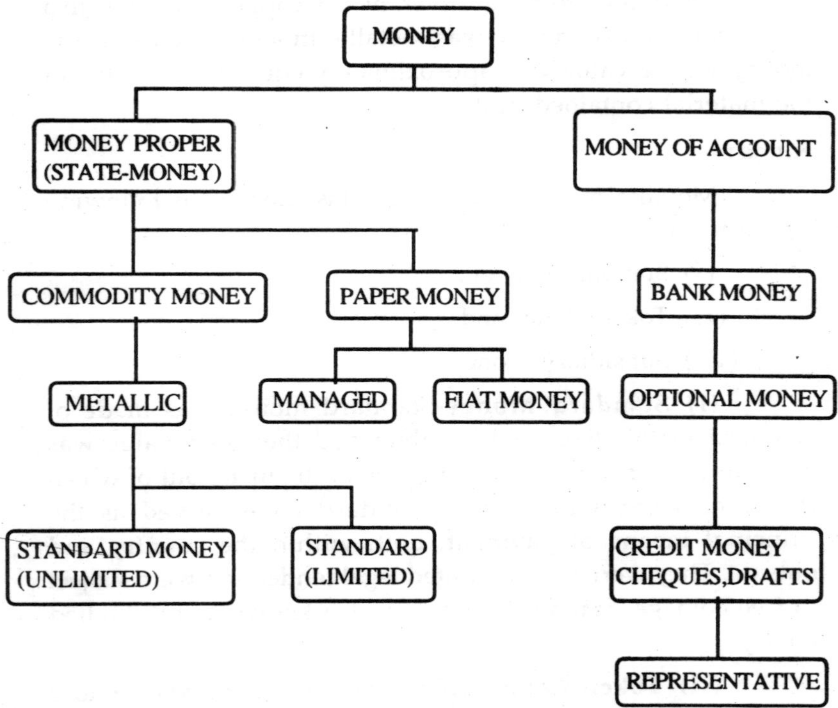

It is called optional money because a creditor may or may not accept it in the discharge of debts *e.g.* a creditor need not accept a cheque from a debtor in discharge of a debt. All credit instruments come under this head, as cheques, postal orders, bank drafts, promosory notes, bills of exchange. As they are issued by banks and non-statutory bodies so they lack of characteristic of being legal money. Technically speaking, this type of money is not money proper as it does not possess the essential characteristic of general acceptability.

III. On the Basis of Material used

On this basis money may be classified as follows:

(1) Metallic Money

(2) Paper Money

1. Metallic Money– Metallic money prevailed for a long time in the economic activity of people. Metallic money consists of coins of gold and sliver, nickel, copper or bronze. In a sense, commodity money was metallic money because it was money whose value was approximately equal to the value of the material contained in it.

Kinds :

Metallic money is further classified in to following sub-head as :

(i) Standard Money,

(ii) Token Money and

(iii) Subsidiary Money.

(i) Standard Money-Standard money was made of standard metals like gold or silver and their face value was equal to their intrinsic value or value of the metal out of which the coins were made. These standard coins served as the principal means of payment, both within the country and outside. They were also unlimited legal tender and were subject to free coinage. Standard money is also known as full bodied money.

(ii) Token Coins– Token coins are those coins whose face value is more than their intrinsic value *i.e.* the value of the material out of which they are made. These coins are characterised by shortness in weight and so they are intrinsically worthless as money. Thus token coins are :

(a) limited legal tender,

(b) not subject to freecoinage, and

(c) have face value more than the value of the material of which they are made.

(iii) Subsidiary Money– Small change as 50 paisa pieces, 25 paisa pieces, 10 paisa pieces, 5 paisa pieces, etc. in India is example of Subsidiary Money. It is used for the purpose of small change while making transactions.

Merits

Although it is not considered to be a good monetary system, yet it has following merits:

(1)*Difficult to copied*- It cannot be copied by the people since it takes a lot of time and technical know-how.

(2)*Check on Un-limited Supply*- It restricts the lust of the Governments to increase the unlegitmate supply of money since the supply of money can not be increased so rapidly. Coinage takes time.

(3)*Longer Life*- It is not subject to a shorter life in comparison to paper currency. It last long.

(4)*Not Harmful*- In case of standard coin the possesser of the money is not harmed by the governments decision of non-monetization.

(5)*Face Value*- It always bears its face value and this avoids any kind of hesitation by the acceptors.

Demerits

Despite of the above merits , it has lost its omnipotency in the modern economies because of reasons mentioned below :

(1)*Inelastic Supply*-The supply of money under metallic system becomes comparatively inelastic. In cannot be responsive enough to fight the immediate need of more money.

(2)*Rigid in Operation*-It brings rididity in the operation of the monetary system.

(3)*Costly* -Coinage is a costly affair.

(4)*Inconvenient* -It lacks quick transportability.

(5)*Wastage of Metal*-It is inconvenient in making big payments.

(6)*Inconvenient* - It involves wastage of costly metals. Difficulties arises when the supply of metals becomes insufficient.

2. Paper Money– Paper money originated as a substitute for metallic money. But later on it became representative money, representing certain weight of gold or silver and ultimately it has become money as we see it now.

Paper money is the money made of paper bearing all the essential char-denomination

Paper money consists of notes issued by the government or banks, generally by the Central Bank. There are three main kinds of paper money *viz.*,

(i) Representative Paper Money,

(ii) Convertible Paper Money and

(iii) Inconvertible Paper Money.

(i) Representative Money– Paper money is known as representative paper money when cent per cent metallic reserves are kept by the issuing authority against the issue of paper money or currency notes.

(ii) Convertible Paper Money– If the issuing authority promises to convert currency notes into standard money on demand, it is called convertible paper money.

(iii) Inconvertible Paper Money– Inconvertible paper money is also know as fiat money. Fiat money or inconvertible money is money by command. Fiat money or Inconvertible paper money is backed by legal force which means that the said currency is enforced by law. Thus Fiat money or inconvertible paper money is not convertible into standard money on demand. This type of money is not wholly backed by the reserve. Only proportional or minimum reserve is kept and so this money is called money by command *i.e.* on the force of law and nobody can refuse to accept it. In most parts of the world, fiat money or inconvertible paper money is the most important form of money now-a-days.

Merits

(1) *Elastic Supply*- Supply of paper money is elastic. It is easy for the government to adjust the supply of money according to the needs of the time.

(2) *Low Issuing Cost*- The cost of issuing the paper currency is far less than the metallic money.

(3) *No Westage of Metals*- It does not involves the wastage of costly metals.

(4) *High-Transportability and Portability*- It has high degree of transportability and portability.

(5) *Easy to Keep*- It can easily be kept anywhere.

(6) *Convenient in Big Payment*- Paper money is convenient in making big payments.

Demerits

(1) *Leads to Inflation*- It often to inflation. It does not provide any check and governments in order to escape monetary crises increase the supply.

(2) *Less Durable*- It is less durable since it is made of paper. It is subject to decay by moisture, rain and insects.

(3) *Non-Monetization*- In the case of non-monetization the possesser of the money always looses.

(4) *Forgery*- Forgery in paper currency is very much possible.

(iv) Credit Money or Bank Money–Modern economists have given another form of money *i.e.* credit money or bank money. The credit money can also be called as 'promise-to-pay' money. Credit money is the most popular form of money in the modern time to meet the transactions safely. It is the swiftest kind of money to meet larger transactions. In the modern days majority of the business activities are undertaken in the form of credit money. Various credit instruments like cheque, drafts and bills of exchange are termed as credit money or bank money. These are also called credit instrument or negatiable instruments.

❐

5

Present Currency System

The Indian monetary system has had a very chequered career-from silver standard to gold exchange standard, to gold bullion standard, to steling exchange standard and finally and presently to I.M.F. Standard or what it may we called 'Gold Parity Standard.' In India, rupee is a unit of account. The Indian rupee is therefore expressed terms of rupee. Development of Indian currency System has had a long history. History of Indian currency in systematic form could be started only after 1880. Since then form of Indian currency may be studied as follows :

DEVELOPMENT OF INDIAN CURRENCY

Development of Indian Currency System passed through several efforts and stages as mentioned below :

(1) *Efforts of East India Co.* : The role of East India Co. has been significant in providing new shape to Indian currency. The credit goes to Co. for manufacturing pure and fixed weight gold and silver coins. These both types of coins were transferable . The Co. fixed the ratio of 1:15 in these coins and provided shape of legal tender.

(2) *Currency Act.1835* : With a view to achieve uniformity in all its rulling areas, the East India Co. enacted the Currency Act in 1835. Under the provision of the Act, only silver coin declared as legal tender. Though during this period gold coins were also in currency but it was not recognised as legal tender. But with the passage time with the discovery of new gold mines and decline in production of silver disturbances arised in the currency of silver.

(3) *Mansfield Commission* : The Mansfield Commission was appointed in 1866. The Commission recommended for issue of paper currency alongwith silver and gold coins. Though the Government had taken steps on the recommendation of the Commission, but because of fall in value of silver, silver standard became out of operation. To study the arised problem in the silver currency system, the Herschell Committee was constituted in 1992.

(4) *The Heschell Committee* : The Committee mainly studied in the context of silver standard. The committee recommended for discontinued free mint of silver and gold coins. With a view to implementation of recommendation of the committee in 1893 the currency Act was enached.

(5) *The Currency Act 1993* : For implementation of recommendation of Heschell Committee, Currency Act was enacted in 1893. The Act terminated both type of coins *i.e.* gold and silver. It was mentioned in the Act that only government can mint silver coins as per requirement. According to provision of the Act rupee declared as token coin.

(6) *The Fowler Committee* : Though with the implemen-tation of recommentation of Heschell Committee, exchange rate of rupee increased but because of varities of problems its value again started declining in 1898. To study the problem, a new committee was constituted under the chairmanship of *Sir Henry Fowler*. The Committee recommended against free mint of silver.

(7) *Currency Act 1899* : With a view to implementation of the recommendation of the *Folwer Committee,* in 1899 a new currency act was enacted.

(8) *The chamberlain Commission* : The Fowler Committee in its recommdation criticised for continution Gold Exchange Standard. With a view to find the solution of the problem in 1913 the Chamberlain commission found Gold Exchange Standard most appropriate for India.The commission rejected necessity of gold money currencies and emphasised for issue of paper currency. The commission also recommdnded for strengthend of gold reserves. The recommendation of the Commission could not implemented because soon after the first world war had taken place.

(9) *Breakdown of Gold Exchange Standard* : Indian currency was badly effected by the first world war. The Government lost the faith of people. Peoples started withdraw their deposits from Post Offices and Banks and demand of gold in lieu of currency note had increased. Though best efforts had been made by the Government to save monetary standard. But the economy was absolutely ruined and Gold Exchange Standard breakdowned.

(10) *The Babiagton Smith Committee,1919* : Soon after war operation, trade relation of India with Europian countries continued resulted which hereculean changes taken place in foreign exchange rate.

(11) *Hilton Young Commission,1995* : Important fluctuation had taken place in the exchange rate of Indian rupee in 1920 and 1925. To study the problem, a commission was appointed in 1925 under the chairmanship of Hilton Young. The Commission recommended for adoption of Gold-Parity Standard. The commission not found any utility of Gold currency in circulation. The other important recommendation of the commission was with regard to establishment of a Central Bank in the country.

(12) *Currency Act,1927* : With a view to implementation of recommendation of Hilton Young Commission, a new currency Act was enacted in March 1927. According to the provision of the Act the exchange value of Indian Rupee determined equal to 1 seling and 6 paisee.

(13) *Sterling Exchange Standard* : With the abandoment of Gold Standard by UK on September 21,1931, the Government of India had to postpone the currency Act on September 22,1931. On September 25, 1931 value of Rupee was linked with sterling. It had ended convertibility of rupee into gold and sterling standard was established in India.

(14) *Establishment of Reserve Bank of India* : To establish central Bank in India, the Reserve Bank of India Act was enacted in 1934. The Reserve Bank of India was established on April 1, 1935. The establishment of Reserve Bank of India is a landmark and an important event in the history of Indian money. The Bank has been enthrusted with the responsibility of exercise control over money and credit.

(15) *Effects of Second World War* : Industrial and agricultural production had increased during world war second. The exchange rate of rupee remained static . During war period paper currencies was issued to face the situation of price rise.

(16) *Empire Dollar Pool* : During the period of war demand for US dollar increased. With a view to make availability of dollar easier, in 1937, British Empire and Commonwealth countries Jointly established 'Empire Dollar Pool.'

(17) *Demonetisation, 1946* - On January 1946, the Government of India demonetise notes of big denomination. It was first demonetised currency notes of 1000,5,000 and 10,000. These currencfy notes were withdrawn from circulation. This step lost the faith of people in paper currency.

(18) *Membership of I.M.F.* : In October 1946 India accetped membership of I.M.F. and the World Bank and announced value of its currency in gold or Dollar in place of serlling. Hence value of Rupee was determined equal to 30.2250 cent and 0.268601 gram of gold.

(19) *Effects of Partition* : The whole economic structure of India adversely affected by partition. In order to establish monetary system in Pakistan, the Reserve Bank of India Act was modified in 1947 under which provision has been made for continution of paper currency and coins in Pakistan upto September 30,1947.

(20) *Devaluation in 1949* : On September 1949 UK devaluated pond sterlling by 30.5 per cent. Hence, the Government of India also announced for devaluation of Indian Rupee by 30.5 per cent. With this devaluation value of Indian rupee fixed in form of dollar equal to 21 cent in place of 30. 2250 cent and 0.186521 gms. of Gold.

(21) *Sterling Balance* : During the period of world war second, goods in large quantity exported to UK. The payment of such exports accumulated in the form of sterling balance. The sterling balance which was 64 crores in 1939, had increased to 1662 crores in 1962.

(22) *Deficit Financing* : The Indian Currency specially affected in the beginning of plan era. Deficit Financing was adopted for fulfillment of development expenditure of the country. Deficit financing increased the prices and several new problems faced in circulation of currency.

(23) *Decimal Coinage System* : In April 1957 decimal coinage system was introduced in India. Under this system rupee was announced as standard unit of money and small unit fixed in the form of paisee. 100 paise announced equal to 1 Rupee. Gradually old coins of this standard were withdrawn from circulation and at the place of which coins of 1,2,3,5,10,20,25, and 50 paise were brought into circulation . This system made measurement of value much easier.

(24) *Devaluation of Rupee in 1966* : Second devaluation of Indian rupee by 36.5 per cent was announced on June 6,1966. With this devaluation value of rupee fixed equal to 13.33 cent or gold equal to 0.1185 gram. The main cause responsible for the devaluation was unfavourable balance of payment of the country.

(25) *Effects of Dollar Crisis* : In December 1971 US dollar was devaluated by 7.9 per cent. Because of devaluation of dollar new value of Indian rupee was fixed equal to 7.279 per dollar in place of equal to Rs. 7.5 per dollar. Hence Indian rupee revaluated by 3.03 per cent. Afterwards US devaluated dollar by 10 per cent in 1973 . Since then system of Fixed Exchange Rate was abandoned and ideology of Flexible Rate of Exchange was developed.

(26) *Demonetisation,1978* : In 1946, though big notes were demonetised but keeping into consideration the need of the country the same have restarted. On January 16,1978 these big note (1,000,5,000 and 10,000 Rs Note) demonetised again. Amount of these notes at the time of demonetisation was equal to Rs. 145.42 crore.

(27) *Devaluation of Indian Rupee in 1991*- In 1991 Indian rupee was further devaluated by 18 percent. The devaluation was thought proper to correct unfavorable balance payment

MONETARY SYSTEM PRIOR TO INDEPENDENCE

The Indian monetary system has passed through various stages of development. In fact, the Indian system has had an eventful career. The silver standard was followed by gold bullion standard, gold exchange standard-sterling exchange standard, and finally by the system of Special Drawing Rights (SDRs)

In 1835, the silver rupee, weighing 180 grains, 11/12 fine silver was adopted as a standard coin and legal tender throughout India. This started the era of silver standard in India. Around 1873, due to the discovery of new silver mines, world supply of silver increased and the old price of silver began to fall from 1874. The Government decided to abandon silver standardd in 1893.

India was on the Gold Exchange Standard during the period 1900-1917 . Although gold coin did not circulate in the country but the rupee coin (silver rupee) was convertible to sterling at the fixed rate of 1sh. 4 d. The Government of India maintained the Gold Standard Reserve and the Paper Currency Reserve in London though a branch of each was located in India also. The Gold Exchange Standard had very intricate system of working. The fixed rate of 1 sh. 4d. was prevented from falling below this rate by the sale of Reserve Council Bills (or Sterling Drafts). The gold exchange standard broken down in the middle of 1917 and was given up.

The Currency Act of 1927 was said to have established Gold Bullion Standard in India. Since the Indian currency could be either convertible to gold or sterling, the standard could be characterised as gold bullion-cum-sterling exchange standard. After September 1931, when England went on the gold bullion standard, India's monetary standard became simply sterling exchange gold bullion standard. India's monetary system became sterling exchange standard.

Between September 21, 1921 and March,1,1947 rupee continued its link with the sterling although sterling was no longer related to gold. In other words, roughly during the period of over 15 years, India's currency was on sterling exchange standard. On March 1,1947, i.e. the date of India's joining the IMF India's monetary system also changed.

PRESENT MONETARY STANDARD IN INDIA

The Reserve Bank of India was set up in 1935, under the Reserve Bank of India Act, 1934. The Reserve Bank was asked to follow the Proportional Reserve System of note issue. Under this system the Reserve Bank had to maintain not less than 40 per cent reserves against note issue in gold coins, gold bullion or sterling securities, provided that a minimum of gold reserve worth Rs. 40 crores was maintained. The remaining 60 per cent of the reserve was backed by one-rupee or rupee coins or approved bills of exchange of the Government of India securities.

After getting the membership of the IMF in 1947, the rate of exchange of Indian rupee was fixed in terms of gold instead of sterling. Indian monetary standard was no longer the Sterling Exchange Standard, it had now changed over to the Gold Parity Standard. Now the Reserve Bank was not under any obligation to back the 40% reserve only in sterling securities, it could now also keep foreign securities other than sterling.

In October 1956, the Reserve Bank of India Act was amended in order to remove the rigidity of the proportional reserve system to meet the growing needs of a developing economy. By the Amendment Act of 1956, it was provided that the Reserve Bank should maintain a minimum reserve of Rs. 400 crores in foreign securities and Rs. 115 crores in gold coins and bullion. Under special circumstances, the unit of foreign securities could be lowered to Rs. 300 crores. In October 1957, an Ordinance was issued empowering the Reserve Bank to reduce the minimum currency reserve from Rs. 400 crores to Rs. 200 crores, of which gold holding were not to fall below Rs. 115 crores. This in effect meant reduction in the foreign securities holding of the Reserve Bank to a small amount of Rs. 85 crores. The drastic reduction was necessitated by the rapid depletion of foreign exchange reserves due to adverse balance of payments.

India's paper currency is an unlimited legal tender money which is convertible. The present thinking in the monetary circles is that it is no use making money internally convertible. So long as the monopoly power of note issue rests with the Reserve Bank of India, there is no need to make paper money convertible into gold or bullion.

PRESENT CURRENCY SYSTEM OF INDIA

Under the Reserve Bank of India Act, 1934 and Banking Regulation Act, 1949, the Reserve Bank of India has wide powers to control and regulate the volume of currency and credit in the country.

The Reserve Bank of India has the monopoly power of note issue.

India has adopted the decimal coinage system which came into operation from April 1, 1957. Under the system, the rupee remains unchanged both in value and nomenclature. The rupee is divided into 100 equal parts. The naya paisa has now become the primary unit of Indian currency and its multiples of 2,3,5,10 20,25 and 50 constitute the different units of the new currency. The advantage of the decimal system of coinage stems from its simple business calculations. There are one-rupee coins, 50 paise coins, 2 paise coins and 1 paisa coins. Originally, the rupee coin was full-bodied coin made of silver, but now it is minted out of nickel, coins are used to perform small transactions.

The Reserve Bank of India has the sole authority of note issue. With the exception of one-rupee note, all currency notes are issued by the Reserve Bank of India. At present, the Reserve Bank of India issues currency notes of the hundred and five hundred rupees. During the period 1950-51 to Sept.1996 the money supply (M_1) increased from Rs. 2,016 crores to Rs. 2,17,225 crores. The currency with the people has increased from Rs. 1,467 crores in 1950-51 to Rs. 1,19,695 crores in September 1996.

Exchange Value of the Indian Rupee : Since the time of joining the membership of the IMF the external value or the exchange value of the Indian rupee is expressed in terms of gold or dollars. On 20th September, 1949, the Government of India decided to devalue the rupee in terms of U.S. dollar. The exchange value of rupee changed from 30.225 cents to 21 cents. The gold parity of the Indian rupee fell from 0.26691 grams to 0.186621 grams of fine gold. The Government of India took this step following the decision of the U.K. and other countries of the sterling area (except Pakistan) to devalue their currencies in terms of the U.S. dollar.

Indian rupee was further devalued by 36.5 per cent on June 5,1966. The main objective of this devaluation of the rupee was to correct the chronic and fundamental disequilibrium of the balance of payments. In June 1966, the exchange rates were Pond 1= Rs. 21, and $1 = Rs. 7.50 . But after the 14.3 per cent devaluation of the pound in November, 1967, the exchange rate stood at $ 1=Rs.18. The continued weakness of the pound and high rate of British inflation forced India to end the rupee link with pound sterling on September 24, 1975. At present, the exchange value of the rupee is determined daily with reference to a basket of selected currencies of 5 countries which are India's major trading partners.

The RBI effected an exchange rate adjustment on July 1,1991 in which the value of the rupee declined by about 7 to 9 per cent against five major international currencies. There was another exchange rate adjustment on July 3,1991 in which the value of the rupee further declined by 10 to 11 per cent against the major currencies . Considering certain other minor exchange rate adjustments, the value of the Indian rupee depreciated by over 20 per cent against the basket of 5 major currencies in July 1991.

After the introduction of the unified system of exchange rate determination, the value of Indian Rupee has stabalised in the International market. As on March 23, 1996 the exchange rates were Pond 1 = Rs 53.90, US $ 1 = Rs. 35.12 and Japanese yen 100 = Rs. 32.84.

In brief, there have been significant changes in the structure and working of the Indian Monetary System over the last few decades. Changes in the monetary system, especially after 1967, have been brought about to meet the requirements of a growing economy.

MERITS AND DEMERITS OF INDIAN CURRENCY SYSTEM

Merits

The Indian currency system is quite old. Its main merits are discussed below :

(1) *Flexible* : One of the important feature of Indian currency system is its flexibility . After keeping reserve funds equal to 200 crores of gold and foreign securities, as much as required. Currencies notes may be issued. Hence it is not required to increase the quantity of reserves to increase quantity of money

(2) *Economy* :The Indian Currency System posesses quality of economy. Neither more reserves are required nor more expenditure are needed on printing of money.

(3) *Legality* : The merit of legality is also found in Indian currency because it is operated by the Reserve Bank of India.

(4) *Public Confidence* : Because legality, Indian currency posesses merits of public confidence.

(5) *Simplicity* : Indian currency system is quite simple. Hence, there is not difficulty for public to understand.

(6) *Suitable in Crisis* : As quality of flexibility exists in the Indian Currency System, it found most suitable at the time of crisis . Whenever in emergency there required to increase in the quantity of money. It can be increased without much of difficulty.

Demerits

Though present Indian currency system is not lacking of merits but it also has some demerits. Some of the important demerits of Indian currency system are discussed below:

(1) *Lack of Convertibility* : The Indian Currency System is lacking of convertibility therefore it failled to obtained much of people confidence. Only for foreign payments and after approval by the Reserve Bank of India, currency of India is convertible.

(2) *Fear of Inflation* : There always exists fear of inflation. It is a major drawback of Indian currency system resulted of which quontam of inflation in the country continuosly rising. Due to rising problem of inflation, severally Indian Currency had demonetised and de-valuated.

(3) *Deficit Financing* : Because of much flexibility exists in the Indian Currency System, severally Government of India prepared deficit financing budget which proved harmful in the longrun.

❑

6

Theories of Value of Money

Meaning

The value of money is its purchasing power, *i.e.*, its capacity to command goods or services in exchange for itself. The larger the volume of goods and services a unit of money can buy in its exchange, greater will be its value. This shows that the value of money depends upon the prices of goods and services. If the level of prices is high, a unit of money will buy less goods and services and if on the other hand the level of prices is low, a unit of money will buy more goods and services. This shows that the value of money or its reverse, the level of prices, does not remain constant. It goes on changing from time to time. Now the question is as to why does the value of money change? The answer to this question is given by the Quantity Theory which explains that the value of money or its reverse, the price level depends upon the quantity of money, *i.e.*, the supply of money (demand of money remaining the same) in the country. Thus whenever there is a change in the quantity of money in the country, the value of money will change.

Definition

The concept of value of money has been defined by economists differently as mentioned below:

D.H. Robertson defines, "By value of money we mean the amount of things in general which will be given in exchange for a unit of money."

J.M. Keynes defines, "Since the purchasing power of money in a given context depends upon the quantity of goods and services which a unit of money will purchase. It follows that it can be

measured by the price of a composite commodity made-up of the various individual goods and services in proportion corresponding to their importance as objects of expenditure."

Irving Fisher defines, "The purchasing power of money is reciprocal to the level of prices, so that the study of the purchasing power of money is identical with the study of price level."

Dissatisfied with the quantity theory of money, *Keynes* developed the Saving-Investment approach of value of money. According to *Keynes* the changes in price level are due to the change in the level of income.

Mr. Davanzatti was the first ittalian economist who expounded the Quantity Theory of Money. but the credit goes to the American economist Irving Fisher for popularised the approach. Irving Fisher given the approach a quantitative form and explained with the help of the equaltion know as equation of exchange. There are two version of the Quantity Theory of money as given below :

(i) The Transaction Approach, and

(ii) The Cash Balance Approach.

The above two approches have been discussed in following description.

QUANTITY THEORY OF MONEY

The value of money means, that what a unit of money can buy in terms of goods and services. We know that the price of goods and services or the general price level does not remain constant. Hence the value of money is always changing. There is inverse relationship between general price level and value of money. When general price level increases , it decreases the general value of money. If general price level decreases, it increases general value of money.

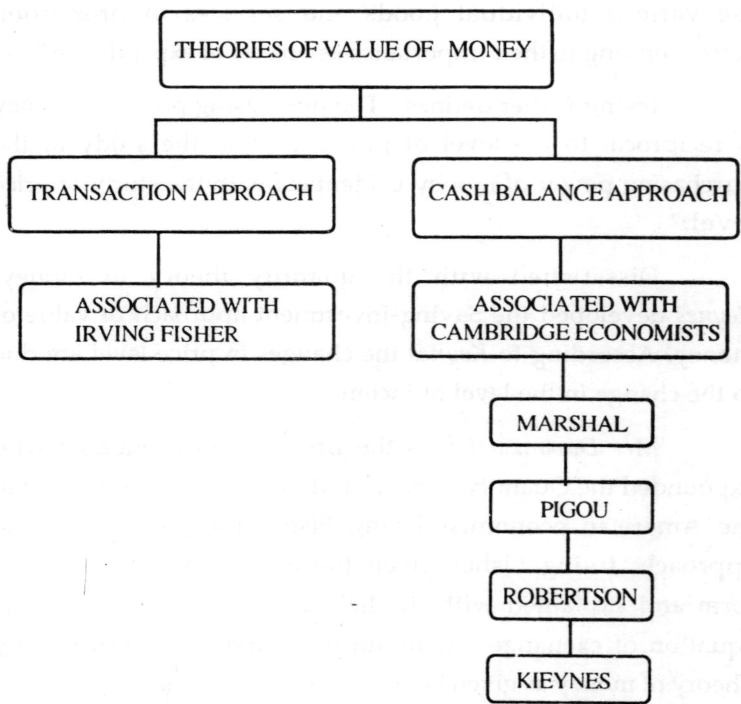

The earliest writers pointed out the close relations existing between changes in general prices and changes in the quantity of money. The idea was developed and came to be known as the Quantity Theory of Money. The theory states that the general price level depends upon the total quantity of money in the country.

The qunatity theory of money explains that the value of money during a certain period depends upon the quantity of money in circulation in a given economy. The quantity of money supply determines the general price level as well as value of money. If there is any change taken place in the money supply, it will leads to change in the general price level directly and the value of money will be affected inversely in the same proportion. If the quantity of money in circulation is doubled, other things remained the same, the general price level will be doubled and the value of money comes to halved. Similarly, if the quantity of money comes to halved the price level will be halved but the value of money will be doubled . Eminient economists explains the aforesaid situation as follows :-

F.W. Tausing Stated, " Double the quantity of money, and other things being equal, prices will be twice as high as before; and the value of money as one half. Halve the quantity of money, and other things being equal, prices will be one half of what they were before, and the value of money double. "

J.S. Mill explained, " The value of money, other things being the same, varies inversely as its quantity ; increase of quantity lowers the value and every diminution raising it in a ratio exactly equivalent."

Benham says, "In its most rigid form theory asserts that any given percentage increase or decrease in the quantity of money will lead to the same percentage increase or decrease in the general level of price.

The phrase "other things being equal" means that there should be no change in velocity of circulation of money, the use of credit instruments as money and barter transactions. At the same time; the demand of money must remain constant.

DETERMINATION OF THE VALUE OF MONEY

The value of money like the value of any other commodity, is determined by the demand for and supply of money.

Demand of Money– Money is the medium of exchange. The demand for money comes from the supply of goods in the country. The supply of goods depends in a given period, on the total volume of production in the country and the total volume of production, in its turn,depends on the efficiency of the factors of production and not on the value of money. Hence during a given period when the quantity of money changes the total volume of production will remain the same and so the supply of goods will also remain constant.

It means that demand for money does not change during a give period when the quantity of money changes. Hence the value of money will be determined by the supply of money, *i.e.,* the quantity of money. Thus if the quantity of money in circulation is doubled the price level will also be doubled whereas the value of money will be halved.

Supply of Money—Let us find out as to what determines the supply of money during a given period. The supply of money is equal to the total quantity of money used to purchase the goods. But we know that each piece of money may be used several times during a given period and each time a piece of money changes hands for buying goods, it increases the supply of money. Let us suppose that a rupee is used five times in a week for buying goods; the total supply will be equal to 5 rupees and not one rupee. The average number of times a unit of money changes hands for buying goods and services during a given period is known as *velocity of money.* Thus the supply of money is equal to the quantity of money multiplied by velocity of money. Change in the supply of money will cause proportionate change in the price level.

This is the oldest quantity theory of money. The theory in its original form stated that demand for money remaining the same, the price level varies directly with the quantity of money in circulation.

Equation of Exchange

Fisher explained the Quantity Theory of Money algebracally . The Equation of Exchange was developed by Irving Fisher as is given below ;

$$MV = PT$$

where M=Quantity of money in circulation.

V=Velocity of money in circulation .

It indicates average turnover of a unit of money in change hands.

P = Price Level

T =Total Volume of transactions of goods and services during a given period of time .

The above equation has two facets, these are MV and PT. MV indicates total supply of money in the economy, M indicates purchase of goods and services on a particular period of time. It changes hands by more than once. Hence total money supply is represented by the quantity of money multiplied by its velocity. It is represented by MV in the above equation. PT in the euqtion represents total demand for money or the money value of all the goods and services brought during a given period of time.

Hence in the euqtion total volume of transaction (T) multiplied by price level (P) which indicates the total demand of money. Thus, MV=PT , or the total supply of money (MV) is equal to total demand of money enable the total transactions at a given price (PT) . The equation is known as the cash transaction equation which can also be expressed as follows :

$$P = \frac{MV}{T}$$

The above equation shows that the price level is determined by the total quantity of money divided by the total transactions. According to this relationship total quantity of money determines the price level provided P and T remained constant.

However, the above equation is criticised by some economists on the ground that the theory absolutely ignores the credit money as well as its velocity, though both are equeally important in the modern economies. *Irving Fisher* realised the mistake and extended his original version of equations considering the credit money as well as velocity of money. The extended form of Fisher's equation is explained below :

$$MV = M'V' = PT$$

or $$P = \frac{MV + M'V'}{T}$$

Here, M' Represents Credit Money

V' Represents Velocity of Credit Money

M,V, P and T represents the same as mentioned above.

The extended version of Fisher's equation explains that the price level (P) is directly related to total quantity of money (original money and bank money) multiplied by its velocity. However, it is inversely related to T. *Fisher* extended his original equation on the basic proposition that the price level and the value of money is a function of money supply provided other things remained the same.

The other things which are mainly supposed to same are mainly includes M', V', V and T. If they remain constant, price level will change directly and proportionately with the change in the money supply. Price level affects the value of money inversely and in turn change in money supply influence the value of money inversely.

Let us explain it through a numerical example. Suppose Total Money in the market is Rs. 100 and its velocity is 5 per unit. Amount of transactions is 500, Total Bank Money is 200 and its velocity is 10 per unit. Now let us find out the price level.

From the above statement

$$M = 100$$

$$V = 5\,;\, V' = 10$$

$$M' = 200$$

$$T = 500$$

The Fishers Formula is $$P = \frac{MV = M'V'}{T}$$

By putting the values in the equation we get

$$P = \frac{(100 \times 5) + (200 \times 10)}{500}$$

Or $$P = \frac{500 + 2000}{500}$$

Or $$P = \frac{2500}{500}$$

Or $$P = 5$$

Hence the price level is 5.

Graphical Presentation

"The Quantity Theory asserts that (provided the velocity of circulation and volume of trade are unchanged) if there increase in the number of dollars whether by renaming coins or by de-basing coins or by increasing coinage, prices will be increased in the same proportion ."

According to *Fisher* version of Quantity Theory of Money, the changes in the value of money as a result of changes in the quantity of money is brought about through. While quantity of money and price level are directly proportional to each other, Quantity of money and price level on the one hand and value of money on the another are inversely proportional to each other.

Hence it is clear that the value of Money is inversely proportional to the quantity of money in circulation in the economy. It may be explained through the help of following diagram :-

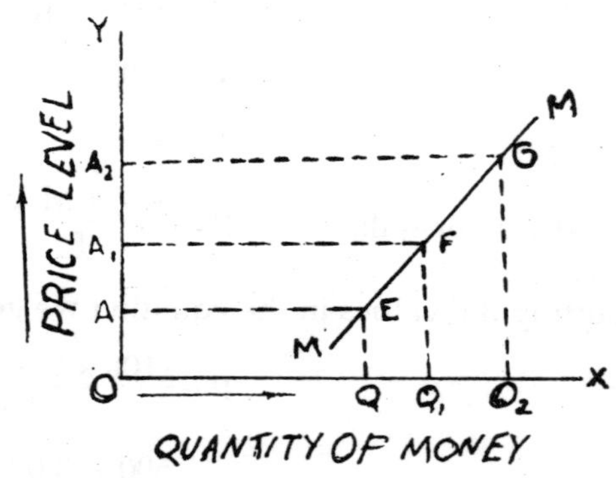

In the diagram the Quantity of Money has been shown on the X-axis whereas the price level has been shown on the Y-axis. General price level in the economy is OA. The supply of money or its quantity is OQ. Suppose the Quantity of Money increase from OQ to OQ^1 the price goes to OA^1 from OA. Hence there is AA^1 change in the price level which is equal to OQ^1 which is the change in the Quantity of Money. This change in price-level has brought down the value of money also in the same proportion. A further increase in the quantity of Money from OQ^1 to OQ^2 the price level goes to OA_2 from OA_1 which further reduces the value of money. The Curve M_1M shows the relation between the change in the quantity and the price level in the economy.

Assumptions

1. **Fisher** assumed that V and V' in the equation do not change with the change in the quantity (M). Regarding T, the volume of trade, he pointed that it also remains constant during a period when M changes. The argument is that volume of trade depends on the aggregate volume of production which in its turn is determined by the supply and efficiency of factors of production. But these things do not change when the quantity of money changes. Hence T would also remain constant. But *Fisher* has assumed a long period of time or V and T to be constant.

2. According to **Fisher,** the velocity of circulation of money depends on the habit of people and methods of business and hence they too do not change over a given period of time. He also assumed that M' bears a constant relation to M, the quantity of legal money.

3. **Fisher** also assumes the existence of full employment in the country. It means that there are no idle resources in the country and as such there is no possibility of increasing goods and services with more money.

Under the above assumption *Fisher* says that changes in M will cause direct proportional changes in the price level. The conclusion may be stated as "other things remaining equal, the general price level varies directly and proportionately with the supply of money and inversely and proportionately with the demand for money."

Criticism of the Quantity Theory of Money

1. *Based Upon Unreal Assumptions* : : The theory is based upon unreal assumptions that other things never remain constant. It has been assumed that certain things will remain constant. But in a modern dynamic society it is not possible to keep these things constant. Irving Fisher, himself has felt that the theory will not held good in the period of transition.

2. *Change in Prices is not due to Money supply only* : It is criticised that theeffect of changes in the quantity of money do not change the price proportionately as is stated in the Fisher's equation. Money supply is one of the causes of bringing a change in the prices of the commodities but not the only cause of increase in the demand which may also raise the price level. Only under very special circumstances doubling of the quantity of money will double the price level. Usually the price level may go up to more or fall down to less than that.

3. *Change in Money Supply may not always change the Price Level* : It has been observed that the money supply does not always tend to effect the price level and consequently the value of money. Sometimes it does not affect the price level at all. According to *Crowther* :

"It cannot even explain why it is that a creation of money will sometime take and start off a rise in prices, while at another time an equal creation may have no effect at all."

4. *Velocity of Money may Increase* : The velocity of money may increase by the rapidity of economic activities like transportation, use of book credit etc. In such cases the price level will also go up.

5. *Increase in Transaction will bring down Prices* : If the economy improves its transportation facilities , with the diversification of industries and greater production which will consequently bring a corresponding decrease in the Price level. In the present day economy the act of modernisation is common which always fluctuates the transactions and every economy non-a-days is busy in increasing its volume of trade. In such conditions this theory does not prove practical in asserting that Money supply will only affect the price level and the value of money.

6. *Increase in Money Supply cannot help in Depression* : A suggestion underlying this theory is that if there is a period of the supply of money should be increased but it cannot always help. It became apparent during the time of great depression of 1929-34 when the money was increased to a great extent but all was in vain. It did not produce the desired result.

7. *The Quantity of Money taken into account is not full without making distinction between the deposit for saving purposes* : It also does not take into account the nature of overdrafting is one of the greatest system of providing credit in the country like Britain.

8. *Price and Transactions Keep on Changing* : Various factors affect the price and trade in the economy. Moreover no economy is a closed economy. Each takes part in the foreign trade which also affects the supply of money and trade. The price of any commodity at present is always under the influence of the price to be in future. Demand and supply of the commodities also keep on changing which makes the transactions unstable. Whereas this theory assumes that at a particular time there will be constancy in the price level or transactions. But this is not correct.

9. *Velocity of Money is a Vague Notion* : The velocity of money has been taken as one of the factors affecting the total amount of money available in the market. It gives a simple mechanical explanation of the V.This theory does not explain as to why in the time of depression the velocity of money will decrease and at the time of inflation velocity of money will increase ? The factors which govern the velocity of money are also not given in this theory.

10. *Transaction in Cash are not the yardstick of Purchasing Power of Money* : This objection has been raised by *Lord J.M. Keynes,* According to him the transactions which takes place in the economy are cash and commodity

transactions both. The quantity of the commodity transaction is comparatively small. But the equation only measures cash transactions and completely ignores the commodity transactions. Thus it does not measure the true purchasing power of money. Looking at this shortfall *Lord Keynes* felt that the Cash transactions approach is an, "unreliable guide to purchasing power of money. "

11. *This Theory does not consider War Time Policy* : It has been generally observed that during the war the prices of certain commodities starts going up. To meet the deficit, large amount of currency notes which are inconvertable are issued by the governments. But this expresses that change in the quantity of money brings a proportionate charge in prices which is not always true. Sometimes Money supply is able to bring proportionately less change in the prices.

12. *Prof. Edwin Cannan's Criticism* : According to *Prof. Cannan* money is not a commodity whose price is affected by its demand and supply but the demand for money depends upon various factors. A person's desire to hold money with him is also a factor . He says that the demand of money depends , " not by the number and amounts of transactions, but by the ability and willingness of persons to hold currency in the same way as we think of the demand for houses as coming not from the persons who buy and sell or lease and sub-lease houses, but from the persons who occupy houses. "

13. *The Quantity Theory offers a long-term analysis of money* : This Theory offers no explanation for short-term , so the theory could become less useful because according to Keynes we are all dead in the long-run.

14. *It is based on wrong assumption of full employment* :: Full employment is a rare phenomenon. Its assumption of full employment is removed, M will not have a direct and proportional relationship with P.

15. *Ignores Rate of Interest:* The quantity theory ignores the rate of interest as a determinant of the price level. Because in actual practice any change in supply of money normal firm affects the rate of interest and then other variables like price.

In face of the above criticism many supporters of this theory have tried to validate the operation of the theory. Noted among them are *Prof. Kemmerer, gustav Cassel.* But the fact remains that this theory excludes the transactions which take place in the economies without the help of money or non-monetary transactions. Further it is rather very difficult to measure the velocity of money. Even then this theory is not without its importance. It shows, at least a promotion factor which fluctuates the value of money *i.e.,* quantity circulating in the market . *Prof. Pigou* has rightly observed :

"The Quantity Theory furnishes a tool which in the skilled hands of Irving Fisher has accomplished great things ."

Cash Balance Equation

Fisher's approach discussed above was based on the medium of exchange function of money. The theory emphasised on the demand side of money. Different approach to the quantity theory of money has been attempted by the Cambride economists like *Marshall, Pigou, Cannan, Robertson* and *Keynes.* This approach is also known as Cash Balance approach of the cambridge version of the quantity therory of money. This theory is based on the store of value function of money. This approach emphasised more on the demand side of the money.

The quantity theory has been presented in a slightly different version by English economists like *Marshall, Pigou, Robertson* and *Keynes.* As these economists belonged to the

Cambridge school ,the equation has come to be known as Cambridge Equation. Since this equation emphasises on cash balances, it is also known as cash balance equation. According to these economists the value of money depends upon the demand for money and that the demand for money does not depend upon the volume of goods to be sold for money but by the ability and the willingness of the people to hold cash in the same way as we think of the demand for house as coming not from persons who buy and resell or lease and sub-lease houses but from persons who occupy house."

According to this approach the value of money is determined on the basis of its demand and supply.Whenever the demand for money is equal to its supply, the value of money, as in the case of other things is determined. The changes in the value of money thus caused by change *either* in its demand *or* in its supply *or* both. Hence , the approach is bassed on the general theory of value and is applicable to the problem of money. The approach consider the demand for and supply of money at a particular time rather than over a period of time as enunicated in the transation approahc.

According to cash balance approach the supply of money and its stock at a particular time, not its flow over a period of time, comprises all the cash and bank deposits subject to withdrawals by cheque. People want to keep some portion of their income in the cash with time or in the bank to meet their personal expenditure or as a precaution for exigencies and likewise merchants and industrialists want to hold cash for business needs.Demand for money according to this approach has been interpreted in a different manner.

Thus at any time people can be assumed to hod a certain amount of cash sufficient to fulfil the above objectives and these balances may be just a fraction of the national income.According to Fisher ,the demand for money is arises not becasue of its own shake. It arises only to purchase the commodities and services. In more clear term, money is demanded because, it serves as medium of exchange . But this theory exphasis that the demand for money is made for meeting day to day requirements of individual business and the government. Thus, the demand for money refers to that quantity of money which the individual, business and the government hold to meet its day to day orequirements . Hence the supply of money, set at the community's aggregate demand (or cash balanc) which determines the level of price level and inversely to the money value. On the other hand if supply of money is constant, the price level will change inversely and money value affected directly with any change in the demand for money An increase in the demand for the money (for store purposes) will lower down the demand for goods and services because in this situation people can have a larger cash balance Just by curtailing their expenditure on good and services . Consequently the price level fall and money value will go up converse will be the case under which there willl be fall in demand for money.

Marshall's Equation

Based upon the above conception of the demand of money, *Marshall* give the following equation:

M = KY

wherein M = quantity of money with the public (Total supply of money).

Y = the real national income.

K = the fractional part of the real national income which people want to keep in cash.

Let us now explain the equation by taking an example:

(a) Suppose the total supply of money = Rs. 1,000.

(b) The real national income = 30,000 units.

(c) K is supposed to be 1/15 or Y

Then since M = KY

Therefore, value of Rs. 1,000 = 1/15 [30,000] = 2,000 units or The value of 1 rupee = 2 units

Therefore, the price level per unit = 50 paise.

Pigou's Equation

Prof. Pigou's equation is as follows:

$$P = \frac{KR}{M}$$

wherein P = The value of purchasing power of money

R = The real national income.

M = Total cash.

and K = The fractional part of R, which people want to keep in cash.

For sake of illustration let us suppose that

M = Rs. 1,000

R = 30,000 units

$$K = \frac{1}{15} \text{ part}$$

Therefore, $P = \frac{KR}{M}$

or Value of one rupee $= \frac{2000}{1000} = 2$ units

or Price Level = 50 paise

Prof. Pigou has also give an extended equation in which he includes bank money or deposits also :

Value of one unit of money $= \frac{KR}{M} [c + h(1-c)]$ in which 'c' is cash held by the people, (1–c) is bank deposits; h is the percentage of cash reserve agaisnt bank deposits.

Robertson's Equation

Robertson has given an equation almost similar to *Pigou's*. But *Robertson's* equation is preferred to *Pigou's* equation because it can be easily compared to *Fisher's equation.*

His equation is :

$$M = PKT$$

or $$P = \frac{M}{KT}$$

wherein P = The price level (the reverse of the purchasing power or value of money).

T = The total amount of goods and services or real national income in terms of goods and services.

K = that part of T which people want to hold in cash.

Keynes's Equation

Keynes has given a cash balance equation on the assumption that people would keep a certain amount of cash in order to buy only consumption goods. He gave the following equation:

$$n = pk$$

or $$\frac{1}{p} = \frac{k}{n}$$

or $$p = \frac{n}{k}$$

in which p = price level of consumption goods.

n = cash with the public

k = proportion of consumption goods over which people keep cash.

Keynes has also given an extended equation to distinguish between bank deposits and cash. He gives the equation as:

$$n = p(k+rk)$$

or $$\frac{1}{p} = \frac{k+rk'}{n}$$

or $$p = \frac{n}{k+rk'}$$

In this equation K is the bank deposits and r is the proportion of cash reserves kept by the bank against their deposits.

It should be remembered that later on *Keynes* gave up to quantity theory in favour of his Income Expenditure approach to the value of money.

Evaluation of the Cash Balances Equation

The cash balance approach of the quantity theory is superior to *Fisher's* equation in the sense that it relates the value of money or the price level to people's demand of money for holding cash balances. Whenever people's demand for holding cash balances increases, they will spend less money on goods and services and hence the pries will fall. On the other hand, if people's demand for holding cash balances falls, they will spend more money on goods and services and as a result of it the price level will rise. In this way cash balances approach of quantity theory gives an explanation for inflation and deflation (rising and falling prices).

But the defect of this approach lies in the fact that it emphasises the purchasing power of money in terms of consumption goods alone. But this is a narrow view since money has purchasing power over many other goods. Again the cash balances approach ignores the influence of important variables like income, saving and investment which cause changes in price level. It simply says that changes in the demand for money cause changes in the value of money.

Fisher and Cambridge Equations Compared

The different between *Fisher* s equation and Cambridge equation is not so important as it is generally supposed. both these equation represent different view of the same things from different standpoints.

Cambridge equation concerns with the amount of money held in the balances of people at any given time with the object of financing their transactions. *Fisher's* equation on the other hand deals with the amount of money required by the people during a given period to finance their transactions.

However, in one sense Cambridge equation is better than that of *Fisher's* because it says that the changes in prices level are not due to the changes in supply of money but due to the habit of the people regarding the holding of a proportion of their income in the from of money.

A COMPARISON OF FISHER'S APPROACH WITH CAMBRIDGE APPROACH

The two approaches i.e. the transaction approach and the cash balance approach of the Quantity Theory of Money described above indicates certain similarties and dissimillariteis. To arrive on the conclusion that which version of the theory is superior and why, it is necessary to first study similarties and dissimilarities between the two versions of the theory and then to conclude.

Similarities

Following is the similarities between the two approaches.

(1) *Determination of Value* - The same conclusion lead in both the theories that it is the quantity of money which determines the value of money and the price level.

(2) *Use of Similar Symbols* : In Fisher's equation MV + M'V', in Robertson's equation as well as in Pigou's equation M, n in Keynes equation refers to the same things i.e. quantity of money. Further the following points also worth -mentioning in this regard:

(i) In Fisher's equation credit money has been represented seperately by 'M' whereas in Cambridge equation it has not been shown seperately because the total quantity of money also implies credit money.

(ii) In Fisher's equation velocity of legal tender money and credit money have been represented seperately by V and V' whereas in cambridge equation there is no mention about velocity of circulation of money.

(3) *No Fundamental Difference* : The cash balance equation as propound by Robertson i.e., $P = \frac{M}{KT}$ and as propound by Fisher i.e. , $P = \frac{MV}{T}$ resemble with each other. These symbols used in two equation are almost the same. The only difference seems in case of V and K. But even V and K are reciprocal to each other. In Fisher's equation $V = \frac{PT}{M}$ where as in Robertson's equation $K = \frac{M}{PT}$, Hence, , K is reciprocal to V in other words $K = \frac{I}{V}$ or $V = \frac{I}{K}$. Therefore, there is no fundamental 'difference between the two equation, rather they represent different aspects of the same phenomenon.

(4) *Different Angles of Presentation* :According to Robertson, Fisher's equation and Cambridge equation are not basically different from each other. He expressed the view that these both equations rather explain the same thing with two different angles. Fisher's equation stresses money as a flow where as Cambridge version emphasies on money as stock.

Dissimilarities Between The Two Approach

No doubt there are some similarities between the two approaches but there are dissimilarities between the two as analysed below :

(1) *Different Concepts* - The two version of equation make use of different concepts of demand for money. In International approach, the demand for money arises because of exchange of goods and services and accordingly it stresses medium of exchange function of money. In cash balance approach, the demand for money is to store and thus it emphasises the 'store of value' function of money.

(2) *Approach toward Money & Cash* - In Fisher's equation, emphasis is accorded on velocity of circulation of money (V) , whereas in the cash balance approach, the stress, is laid on the idle cash balance which is a fractional part of the national income (K) . It should be noted that (V) is exactly opposite (K).

(3) *Value of Money* - In Fisher's equation value of money is explained over a period of time, whereas cambridge equation explains the value of money at a particular point of time when period of time is considered , velocity becomes important factor because money during that period is expected to perform variety of functions. On a given point of time money simply represents some goods and services. In this process K plays an important role. It is because that vis. emphasised in Fisher's equation whereas K is emphasised in Cambridge equation.

(4) *Two Equations Are Not Identical* - In its meaning, symbol P is not used identical in meaning in both the equations. P in Fisher's equation represents general price level and in Cambridge equation it refers to only the price of consumption goods.

Which Version of Theory is Superior and Why ?

An analysis of similarities and dissimilarities of in the two version of the Quantity Theory of Money - Cash Transaction and Cash Balance establishes the superiority of the Cambridge version i.e. cash balance approach. the following arguments can be offer to support the view :

(1) Fisher's version is mechanical, against it Cambridge version is realistic. Fisher's version is mechanical in the term it treats price level as the exclusive function of the quantity of money in circulation . It provides no recognition to human motives . On the other hand , Cambridge version make consideration of human motives by emphasising on K in determining the price level. The size of K is almost determined by human motives i.e. store value of money.

(2) As the sole determinant of the value of money, Fisher's version considers only the quantity of money (i.e. supply of money). The Cambridge equations consider both demand and supply aspect of money in determination of value of money. Hence, the cambridge version seems to be more comprehensive as compared to Fisher's version. In this way, Fisher version is also considered as incomplete.

(3) There is another point of view from which Cambridge version is also considered more wider and comprehensive . Fisher's version does not consider the income level as a determinant of price level. According to the Fisher's version the price level is determined by the quantity of supply (supply of money) and the total number of transactions. On the other hand in Cambridge version, price level in influenced by the income level and the changes have taken place in it.

(4) Fisher's equation propounded on the basis that price level changes only when there is a change in the supply (total quantity) of money in circulation. But the Cambridge version explains that price level may change even without any

change in the quantity of money, if K undergoes change. If people starts holding more cash balance (if K changes), the price level will also undergo a change without any changes in the qunatity of money . Thus K is more important determinant as compared to M.

(5) As the main determinants of the demand for money , the Cambridge version stresses on subjective factors. Fisher's version considers only objective factors while discussing the demand for money.

On the above discussion, it may be concluded that Cambridge version obtained superiority over Fisher's approach to the Quantity Theory of Money.

Value of the Quantity Theory of Money

Inspite of its criticism the quantity theory of money states some important facts.

First of all it states that whenever the supply of money has been increased in large quantity, the prices have gone up.

Secondly the quantity theory assets that prices can be controlled through the control of volume of money in the country. Thus monetary policy in all countries operates on this important fact.

INCOME THEORY OR SAVING-INVESTMENY THEORY OF MONEY

In the present modern economic world of dynamism, the two version of the Quantity Theory of Money- Fisherian and Cambridge have lost their importance. It happens because both these version have failed to explain the value of money and other relationship. The two approaches have reached on the conclusion that it is the change in the quantity of money which results in the change in level of price or in the value of money. These approaches have absolutely ignore other determents of price level such as saving, investment, expenditure etc. Similarly these approaches also fail to explain the reason as to why these changes in price level take place in the economy.

There is another theory explaining the process as to how the price level changes occurred. The theory was developed by J.M. Keynes known as 'Income Theory of Money. Contrary to the Quantity Theory, the income theory established relationship between price fluctuations and other elements such as income, expenditure, savings, investments etc. Crowther, Hayek, Heberler are other economists who have made valuable contribution to the income theory for further development. The theory is also known as 'Saving-Investment Theory of Money' because there are two factors which simultaneously influence the price level. The theory in its analysis consider the whole of the economy.

The income theory explains that changes in income results in the change in aggregate demand of goods and services . It is not the volume of money which results in changes in the price level. The theory explains that the aggregate money income of the society is determines by the aggregate demand of goods and services. Whenever there is an increase or decrease in the aggregate money income , it implies a similar change in the purchasing power of the money which in turn affects the price level in the same duration provided there is no change occurred in the volume of production. Thus changes take place in money income and not in money supply. These changes bring about changes in price level due to changes in aggregate demand . In fact money supply itself may change because of changes in the level of aggregate income, savings, investment , price and other similar activities. The theory may be explained in precise words as "The value of money or the price level is the consequence of the aggregate income rather than the supply of money.

Explanation of the Theory

The term money may be interpreted in two sense i.e., (i) money income , and (ii) real income. Money income of the society belongs to sum total of the monetary reward obtained by various factors of production during a particular time period. The monetary reward of the different factors of production is equal to the value of goods and services produced during a particular period. Hence money income represents the value of goods and services produced during a particular period of time. On the other hand, the real income implies the aggregate output of goods and services produced during a particular time period. .

It is determined by the following two elements : -

(i) Available factors of production to the community for productive purposes, and

(ii) The effective demand of the Community for goods and services without which no entrepreneur would like to engage various factors of production.

The income of the community will be used in satisfying the aggregate effective demand that will result in expenditure which may be either on consumption of goods or on capital or in investment of goods. The expenditure may be either consumption expenditure or investment expenditure. The aggregate expenditure of the community (consumption and investment both) will tends to be equal to the aggregate value of output. Again , the aggregate expenditure of the community will be equal to aggregate income of the community because one man's expenditure's will be other man's income. Here aggregate expenditure is always tends equal to aggregate income. In other sense aggregate income generate from the investment and sale of goods. Thus every expenditure generate income which after being spent generate another income. Hence aggregate income of the community must be equal. It can be concluded from the aforesaid analysis that level of income of the community determined by the level of expenditure . Larger the expenditure will generate larger money income and likewise larger aggregate income will demand for larger the aggregate expenditure.

The aggregate expenditure defines the effective demand and determines the real income or the level of output and employment in the community. In this situation aggregate expenditure is the real determinant of output, employment and prices. Hence aggregate expenditure has the direct relation with output ,employment and prices and the whole economic activities is governed by the aggregate expenditure. Thus, the income theory explains how aggregate demand, aggregate expenditure and aggregate income determines the value of money or price level. The price are determined by the money income and real income (or output of good and services). On the basis of the aforesaid explanation, the income theory of price can be expressed algebraically in the following form :

$$P = \frac{Y}{O}$$

Where P represents the general price level.

Y represents money income, and

O represents total output of goods and services *or* real income

According to this equation the general price level (P) can be found out by dividing the total money income by the total output of goods and services. If money income increases faster than the output of goods and services, the prices will depict an upward trend. If money income does not increase or increase slowly or it does not change at all as compared to the increase in output, the prices will fall. If output increases more rapidly as compared to the money income, there will also be fall in the price level. Therefore it is required to compare the money income and the real income (output of goods and services) to arrive at the general price-level or the value of money.

The above idea of the Investment Theory has presented by J.M. Keynes in his Saving-Investment Theory. According to Keynes disequilibrium in the saving and investment causes price fluctuation through changes in the income level. If there is equalibrium in the saving and the investment there will not be occurred any change in the price level or value of money. Keynes has given the following equation for explaining the theory.

$$Y = C + S \text{ ---------------------(i)}$$

Where Y represents income

C represents consumption

S represents Savings

Keynes holds the view that total income is not possible to consume. A part of its saved which is normally invested. Thus, the equation may be put in the following form.

$$Y = C + I \text{----------------------(ii)}$$

(Here I represents Investment) . By combining the above two equations, we obtained,

$$Y = C+S$$

Or $Y = C + I$

Or $C + S = C + I$

Or $S = I$

The following inferences may be drawn from the above equation of Keynes.

(i) Saving and investment are equal at the point of equilibrium. Hence S = I

(ii) Money income is always equal to the amount spent for consumption and money saved during a particular period.

(iii) Total money supply in the market is equal to amount spent on consumption + amount spent by the entrepreneurs for investment.

Thus every increase in savings will be available for investment. If saving exceed investment, the price level will fall or value of money will increase . Contrarily , if investment exceeds saving, the price level will go up but money value will come down. Thus any disequilibrium will prove harmful to economy. Therefore efforts should be made to establish a balance between the two.

Importance of Theory

Or

Superiority of the Theory over Quantity Theory of Money

It has been claimed that saving investment theory or income theory is superior to the traditional theories of value of money. Following points made an effort in explaining merits of the Saving Investment Theory over the Quantity Theory of Money.

(1) *Goods Combination Two Theories* - The Savings - Investment theory has a good combination of the two theories- the general theory of value (the theory of individual price)and the theory of money (the theory of general prices) . Therefore it presents a more comprehensive view of price fluctuation as compared to the classical theory of the value of money (or the quantity theory of money)

(2) *Explain Simple Relationship* - The older quantity theory of money discloses the fact that any changes in the quantity (or supply) of money will affect the price level directly and proportionately, if other factors remaining constant. Thus, the theory depicts a very simple explanation of money-price relationship.

(3) *Complicated Theory* - The saving - investment theory is rather complicated because it describes a series of events that in turn lead to the change in price level. If there will be any change in the supply of money, it will lead to changes in the rate of interest. It also brings a change in the relationship between savings and investment. The change in the relationship in turn, influence the level of income, employment and output which ultimately bring about a change in price level. Investment exceeds saving resulted price rise and saving exceeds investment resulted fall in prices. Hence it establishes a better relationship between money and price.

(4) *Describes Cyclical Fluctuation* - The Saving-Investment theory provides a tool for analyzing the cyclical fluctuations in price, employment and output. The theory explains that business cycles is nothing but an altering expansion and contraction of national income. Therefore, Saving - Investment Theory is a distinct improvement over the quantity theory of money.

(5) *Situation of Full Employment* - The Quantity Theory of Money has assumed the situation of full employment. This assumption not seems to be realistic because the situation of full employment does not exist in any economy of the world . The Saving - Investment Theory does not assume full employment as the basis of theory.

(6) *Fails to Point -out about change in Velocity of Money* - The Quantity Theory of Money does not explain as why the velocity of money change or the factors that change the velocity of money. The Saving - Investment Theory clearly explains changes in the velocity of circulation of money from time to time. Therefore, the theory recognized better than the quantity theory of money .

Despite certain proven merits, of the Saving - Investment Theory, the theory suffers from some serious limitation that the theory answers only with regards to the short - term fluctuations in prices and employment. It also does not provide any information about the long-term fluctuation in price and employment, whereas the quantity theory of money explains the long term fluctuations in price in the situation of full employment. Thus , the suitability of the quantity theory of money also cannot be support out rightly.

MILTON FRIEDMAN'S

QUANTITY THEORY OF MONEY

Prominent economist of Chicago University, and Noble Prize Winner of 1976 *Professor Milton Friedman* accepted the importance of Quantity Theory of Money and tried in 1936 to provide new shape to it. In his one of the published research paper in 1959 entitled The Quantity Theory of Money : A Restatement.

Friedman presented modified version of Quantity Theory. Professor Friedman is of the view that Quantity Theory of Money is virtually theory belongs to demand for money. Friedman tried to resurrections to the theory an propounded by Fisher by providing new shape to the demand for money.

Friedman's Equation

According to Milton Friedman, demand for money only influence to value of money and given the following equation for demand of money.

$$M = f\ (P, Y\frac{I}{P}\ \frac{dp}{dt}\ rb,\ re\ W,\ U)$$

Where M = Aggregate Demand for Money.

P = Price Level.

Y = Total National Income

rb = Interest rate on Bonds

re = Yield on Equities

W = Ratio of Assets in human Assets.

U = Utility Determining Variables. It tend to influence tests and preference.

$\frac{I}{P}, \frac{dp}{dt}$ = Quantity of Physical Goods in lieu of Unit of Money

According to Milton Friedman demand for money is the result of price level, total income and income obtained from various sources (Bonkds , Shares etc.)

❐

7

Elementary Study of Monetary Standards

MONETRY STANDARD

Meaning

In every economy Monetary Standard refers to explanation of the form of standard money in circulation. The monetary authority of every country adopts certain standard money for the discharge of its official obligations and for circulation in the entire economy. It is a system under which value-basis of money in circulation is fixed in term of some metal or in any other form so that purchasing power of money is created. This standard money is actually the legal money which is of national character. This legal money, if made of gold the country is said to be on gold, standard. A monetary standard, not only provides for medium of exchange and store of value internally but it also facilitate international payments.

Definitions

George N. Halm defines , "Monetary standard (may be defined) from the viewpoint of economics as the principle method of regulating the quantity and the exchange value of standard or definitive money."

Shapiro and Others defines, "The Monetary standard of a nation involves the overall sets of laws and practices which control the quality and quantity of money in the system."

Objectives

A sound monetary standard has thus two main objective—

(a) To maintain stability in the external value of its currency or money;

(b) To maintain stability in the external value i.e. value of internal currency vis-a-vis the foreign currencies.

Kinds of Monetary Standard.

Monetary Standard can broadly be classified into two categories as follows :

(I) Metallic Standard, and

(II) Paper Currency Standard.

These can be explained in detail as follows :

(I) *Metallic Standard*—There are two kinds of metallic standard viz.,

(a) Monometallism—It has two standard examples.

(1) Silver Standard, and

(2) Gold Standard- It is mainly of two type as follows :

(i) Direct, and

(ii) Indirect—It can be further classified in four categories :

(i) Gold Bullion Standard,

(ii) Gold Exchange Standard,

(iii) Gold Reserve Standard,

(iv) Gold Parity Standard.

(b) Bimetallism : It can be classified as

(i) Gold

(ii) Silver

(II) *Paper Currency Standard*—It can be classified in following two categories :

(i) Free;

(ii) Managed.

Monetary standard can broadly be classified into two categories -(1) Metallic standard and (2) Paper currency standard. There are two kinds of metallic standard viz (a) Monometallism and (b) Bimetallism (Gold and Silver). Monometallism has two standards example (i) Silver standard and (ii) Gold standard. Gold standard in terms is of two types -(i) Direct (ii) Indirect. Indirect monetary standard can be classsified in four types:-(a) Gold Bullion Standard-(b) Gold Exchange Standard, (c) Gold Reserve Standard, (d) Gold Parity Standard.

Paper Currency Standard may be classified in two categories as follows :

(a) Free Paper Currency,

(b) Managed Paper Currency.

The whole description of the kinds of Monetary standard can also be shown with the help of the following chart—

Monometallism is refers to that type of monetary standard in which only one metal is used as standard or legal money throughout the country. The coin of this particular metal is a full bodied coin and also an unlimited legal tender. For example -India was on Silver Standard till 1893 and Great Britain was on Gold Standard till 1931.

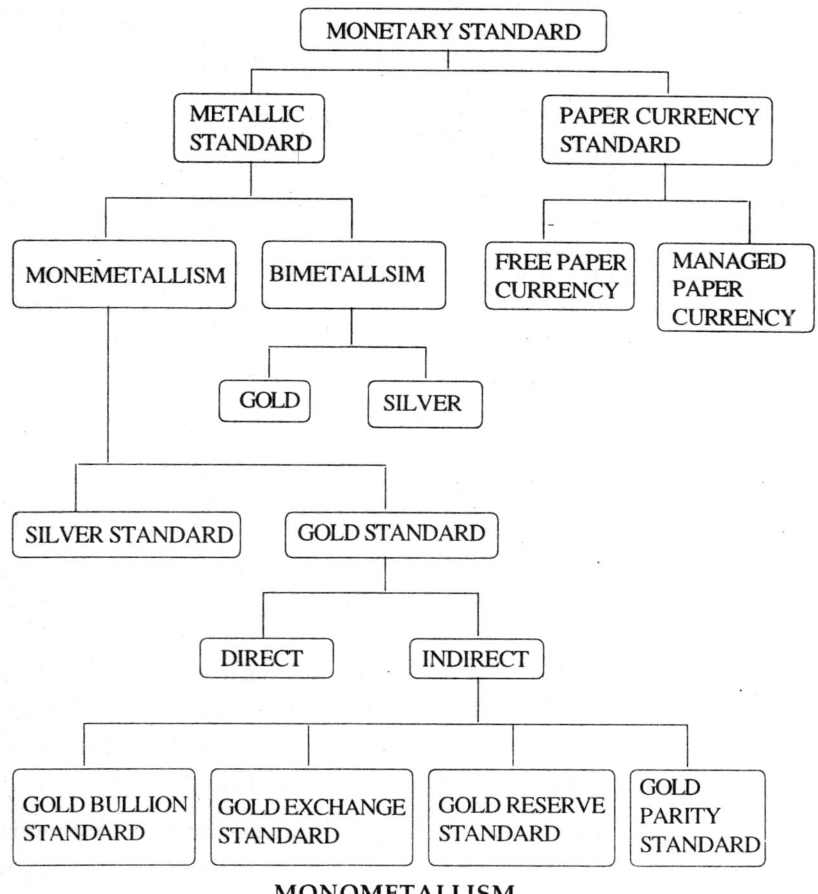

MONOMETALLISM

Charactristics

The important charactristics of Mono-metallism are discussed below :

(i) *Standard coin either in Gold*: Under the system of mono-metallism principally standard coin may be in any metal but in practice due to because of some specific reason they found normally *either* in gold or silver.

(ii) *Un-limited Legal Tender* : Money made of metals (Gold/Silver) marked as main or standard money and the same are also recognised as legal tender.

(iii) *Token Money* : Under monometallism, in addition to standard money of one metal there may be in circulation token money of other metal. But these are recognised as limited legal tender and the same having relation with standard money.

(iv) *Free Coinage*: Under this monetary standard, standard coins or primary money are allowed for free coinage. Any person may obtained money from mint by just paying metal equal amount of money required.

(v) *Name* - If primary money of the country is made of gold then the system is named as 'Gold Standard' and if it is made of silver then it is named as silver standard.

Advantage

Monemetallism is equipped with following advantages :

(1) *Faith*- Since under the system of mono-metallism most costlier metals like gold or silver are use and their internal and external value tends to remain equal. Therefore, people express utmost faith on this standard.

(2) *Simplicity* : It is the simplest form of monetary standard. Since only one metal is used as money, it is quite convenient for the common people to deal with it.

(3) *Uniformity* : Under mono-metallism quality of uniformity is found in the standard since coinage made of single metal are used. Even illiterate person can recognised this standard without much difficulty.

(4) *Convenient* : Mono-metallism is convenient for both the Government as well as public. It is coinage. At the same it is convenient for the Government as under the system there arise no problem regarding safety of reserve is arised.

(5) *Greatest Public Confidence* : Since this type of money is a full bodied money made either of gold or silver, it is still greater public confidence.

(6) *Helpful in International Payments* : When monometallism is used on an international scale, there is no problem associated with determination of exchange rate of various currencies. Besides , it makes the task of international payment easier and simpler.

(7) *Prohibits the Gresham's Law to operate* : According to this law bad money tends to drive out the good money from circulation . Since standard coin under this system is made up of only one metal, there is simply no question of bad money or good money and thus this law will not operate.

(8) *Control of Inflation* - There is no fear of inflation under this system as primary money is made of either gold or silver, because only money can be issued equal to available metal.

Disadvantage

Following are the important disadvantage or demerits of Monometallism :

(1) *Lack of Adequate Supply* : The precious metals like gold and silver are always in short supply due to which it cannot be adopted world wide.

(2) *Lack of Elasticity* : Monometallic standard is inelastic in nature i.e. its supply cannot be increased according to the requirements. It was because of this difficulty that all the countries of the world abandoned the gold and silver standard.

(3) *Retareds Economic Growth* : A metallic standard due to its inelastic nature retards economic growth of the country. The economic growth necessitates expansions in money supply from time to time according to the requirements of the country. Monometalic restricts expansion in money supply due to limited stock of the precious metals.

(4) *Lack of Price Stability* : The price of metal is subject to fluctuation due to fluctuation in its demand and supply . With frequent changes in the price of metal the value of money changes and thus the price level also does not remain stable.

BIMETALLISM

Meaning

Bimetallism is a monetary system under which both gold and silver are subject to free coinage and both are given full legal tender powers. A small charge may be made to cover the cost of coinage, including the cost of any alloy that may be added to the gold or silver; such a charge representing a very small part of the value of the coins, since the essence of free coinage is the parity between the value of the coins and the metal from which they are made, and this charge at all is made, coinage is said to be not only free but gratuitous. Gratuitous coinage of both metals is not essential to bimetallism , but free coinage is allowed.

Since under bimetallism neither the gold nor silver coins can have a value greater than the value of the metal from which they are made and since it is the intention of the State to make the gold and the silver units equal in value, the gold coins must be smaller in size than the silver coins of the same denomination, the difference in size being determined by the difference in the market value of the two metals. If, for instance, an ounce of gold is worth as much as 20 ounces of silver on the metal market then silver coins of a given denomination must be made to contain 20 times as much silver as gold coins of the same denomination contain gold.

The ratio between the weight of the silver coin and the gold coin of the same denomination is called the mint ratio while the ratio at which the two metals in bullion form exchange on the metal market is called the market ratio. These two ratios must be the same if bimetallism is to work.

A Brief History of Bimetallism

Bimetallism worked in European countries for many centuries. Bimetallism was adopted by France in 1803. The ratio between gold and silver was fixed at 15 oz. of silver for 1 oz. of gold. France was able to maintain this ratio for about 50 years. Due to discoveries of gold in 1848-50 the supply of gold had increased and its market value relative to silver fall. France was then compelled to change its original ratio and give silver higher value in order to save it from the melting pot under the operation of Gresham's Law. In 1865 it was prevalent in the Latin Monetary Union consisting of France, Belgium, Switzerland and Italy. A few years later , Greece, Servia, Rumania and some Sourth American States also joined this union. But this union was also not able to maintain bimetallism and broke down in 1874 when the price of silver fall in terms of gold. In the U.S.A., bimetallism was adopted in 1792. After various controversies it was abandoned in 1900.

Merits

Bimetallism is refers to that monetary standard where two metals viz gold and silver are used as standard of value. Both these metals are standard coins and are full bodied legal tender money. Both the coins circulate simultaneously. The rate of exchange of two coins are fixed in advance by the government. There is free and unlimited coinage of both the metals into standard monetary units. There is no restrictions on the imports and exports of these metals. However due to operation of Gresham's law i.e. silver coins pushed out the Gold coins out of circulation. Now-a-days bimetallism remains only a historical fact.

(1) *Flexibility in Money Supply* : Since there are two types of metals in circulation, a reasonable level of flexibility in its supply is assumed to the public.

(2) *Price Stability* : Under bimetallism price stability can be ensured if it is adopted on an international scale. Because shortage of one metal can be met with the increase in output of other metals.

(3) *Encouragement to Foreign Trade* : Trade can take place between countries adopting two different standard viz, Gold and Silver. Free imports and exports will further fillup to the international trade.

(4) *Economical Maintenance of Bank Reserves* : Under this system shortage of one metal can be compensated by other because banks are free to keep their reserve in any metal. Therefore, it is easy and economical to maintain the reserves.

(5) *Low rate of Interest* : Since there are two metals in circulation, generally supply exceeds the demand for money. Hence the rate of interest is generally low and it is easy for banks to extend loan for business purposes.

(6) *Smooth functioning of Monetary System* : There is great public confidence in this system. There is stability of price level and exchange rate . Thus this monetary system works very smoothly in this system.

Demerits

Though Bimetallism has several advantages but it has following disadvantages :

(1) *Operation of Gresham's Law* : If bimetallism is adopted by only one or two countries and not on international scale it soon leads to the operation of Gresham's law in which gold coins are pushed out of circulation by the silver coins.

(2) *Fear of Inflation* : Since money of two metals found in operation, therefore there may be every possibility of all danger of excess money supply resulting inflation.

(3) *Speculation* : It is common phenomenon to have difference in the mint rate of two metals . Such incidence may encourage speculation.

(4) *Abrassing* : There is every possibility of abrassing metal since money of only two metals found in operation.

(5) *Mint Rate* : Difficulty in maintaining mint rate and marvel rate particularly when supplies of both metals change in the same direction.

(6) *Foreign Trade* : Little stimulus to foreign trade unless bimetallism is adopted by all countries of the world.

Arguments for Bimetallism

Despite of several disadvantages against Bimetallism, the following arguments may be given in its favour :

1. The first arguments of expansion of monetary reforms favouring bimetallism seems to be less convincing now than it was before and immediately after the First World War when the world's monetary gold stock was thought to be inadequate. But the arguments still keeps some meaning assuming, that in the future, government will desire to maintain metallic foundations for their currencies. A monetary reserves rise in size, monetary systems grow in security. Governments have frequently been forced to suspend the metallic redemption of credit money because their reserves of gold were depleted. If it is desirable to maintain metallic redemption, one would suppose that reserves for this purpose should be very large. The stock of gold in the world is not enough to cope with the demand for gold for monetary purpose. Hence, the addition of silver to the monetary reserves to make redemption more certain would seem to be a right step.

2. The arguments that bimetallism promotes stability in the price level goes as follows. Changes in the quantity of gold cause change quantity hoarded and dishoarded, and in the use of gold cause change in the demand for and supply of gold and therefore cause changes in its value. Now similar supply and demand forces affect silver, and its value too, must be subject to changes resulting from changes in these forces. But

to the extent that changes in the supply of and demand for one metal are neutralised by changes in the supply of and demand for the other, a combined reserve, of both metals would be subject to less severe fluctuations than would a reserve of either metal held singly. What is more, any net addition to or subtraction from a comgined reserve has a smaller proportionate effect than an equal net addition to or subtraction from a single reserve.

As bimetallic reserve are likely to be subjected to smaller proportionate changes than either gold or silver reserve held separately, changes in the value of money must be fewer and less drastic in a bimetallic country than in countries which employ the gold standard or the silver standard.

3. Because a bimetallic nation express the value of its monetary unit in terms of gold and silver simultaneously the mathematical relationship between its unit and the gold monetary units of some foreign countries and the silver monetary units of other may easily be fixed : and the day-to-day rates of exchange change far from the mathematical parties so long as the free movement of the precious metal is allowed by the various nations. Between a gold standard country and a silver standard country, on the other hand exchange rates be subject to wide fluctuations , in accordance with change in the market value of silver bullion in the gold standard country.

4. It is also argued that if all the countries adopt gold standard, the output of gold will fall short of the currency requirements. As a result a period of falling prices and trade depression will ensue. The adoption of bimetallism by tapping the supply of silver for monetary purposes will stop this fall in the price of silver, as well as general prices.

Arguments against Bimetallism

The opponents of bimetallism generally base their case upon its alleged unworkability . They contend that*(i)* a single country, unless it has unlimited metallic reserves, cannot, successfully maintain a bimetallic system and, *(ii)* the adoption of a bimetallic system on an international scale, with the co-operation of all important nations, is not within the realm of possibility.

Bimetallism and Gresham's Law

(1) The belief that a single nation cannot succeed in maintaining the bimetallic standard is based upon the principle of Gresham's Law. No government, it is contended is able to select a mint ratio for gold and silver which will continue to equal the ratio between the values of the two metals in foreign market within the bimetallic country. It is true, the market ratio to depart from the mint ratio fixed in the bimetallic country. Sooner or later, foreign market developments make exportations of gold or silver from the bimetallic country to a profitable undertaking; and when the exportation continues for a time, the bimetallic country is likely to find itself with only one metal. There is only one force powerful enough to counteract the tendency for the market ratio of the value of gold and silver to fluctuate and that is the so-called compensatory action which can be made effective only by practically world wide international co-operation.

While it is practically true that no individual country alone can successfully establish and maintain the bimetallic system . It seems just as certain that the important countries acting in concert to establish and maintain a system of international bimetallism provided only that they fix the mint ratio which needs to be the same for all the countries cooperating , not too far above the market ratio at the beginning. Under such a system the compensatory action would operate as a powerful force and would in all probability keep the market ratio in harmony with the international mint ratio.

Bimetallism therefore, practicable only is the case of international bimetallism. And therein lies the greatest hindrance to the introduction of bimetallism.

(2) There are also other difficulties of bimetallism. It would introduce great confusion in all business transactions. If one of the metal is undervalued in the market , the debtors will want to pay in that metal , while the creditors will of course want payment in the over-valued metal. As a result , all transactions will become uncertain and confused.

(3) Moreover, though ultimetaly the mint and the market ratios would come together , yet there might be intervals when the two ratios will not equal. The speculators will then hold the undervalued metal in the hope of profiting from the latter's rise in its price. Thus, there would be constant speculation in the bullion market. The fact is that whether under gold or silver the monetary standard would have to be managed by the central banks so that its value might be stable. We have enough trouble in linking our fate to one metal. It is no use complicating the mechanism and increasing the troubles of management by tying us on two metals.

GOLD STANDARD

Gold standard is a system of currency wherein the value of the monetary unit of a country is *regulated with reference to gold.* Gold Standard is a copy of Mono-Metallism in which gold is used as standard metal under the system of Gold Standard either the coinage is in gold or the money is convertible into gold on demand. The value of currency is determined in gold standard because gold is the most standard metal. Gold Standard is quite old. It was discovered by mercantalists who were in favour of gold because it was only metal having the quality of having universally durable price. Therefore, it was very much in practice even the First World War.

DEFINITIONS OR OPINIONS ON GOLD STANDARD

Some of the definitions or opinions expressed on the concept of Gold Standard are discussed below :

Crowther Outlined in *An Outline of Money* as" The gold standard is " a device for maintaining the stabilities of the exchange rate."

Prof Benham in *Benham's Economic* pointed out that, " A Country is on the gold standard when the purchasing power of a unit of its currency is kept equal to the purchasing power of given weight of gold."

Lord J.M. Keynes in *A Text on Monetary Reform,* illustrated the Gold Standard ," in its essence is an abstract standard where the price of gold has been fixed not absolutely but for that variation of the prices are restricted whithin very narrow limits, or what amounts to something, where the unit of currency has an approximately gold value."

D.H. Robertson in *Money* described Gold Standard as a ,"A state of affairs in which a country keeps the value of its money unit and the value of a defined weight of gold in equality with one another."

W.A.L. Coulborn in *A Discussion of Money* explained as,"The Gold standard is an arrangement where by the chief price of money of a country is exchangble with a fixed quanity of a specific quality."

The above opinions expressed about Gold Standard though are quite different in words but common in essence. There is no hesitation in accepting the fact the standard of measurement of value under the system country adopting Gold Standard will be gold. Though it is not compulsory in the system that money is also to be made of gold, it may be in any metal but is bound to be unlimited legal tender money.

Characteristics

From the aforesaid one can easily described the charactristics of Gold Standard as follows :

(1) *Free Coinage* : Under Gold Standard free coinage prevail in most of the economies.

(2) *Determination of Value in Gold* : Money in circulation is either made of gold or its value is determined in gold.

(3) *Quality of Gold*-Under Gold Standard, specific quality of gold is also fixed-up.

(4) *Free Trade of Gold* : No restriction is imposed on the import and export of gold but free bargaining in allowed.

(5) *Unlimited Legal Tender* : Under Gold Standard coinage in circulation are of unlimited legal tender quality.

(6) *Role of the Government* : The Government is issuing authority i.e., Central Bank (for instance Reserve Bank of India in India) is bound to sell and purchase the gold in the free market at pre-determined fixed rate

Kinds of Gold Standard

Gold standard has following five kinds :

(i) Gold currency or circulation standard.

(ii) Gold Bullion Standard.

(iii) Gold Exchange Standard.

(iv) Gold Reserve Standard.

(v) Gold Parity Standard.

A brief description of each one of above may be presented as follows :

(i) Gold Currency Standard - Prof. R.G Howtrey has called it as "Gold specie standare", in his book, "The Gold Standard Theory and Practice. In this system the currency and

coins are made of gold. At first gold standard took the form of gold currency standard. For a long time the term ' *gold standard' implied gold currency standard. Under this standard, gold acts both as a medium of exchanges and as a measure of value.*

Main Features

Following are the main features Gold Currency Standard :

(1) *Free Coinage* : Under this system , free coinage exists in the country. Gold coins are found in actual circulation.Mint is also open to public for coinage.

(2) *Legal Tender* : All coinage under the system are unlimited legal tender because they are standard coins.

(3) *Convertibility* : Under this system money is convertible either in gold coins or gold. Any other currency, if it is in circulation is also convertible into gold.

(4) *Kind of Standard* : Under the system specific kind of gold is adopted as standard.

(5) *Foreign Trade* : There is no restriction on the export and import of gold.

This standard was first adopted by Great Britain in the year 1816. It was later on adopted by several other countries, and gradually came to be regarded as an ideal standard all over the world.It gave way, however , during and after the war o f 1914-18: and when currencies were restored to gold after sometimes, another form of gold standard had come in vogue. In England it was at the liberty of a person to take gold bullion or ornaments to the Bank of England to get it changed into gold coins of the similar value.The reason of its predominance before the First World War was the availability of gold in the countries.

Merits

The popularity of Gold Currency Standard is due to its following merits :

(1) *Price Stability* : Gold Currency Standard stablises the price level in the country.

(2)*Automotion* : It was automotion to the economic development and money expansion; since it depends upon the amount of gold available.

(3) *Public Trust* : It posesses relatively more public trust.

(4) *Easy*-Gold Currency Standard posesses the merit of easy to follow and determine the value of gold.

Demerits

Gold Currency Standard posesses several merits but it is not free of demerits. Following are the demerits of gold currency standard—

(1) *Rigidity* : Sometime Problem of rigidity in the money supply arises under Gold Currency Standard because of the scarcity of gold.

(2) *Lacking International Co-operation* : It becomes difficult under this system in promoting international co-operation on monetary lines.

(3) *Economic Development* : To achieve economic development for a poor economy becomes difficult due to shortage of gold.

(ii) Gold Bullion Standard : This kind of gold standard was proposed by David Ricardo: published wrote an essay entitled, proposals for an Economical and Secure Currency with Observation on the Profits of the 'Bank of England', in 1816', which was adopted by the British Parliament in 1819 to this effect.

After the First World War it became impossible for the leading economies to adopt Gold Currency Standard . Money circulation crossed the Reserve, and it became impossible to reduce the circulation and to increase the volume of Gold , then the system was adopted in which money was convertible into gold and the Central Banks were to keep gold for some portion of total money in circulation.

Gold bullion standard is a modified form of gold standard first adopted like gold currency standard by Great Britain in 1925. Under this *system while gold is the measure of value, it no longer circulates as coins.* It is gold standard without a gold currency . The government herein , does not issue gold coins, but binds itself to purchase and sell gold bullion in exchange for internal currency which may consist of paper money and coins of base metals at fixed rates. This provides a true link between the circulating media and gold , between which the maintenance of a permanent ratio is ensured for ever. Export and imports of gold are also allowed without any restriction whatsover. The example of Great Britain was later on followed by several other countries.

Essential Features

Following are the main charactristics of this kind of gold standard :

(1) *Circulation* : Under this system currency was to circulate in any metal other than gold.

(2) *Legal Tender* : It is a full legal tender money convertible into gold.

(3) *Free Trading* : There is no restriction on imports and exports of gold.

(4) *Role of Central Bank* : Under the system , Central Bank was to purchase gold from the public at a fixed price.

(5) *Operation of the System* : The Central Bank of the country was to operate the system by keeping part of the circulated money in Gold Reserve.

The essential features of gold bullion standard are also the same as those of a gold currency standard, with the only difference that the currency does not consist of gold. Instead, it is exchangeable with a fixed quantity. Evidently, it does not matter much, whether the currency consists of gold or something else, provided it is exchangeable with gold, as we know that money is not an end in itself but a means to an end and anything which is exchangeable with gold will serve the same purpose as gold coins. A pound note purchased as much as a sovereign (gold pound) so long as it was exchangeable with sovereign or gold contents of sovereign. Such was the condition obtaining in Great Britain during the regime of the gold bullion standard from 1926 to 1931.

Merits

Following are the merits of Gold BullionStandard :

(1) *Stable*-It establishes relatively more stable exchange rate.

(2) *Elastic*-It posesses more elasticity to supply of money.

(3) *Adjustment*-It helps in proper adjustment according to the monetary conditions of the economy.

Demerits

Following are the demerits of this kind of Gold Standard :

(1) *Government's Interference*- It increase interference of government in the monetary conditions of the country.

(2) *Lack of Public Trust*-It creates uncertainty in the public trust due to overflow during the time of emergency.

(3) *Non-Economic Activities*-It increases in the non-economic activities ; as it took place when Bank of England sold only 400 ounce of gold to businessmen; they took the gold bars, it was cut into small pieces by them and further gold to the persons interested in hoarding gold.

A report of the Bank of International Settlement says that in 1936 the hoarded amount of gold was nearly 50 million ounce.

(iii) Gold Exchange Standard. Gold exchange standard resembles gold bullion standard in many points. Under this standard as well, the circulating media does not consist of gold currency. It may consist of poper money and coins of metal other than gold. *This currency is exchangeable with gold for delivery in a foreign country or it is exchangeable with a foreign gold currency. In the latter case, some people prefer to call it gold courrency exchange standard.*

This system replaces the reserve as gold with some hard foreign currency namely, sterling or dollar. It it is kept in dollars then it is known as *Dollar Exchange Standard* and it it is attached to sterling then it is known as *Sterling Exchange Standard*.

The one essential difference therefore, between this standard and the gold bullion standard is that while under the latter, currency in circulation and gold bullion are exchangealbe for delivery within the country. They are exchangeable under the former only for delivery of gold outside the country.

In this case gold stocks need not be maintained, maintenance of sufficient balance with banks in foreign countries having gold standard serves the purpose.

This system was first adopted by Holland in 1877 and then by Russia and Austria-Hungry in 1892.

India and several other countries adopted it later on. This was the standard which was adopted after the war of 1914-18 by those countries of Central Europe as well whose currencies had to be entirely reconstituted due to their unlimited depreciation. It was recommended at the Geneva Conference of 1922 and its fundamental principles may be said to have affected almost all the monetary systems .

Main Features of Gold Exchange Standard

Following are important features of Gold Exchange Standard :

1. *Relationship* - It has no relation of national currency with gold.

2. *Market Restriction* -It restricted market of gold.

3. *Transation* -Dealing in draft are undertaken to stabilise the rate of exchange.

Merits of Gold Exchange Standard

Gold Exchange Standard has following Merits :

1. *Price Level* -It assists in Stabilisation to the price level.

2. *Rate of National Currency*- It provides stabilisation to the exchange rate of national currency.

3. *International Trade* -It provides encouragement to international trade.

4. *Favourable*-It is most favourable to under-developed countries.

5. *Market Stability* -It provides opportunity for a stable market of silver.

Demerits of Gold Exchange Standard

Following are the Demerits of Gold Exchange Standard.

1.*Bilateral Maintenance* -Bilateral maintenance of Gold Reserves makes this system responsive.

2. *Automatic*- Automatic development of the money is lost under Gold Exchange Standard.

3.*Motivation* - Under this system motivation is found for inflation due to easiness in circulation.

4. *Difficulty*- Difficulty realised in maintenance of exchange rate and stability.

5. *Dependence*- It has too much of dependence on gold causes retardation to the economic development.

Advantage of the Gold Standard

The following are advantages of Gold Standard :-

(1) *Promotes Confidence in the Monetary System* - The gold standard promotes confidence in the monetary system because gold being universally desirable has value in itself aside from its monetary use. This is not true in irredeemable paper money. If gold loses its acceptability as money, it can still be used as a store of value or it can be fabricated as jewellery, and the like : but if irredeemable paper money loses its monetary character, it will immediately become worthless. In a gold standard economy, the public is not only confident as to the quality of the gold money itself but they willingly accept other kinds of money such as hand to hand paper money and bank demand deposits, because these types are redeemable in gold.

(2) *Automatic Monetary System* - All that is essential is to make an internal monetary system automatic under a gold standard to fix certain requirements as to gold reserves in the monetary law and then to observe the rules of the game so determined. When bank notes and other types of hand- to hand money are issued a certain percentage of their face value must be held in the form of gold reserves.

(3) *Price Stability* - Perhaps the most cogent argument which can be presented in favour of a specific monetary standard, from the domestic as apart from the international point of view, is that it makes possible a seasonable degree of stability in the price of view, is that makes possible a seasonable degree of stability in the price level over a long period of time.

(4) *Exchange Stability* - Another important merit is that gold standard secures the stability of foreign exchange rates. The great merit of this stability becomes at once clear when we see how its absence owing to the break down of the gold standard, has checked the development of international trade in recent times. The stability of exchange rates, also secured a certain harmony in the movements in the price levels of different countries.

Disadvantages of the Gold Standard

The critics of the gold standard hold that the advantages which have been disucssed above are likely to be more visionary than real. The alleged disadvantages of the gold standard are chiefly given ahead:-

(1) *Fair-Weather Standard* - The claim that the gold standard is a fair weather standard, is offered by its critics in refutation of the claim that it promotes confidence in the minds of the people . A gold standard prcmtoes confidence in the stability of an internal monetary system only in times of normalcy or prosperity, good wages, high profits, and full employment. When an economic crisis develops, the gold standard is immediately threatened. Despite the presence of gold reserves, the confidence of the people in the safety of the monetary system suddely begins to wane. "Runs on the banks" develop and great amounts of gold are withdrawn for hoarding. At the very time when the gold standard should strengthen the faith of the people, its suspension takes place in order that the

remaining gold reserves may be protected. Thus the gold standard engenders confidence only when confidence is not needed; and in times of war and economic crisis, the suspension of the standard is too easily accepted as the way out.

(2)*Grave Disorders* - The argument , that the gold standard permits the internal monetary system to operate automatically, is untenable in view of the fact that monetary system have been managed by governmental authorities or the officials of central banks in all gold-standard countries since the restoration of the standard following the First Great War.

(3)*Surrenders Price Level to all Forces of Blind Chance.*-Many critics of the gold standard feel that the serious fluctuation in the price level result from the policy of making the value of a country's monetary unit equal to that of a specific quantity of gold. Such a policy , they hold, surrenders the price level to all the forces of blind chance, for variations in the price level may be expected to result from all chances in the supply and demand factors affecting gold, the discovery of new mines and the closing of old ones, developments in mining techniques, changes in wage rates and other costs in the mining industry, variations in the use of gold, in the art of hoarding and dishoarding and importation and exportation.

CAUSES FOR THE BREAK-DOWN OF THE GOLD STANDARD.

The important causes, that led to the breakdown of the gold standard after 1920, are as follows :-

(1) *Violation of Rules of the Game* -The most cogent cause of the breakdown of the gold standard was a failure to observe the fundamental rules of the gold standard. Almost all nations violated these rules. Gold movements were not permitted to have their natural influence on prices. England which was continually losing gold during this period, took steps to offset effects of these movements on the domestic price-level through the purchase of securities. The U.S.A. which

was receiving large imports of gold, sterilised the imports with a view to keep prices stable. The second rule was also violated by the three most important countries, England, France and the United States.

(2) *Obstructions to Foreign Trade* - The First Great War engendered in most countries a strong feeling of nationalism and the policies adopted by government came more and more to reflect a selfish point of view rather than the internal viewpoint. Great Britain lost her pre-eminent financial position, and self-interest prompted her to forego her former free trade policy and to promote intra-empire trade at the expense of non-British countries. Other countries, such as the U.S.A. raised tariff barriers to extraordinary levels and some established embargoes, granted exports subsidies, and entered into barter arrangements the direct exchange of goods. All the added restrictions to trade made possible a disparity of price levels in the different countries which gold movements did not correct.

(3) *Stickness of Prices* - The adjustment of price levels in keeping with the size of golds reserves was also, prevented internally by the development of great consolidated corporations, holding companies which controlled many subsidiaries, trade associations, and labour unions which resisted reductions in prices and wage rates and which instead constantly strove to raise them: and internationally, by powerful cartels which controlled the distribution and price of certain commodities in all parts of the world.

(4) *Maldistribution of Gold* - The war and post-war adjustments led to the maldistribution of the gold reserves of the world. The Central Powers were largely deprived of their gold holdings; many of the new countries of Central Eastern Europe found it very difficult to accumulate adequate reserves: and the U.S.A. and France had excessive reserves, at least as judged by comparison with their pre-war holdings.

(5) *Use of the Gold-Exchange Standard* - The establishment of the gold exchange standard by many countries was also a source of weakness in the international standard for the reason that gold movements which would ordinarily have occurred were no longer necessary. Payments by Indians to foreigners and by foreigners to Indians, for example, did not disturb the gold reserves of India, so long as the foreign countries held bank deposits there which they regarded as part of their gold reserves.

(6) *Political Instability* - Political instability in many of the post-war countries undermined the gold standard. Rumours of war, civil strife, and political agitation threatened the safety of monetary systems and panic movement of funds from country to country took place. When internal conditions looked unsound, individuals banks, and corporations sought to safeguard themselvges by selling their assets at home, and by opening deposit accounts with banks in other countries.

(7) *International Indebtedness*-Finally German reparations, the war debts owned by the Allies to the U.S.A. and a large volume of international lending, all served to prevent the smooth operation of the post-war gold standard. The payment of reparation and of instalments on the war debts caused movements of gold which had little relation to the direction of trade and to the price levels prevailing from country to country.

Thus after the termination of the Second World War the gold standard also got suspended. The effect, was made to create an international organisation to bring stability. However International Monetary Fund was created in 1945, and a new gold standard was adopted which was Gold Parity Standard.

❑

8

Inflation, Deflation Stagflation and Devaluation

Changes in the value of money or purchasing power is a continuous process which goes on taking place from time to time. Whenever the volume of money in the country expands (other things remaining constant) its value falls or the prices rise. The period of rising price is known as inflation. Inflation means continuous rise in the circulation of money which exceeds requirements of all activities. It results in continuous rise in prices which is another aspect of inflation. It simply means that when there is rise in prices because of the gap between money supply and transactions in the economy and where money supply exceed the requirement is called inflation.

On the otherhand, when the volume of money in the country contracts (others things remaining constant) the value of money rises or prices fall. The period of falling prices is known as deflation. In this chapter, we shall discuss inflatiions and deflation. This discussion will be followed by situation of inflation and devaluation in India.

INFLATION

Definition

Inflation is of different types and it is difficult to give a generally accepted definition. Technically the term inflation refers to rise in price due to an increase in the supply of money without a corresponding increase in demand. But generally it means a rise in the general level of price which has been brought about either by an increase in the supply of money or any other reason *i.e.,* shortage of supply of goods increased volume of currency increased supply of gold, etc. Inflation take place "whenever the supply of money and of bank deposits circulating through cheques so called 'Deposit currency' increases, relatively to the demand for media of exchange in such a way as to bring about a rise in the general price level".

Various economists have defined Inflation. Some of important definitions are as follows:

Crowther defines, "Inflation means a state in which the value of money is falling, *i.e.,* prices are rising."

Prof. Edwin Walter Kemmer defines, "Inflation is too much money and deposit currency, *i.e.,* too much currency in relation to the physical volume of busines being done."

Prof. A.C. Pigou defines, "Inflation occurs, when money income is expanding relatively to the output of work done by the productive agents for which it is the payment."

Sir R.G. Hawtrey defines, "Inflation is the issue of too much currency."

Dr. T.E. Gregory defines, "Inflation is the state of abnormal increase in the quantity of purchasing power."

Cause of Inflation

(1) Expansion of Currency and Deposits Money– The monetary authority deliberately expands the currency during deflationary period to lessen the burden upon the debtors and to provide relief to poor agriculturists. This policy is also adopted to finance development plans and achieve the full employment of productive resources. The low interest rate policy of the government also brings about an expansion of bank loans which increases deposit money.

(2) Increased Output of Gold– Inflation sometimes occurs due to a sudden increase in supply of gold. Such an increased supply may be due to the discovery of gold mines or heavy importation of gold from foreign countries.

(3) Scarcity of Goods and Services– The scarcity of goods and services cause inflation. It happens when the supply of currency increases faster than that of the growth of commodities and supply of services. As a result of it the commodities and services will become scarce and their prices would go up.

(4) Raising the Velocity of Money– Inflation also occurs when there is a great increase in the velocities of bank deposit currency. It happens when people stop preferring liquid money and their consumption function dominates the saving attitude.

(5) Deficit Financing– Inflation sometimes occurs due to the fact that the Government has to create money as a means of providing itself with funds for paying Government expenses. It happens when the government issues more currency in the market to meet its expenditure on monetary lines or government borrow money from the foreign countries to increase money supply. This device of the Government to finance itself with funds is known as 'deficit financing'.

(6) International Price Rise– It is said that inflation may be imported; for example rising prices in one country may bring sympathetic rise in the prices in the other country.

(7) Devaluation– Devaluation may cause inflation. After devaluation exports are encouraged. More goods are exported and thus there is scarcity of commodities at home. Hence the prices rise and induce inflation.

(8) Increase in Taxation - Though increased taxation is as a rule disinflationary . It is because suce increase reduce the purchasing power of the people. However, it taxes imposed are on production and sale of such goods which they can be passed on to consumer, price of such goods rise may augment inflation.

TYEPS OF INFLATION

Inflation is of different types classfied on various basis. Some of the basis on which inflation is classified are discussed below :

(A) *On the Basis of Full Employment*

1. Semi-Inflation (bottleneck).
2. Full-Inflation.

(B) *On the Basis of Causes*

1. Credit Inflation.
2. Currency Inflation.
3. Purchasing Power Inflation.
4. Taxation and Budgetory Inflation.
5. Over-Investment Inflation.
6. Dis-Saving Inflation.
7. Devaluation Inflation.
8. Commodity Price Inflation.
9. Imported Inflation.

(C) *Inflation in a Complete Metallic Currency System*

It is caused due to following reasons :—

1. Increase in the Metallic coins' output.
2. Further Monetization of other metals.
3. De-Hoarding of Metals in circulation.
4. Import of the Metal.
5. Issue of more token money.
6. By Monetization of Foreign Coins.

(D) *On the Basis of Inducing Causes:*

1. Profit-Induced Inflation.
2. Wage-Induced Inflation.
3. Deficit -Induced Inflation.

(E) *On the Basis of Rapidity :*

1. Creeping Inflation or slow Inflation.
2. Hyper-Inflation or Galloping Inflation or Jumping Inflation.

(F) *On the Basis of Control :*

1. Open Inflation.
2. Controlled Inflation of Suppressed Inflation.

(G) *Classification on the Basis of Nature :*

1. Demand -Pull Inflation.
2. Cost-Push Inflation.

(H) *On the Basis of Area of Activity :*

1. National Inflation.
2. International Inflation .

Description of each type of inflation given below—

(i) Semi Inflation -According to Lord Keynes if an increase in the price is partly due to increase in the cost of production and partly due to increase in the supply of money before the point of full employment, it is called semi-inflation or Bottleneck Inflation.

This kind of inflation is chronic to the countries which are below the full employment level. This inflation causes increase in the employment opportunities.

(ii) Full-Inflation-This is a kind of inflation which prevail after an economy has achieved the level of full employment. Any increase in the money supply will only result in the rise of prices, since there is full employment in the economy.

In full inflation every unit of more money in circulation will directly increase the prices. It is not good for economy according to Lord Keynes.

Credit-Inflation-It is a kind of inflation which originates due to expansion of credit money which further increases the purchasing power of money without any further increase in the production.

Currency -Inflation -When inflation is caused due to the excessive flow of currency it is currency inflation. It happens when government issues more currency without any ligitimate demand of currency in the form of goods and services.

Purchasing Power Inflation-When the restrictions on the wages and salaries are lifted and more money is paid to these people whose purchasing power increases, causing increase in the prices. It is called purchasing power inflation.

Taxation and Budgetory Inflation-Increase in the taxes whether direct or indirect raises the price of the commodities which result in inflation. To meet the gap between revenue and expenditure some time government adopts the technique of deficit financing, which further increases the money supply and consequently raises the prices.

If this kind of inflation is not checked it results into galloping inflation.

Over investment Inflation-When the investment exceeds the production done by the units, them economy faces inflation due to the increase of money supply in the market due to over investment.

Dis-Saving Inflation-When saving starts falling down, the purchasing power of the individual goes up. This results in increasing the expenditure which causes inflation.

Devaluation Inflation-This kind of inflation occurs when there is decrease in the value of money. This act is called as devaluation. The inflation caused due to this act is called Devaluation Inflation.

Commonly Inflation-When the inflation is caused due to the increase in the commodity price, it is called commodity price inflation.

Imported Inflation-When there is inflation to meet the repayment of the imports, it is called imported inflation . It generally happens when imports goes up very quickly.

Inflation under a Complete Currency System

Now-a-days no economy prevails with the complete currency system. In theory , in such a country the inflation occurs due to varioous reasons. If currency supply goes up or if the government accepts some other metal as currency metal then the supply of coins will go up. In case if more token money is issued more currency will flow into the market and that will further cause inflation . The same thing will happen if foreign coins are monetized.

Profit Induced Inflation-When the sellers want more and more profit; this they do either by reducing they per unit cost or by increasing the selling price. When they want to earn by increasing the selling price then inflation occurs. This is called Profit Induced Inflation.

Wages Induced Inflation-When workers demand more wages and it is increased without any increase in the production of the commodities; then it creates inflation. Because increase in the money-wages ; automatically boosts up the purchasing power of the workers.

Deficit Induced Financing-It occurs when the money supply goes up without any legitmate increase in production through deficit financing. Deficit Finance is the printing of new currency and circulating it in the market, to meet the excess of expenditure over its revenue on the part of the government.

Creeping Inflation-Creeping inflation is the inflation with slow speed. This inflation is helpful to those developing economies which fear a kind of stagnation or breakage in the course of economic transition. It is sometimes inevitable for the economy. As the economy has to divert its resources towards productive field with less amount left to meet the increasing demand for goods and services.

However economists have warned that if such type of inflation is allowed to prevail for long then it would result into galloping type of inflation which will uproot the development of economy.

Creeping inflation can be explained through following diagram.

Diagram

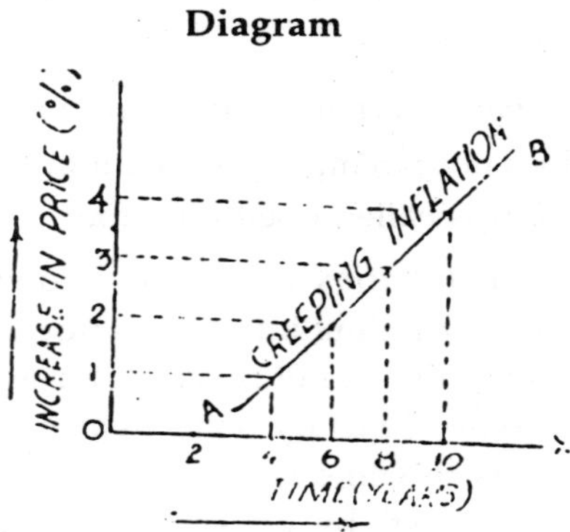

Line AB explains the slow movement of prices upward with the passage of the time shown on Y (axis).

Galloping or Hyper Inflation-It is wrost type of inflation which lies beyond the normal conditions and may end in the ruin of Monetary System of the affected economy. It is a kind of inflation in which prices starts going up, quite rapidly within a very short period. The ratio of increase in price level is higher than that of the ratio of change in the time. It all happens at galloping speed. Lord Keynes has called it as the full inflation in the sense that it is the final stage of inflation.

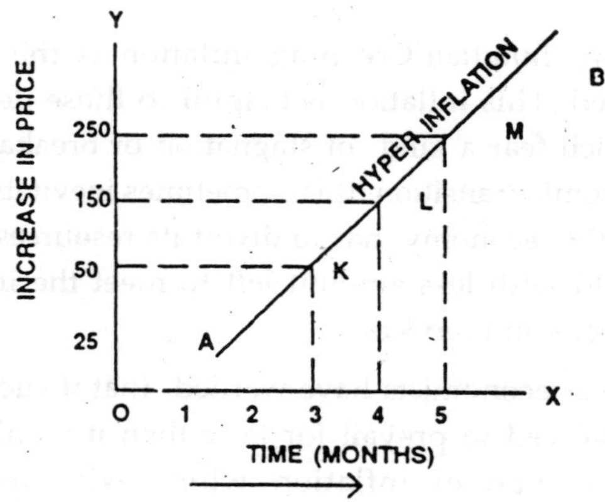

Line AB shows the hyper inflationary urend. At the end of 3rd Month by price level went up by 5% at the end of 4th Month the prices went by 150% and at the end of the 5th the price went up by 250% .

Open Inflation-When an inflation is out of control and government does not attempt to check it or if it goes out of the controlling rein; it is called open inflation.

Controlled Inflation-It is also known as suppressed Inflation. When a prevailing inflation is put under control for a time being. The inflation is not checked for ever, but it is under the pressure of some Monetary policy which does not allow the inflationary trends to come up. To quote Paul Einzing, if the inflation ,"is prevented by governmental measures such as rationing , price control, etc., from producing its effects on prices, it is suppressed inflation."

Demand Pull Inflation-When demand for the commodity increase and exceeds the supply the prices of the commodities starts going up. Demand exceeds the supply and thus purchasing power goes over the commodities available in the economy. It happens , according to experts on the subject due to increasing expenditure of the government and small volume of taxation. This can be explained with the help of the diagram given in the following page.

In the diagram on OX axis demand and supply have been represented. On OY axis prices level has been shown. At the first stage DD demand curve cuts the SS supply curve at *e* : the price level is OP (on OY axis). Further demands goes up by OM cutting the supply curve SS at *e*'.

The price level goes from OP to OP'. Hence the inflation has started in the economy again the demand of the commodity increase and the price level goes to P_2. After a certain period of time, supply becomes inelastic. A further increase in demand (shown by D_3D_2 curve) which meets the supply curve SS' at e' raises the price level to OP_2 . Hence the increase in the prices is only due to the increase in demand. Price level is going up because supply of the goods at the current prices is unable to meet the demand , which is increasing rapidly.

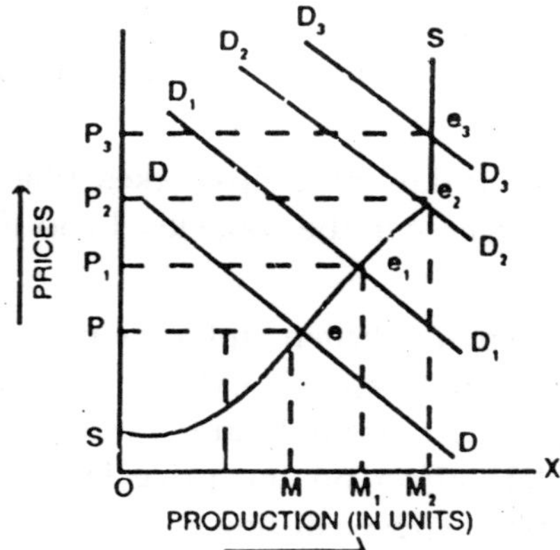

Cost-Push Inflation-Cost Push inflation occurs when less supply is available at higher prices due to the increase in the cost per unit of the product. The push in the cost may be due to various reasons like increase in the wages of the labourers , increase in the price of the raw-material or manufacturing.

This inflation can be explained with the help of the following diagram.

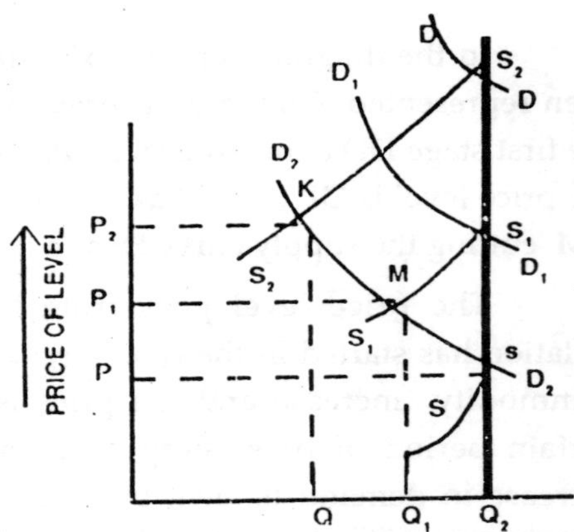

In the diagram demand curve D_2D_2 cuts the supply curve SS at point S. The price level (on Y axis) is OP. The demand and supply are both OQ. Points is the point of equilibrium. A further rise in the cost pushes up the supply curve to S_1S_1 position which cuts the demand curve D_2D_2 at M. OP is the higher price level. A further shift is supply from S_1S_1 to S_2S_2 cuts the demand curve at point K. Price level again goes to P_2.

Cost push inflation chiefly takes place when trade unions press for increase in the wage level and if their demand is accepted.'

National Inflation-When inflationary process attacks national economy only then it is called National Inflation. In such an inflation prices rise only in the economy. They do not have any parallel effect on the price level of the trading countries. This often happens during war.

International Inflation-When the rise in prices becomes common for the whole world it is called international inflation. The National Inflation affects the other economies through trade which bibles the whole world. 'The price-rise becomes the talk of the town', every where without caring for any country as an exception.'

This may happen in case of World War. A World War creates acute shortage of certain essential commodities in the whole world.

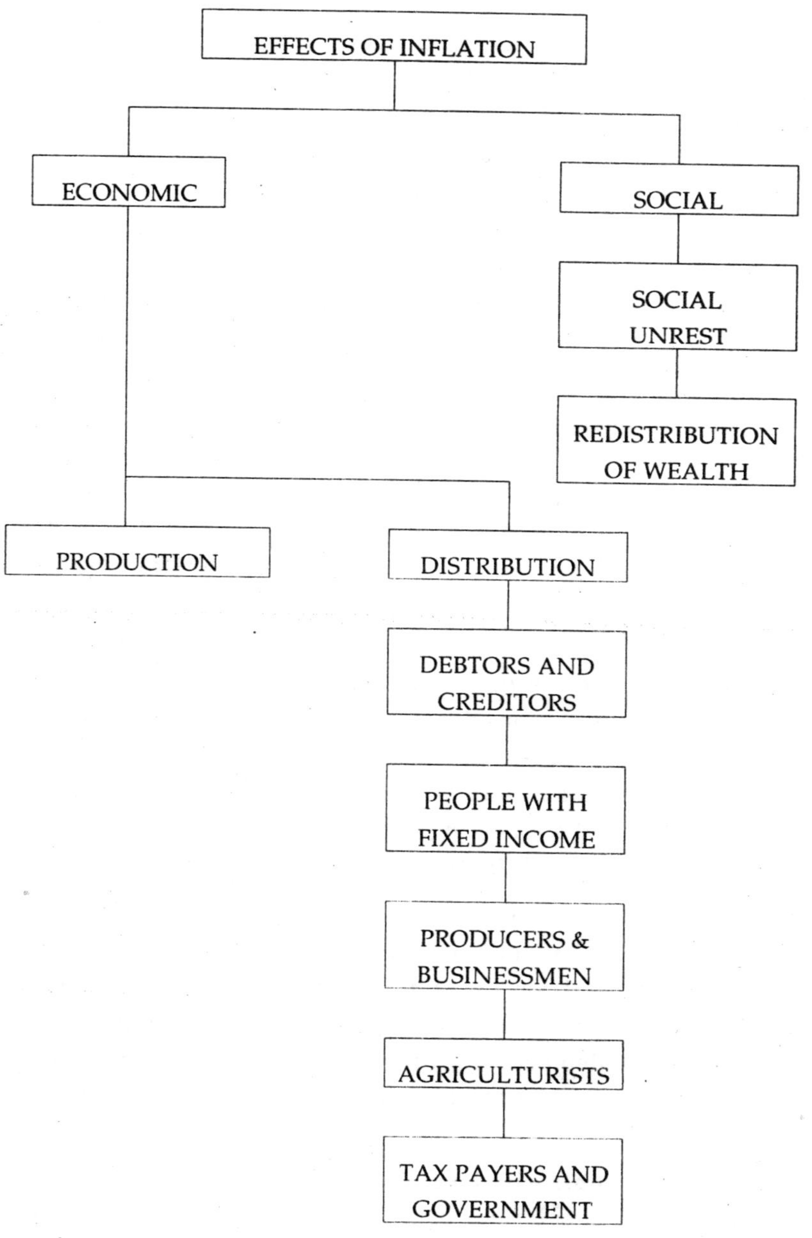

EFFECTS OF INFLATION

Inflation has its multifarious effects on the different sections of the society . Different section are affected by it in different ways. But inflation does not affect all the people euqally. Its effect on the various sections of society and also on different activities are mentioned below:

1. Effect on Production– As observed by *Keynes*, inflation beyond full employment level, affects production adversely. It leads to reduction in production and increase in unemployment. During inflation producers or firms do not find it profitable to produce and sell. They prefer to hoard. Production may also be interrupted by labour unrests and strikes. Similarly agriculturist do not sell but hold their stocks in the hope of getting higher prices. Thus, during inflation or rising prices or falling value of money stocks accumulate, profits fall, production declines and income falls and unemployment ensues.

2. Effects on Distribution– Inflation affects different classes of the society in different ways. It brings about changes in the distribution of income between different sections of the people. Inflation is considered unjust and cruel as it transfers money from the poor to the rich classes. Some people are affected more favourably than the other classes in the community. In the following description the effect of inflation on each class of people in the community has been examined.

(i) Debtors and Creditors– During periods of rising prices debtors gain and creditors lose because the money was borrowed when it was dear but it is paid back when it is cheap. During rising price money buys less goods so it becomes cheap. Thus, though debtors return the same amount of money, they return less in terms of goods or services. Hence the creditors are adversely affected and the debtors gain.

(ii) People with Fixed Income– In this group we include wage earners, salaried people, pensioners, renteers and receivers of interest. This group of people lose since wages, salaries, interest, rent etc. do not increase in proportion to the rise in prices. Thus, the purchasing power of this group of people diminishes during periods of rising prices and they are hard hit.

(iii) Consumers–People as consumers are also hard hit during rising prices. The cost of living rises more than the income and savings are wiped out. But they are required to pay higher prices for articles of consumption. They feel miserable and desperate.

(iv) Producers and Businessman–The entrepreneurs, producers, wholesalers and retailers earn during inflation period of rising prices. This class of people gain because of three reasons :

(i) They are mostly debtors and debtors gain during rising prices,

(ii) They buy raw materials and other goods at old and lower prices with the object to sell at higher prices; and

(iii) Wages, interest, rent etc., do not increase as they are usually fixed by way of contracts made earlier. Thus producers and businessmen earn surplus profits during rising prices.

(v) Agriculturists–Agriculturists gain during the period of rising prices because the agricultural commodities fetch more money in the market but rent on their land is not increased. Moreover wages of the agricultural labour do not increase proportionately.

(vi) Tax Payer and Government–During the period of rising prices, tax payers gain because though they pay slightly higher taxes they give less amount in terms of goods and services than before. Income-tax payers gain because they pay in the currency units whose value has depreciated as compared to the value when it was earned. The burden of land revenue is also decreased because those who pay it, pay less in term of goods to the Government. The burden of public debt, both external and internal, also decrease during the period of rising prices.

3. Social Effects– Social effects of inflation are not less dangerous as explained below:

(i) Social Unrest– The situation of rising prices are always accompained by distress and social unrest. Due to rise in their cost of living wage earners demand for increase in wage. They pressurise their employer through a variety of labour problems and create social unrest.

(ii) Re-distribution of wealth– During rising prices or inflation there is a re-distribution of wealth. Speculators and profiters rob wage earners and fixed income group blindly and become rich people.

We may sum-up the effects of inflation by saying that inflation is economically unsound, politically dangerous and socially and morally disastrous. It creates inequalities of wealth and distribution and paralyses entire machinery of wealth production.

Control of Inflation

Inflation is considered like cancer for economy. It creates inequalities of wealth distribution and paralyses the machinery of wealth production. It must be controlled at all costs.

Inflation is caused when the total expenditure is more than that of the total volume of goods. Hence the best way to control inflation is to limit the amount of the total expenditure incurred by the community. It is not possible to cut the public expenditure on essential services *e.g.*, on education, medical relief, health etc. But all other expenditures can be easily curtailed. The following methods are adopted to control inflation :

1. Fiscal Policy–During inflation the Government should raise the rates of all taxes. This would reduce the money income of the people and they would be left with less purchasing power. As a result of this people would buy less goods and services. But if too high rate of taxation are levied, the capital formation would be retarded. The Government can also initiate schemes of compulsory savings.

2. Monetary Policy–In a modern economic society credit plays a vital role. The commercial banks create money which circulates side by side with currency notes issued by the Central Bank. In order to eliminate huge monetary fluctuations and stablise prices and business activities must control the volume of currency and credit in circulation. The Central Bank is the ultimate monetary authority in a country. To achieve this end the Central Bank raises the bank rate and thereby raises the rate of interest to limit both personal expenditure and private investment. High rate of interest reduces the expenditure on consumption and also leads to decline in private investment. In this way the total expenditure is kept limited.

The other monetary measures are raising the reserve ratio of the scheduled banks, quantitative control of credit to certain limit, control against giving loans for speculative purposes, etc.

3. Monetary Reforms and Blocking Liquid Assets–After the World War there was an excessive note issue in many countries. these countries introduced a new currency in which one new note was given in exchange for a number of old ones. The old notes were either cancelled or blocked. Even the bank deposits were blocked and the depositors were allowed to withdraw only a part of their deposits. Through these devices a large portion of the excess of money was eliminated. The countries which adopted the above devices were Belgium, France, Denmark, Netherlands, Norway, Czechoslovakia and U.S.S.R.

This method has its limitations too, *i.e.*, blocking of notes and bank deposits would cause a good deal of injustice particularly in case of a parent who saved money out of his hard earned money for the education or marriage of his children.

4. Price Control and Rationing–Another method is to introduce a comprehensive system of price control and rationing. The Government fixes the prices of essential commodities and through rationing of essential commodities the demands for these is adjusted to their supply. But the control must be a full and rigid one otherwise the situation would be worse than no control. It will develop black market for the commodities controlled and rationed.

5. Control of Investment–During inflation all types of investments should be curtailed and brought within the control of the Government. A system of licensing would be the best method for it. Only essential industries are permitted to invest while investment in all non-essential channels is stopped.

6. Increase in Production–The most effective method to control inflation is the increased production of commodities. During inflation there is scarcity of goods. It is said that during inflation people go to the market with baskets full of money, but return only with their pockets full of commodities. Hence when production is increased the prices will come down and inflation will be controlled.

DEFLATION

Deflation means a fall in the general level of prices which has been brought about either by a decrease in the supply of money or any other reason, *i.e.*, increase of the supply of goods, decrease in the volume of currency etc. In other words, deflation is said to occur whenever the supply of money and of bank deposits (deposit currency) decreases relating to the demand for media of exchange in such a way as to bring about a fall in the general price level. It leads to fall in prices and therefore, a rise in the value of money or increase in its purchasing power.

Deflation is a state of disequilibrium in which a contraction of purchasing power tends to cause, or is the effect of, a decline of the price level."

Deflation regenerates into depression in the economy. It creates unemployment slackens the economic growth and distracts the economic structure of the country. During deflation velocity of money falls down with the reduction in the purchasing power of the people.

Deflation occurs when checks are applied to remove inflation and when these checks are not controlled at the particular point, then it paves the way for Deflation.

Causes of Deflation

Following are the factors which lead to deflation in an economy:–

(1) Increase in Production–A rapid increase in production over flows the demand in the economy. Supply of goods exceeds the demand at a particular time, which consequently brings the price level down. Increase in production occurs, in the bid to remove inflation, and it steps at the point of over production. This over production results into deflation.

(2) Anti-Inflationary Measures–The measures taken to check up inflation creates the condition of deflation in the economy like:–

(a) Higher Bank Rates–The 'Bank Rate' raised to reduce the credit during the time of inflation proves as a disincentive to savings and investments.

(b) Open Market Operations–These are also responsible for taking away currency from the market.

(c) Higher Taxation–It weakens the entrepreneurial skills to earn more profit. It retards the capital formation.

(d) Reduction in Public Expenditure–Any suspension of public works creates unemployment which reduces the general demand in the economy. It not only reduces the employment but also decreases the 'effective demand'.

(3) Unfavourable Balance of Payments–Unfavourable balance of payments also makes it obligatory for the economy to pay the balance in huge amount of gold. This affects the money circulation which is curtailed in the national market.

The steps of devaluation taken to remove the unfavourable balance of payments also paves the way for deflation in long-run period.

Effects of Deflation

1. The Gainer and the Losers–The people who gain during the time of inflation are the ultimate losers during the time of deflation.

The Gainers

During the time of deflation following group of persons gain:-

(i) Consumers–Due to the fall in prices they are able to by more with less money. For them, the value of money goes up. Due to the fall in the cost of living, their standard of living goes up.

(ii) Land Lords and Property Owners–This group also gains during the time of deflation. The rent of their property being fixed now they get more money, in terms of goods.

(iii) Salaried People–Those getting fixed income or salaries gain during the time of depression. Their purchasing power increases with the fall in the prices.

(iv) Creditors–Those getting fixed income or salaries gain during the time of depression. Their purchasing power increases with the fall in the prices.

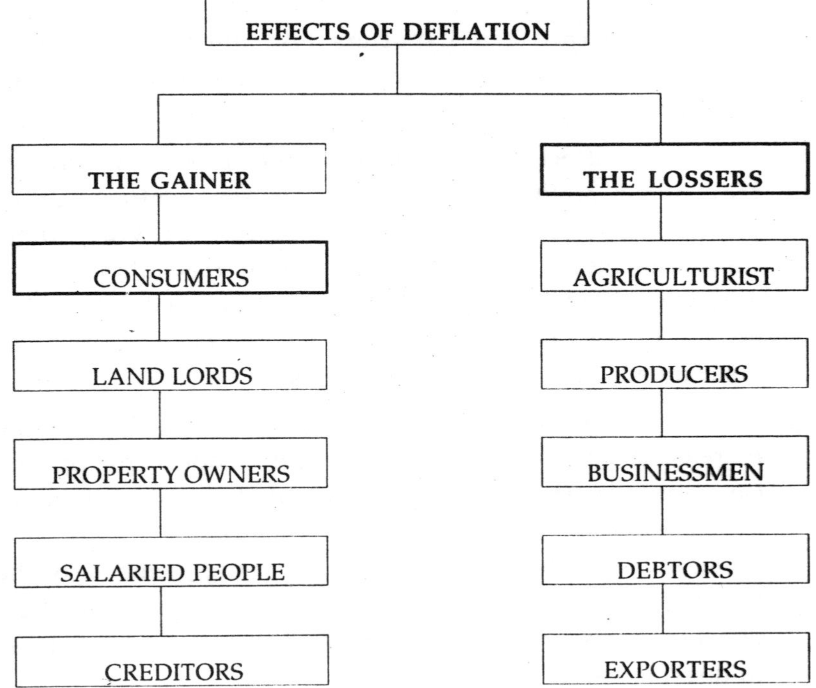

The Lossers

(i) Agriculturists–They lose because they have to pay fixed rent. The purchasing power of rent is higher during deflation than paid during normal times and or during the times of inflation.

(ii) Producers and Businessmen–Profit margin is reduced during the time of deflation. Producer's profit is curtailed. Velocity of money falls down which proves harmful to the businessmen. They close down their enterprises due to continuous loss.

(iii) Debtors–During the period of deflation debtors also lose because the money which they return to the creditors command higher purchasing power. In the sense of goods and services they return more money to the creditors.

(iv) Exporters–Exporters lose during the time of deflation due to an increase in the value of money. Exports are discouraged whereas imports find encouragement.

2. Effect on Employment Level–Due to the ultimate reduction in profit margin the producers start contracting their production. The fall in the prices provide them discouragement. The ultimate result of this fall in prices creates involuntary unemployment. The industrial units which are not capable of reducing the cost to the falling price-level, are compelled to close down their units.

3. Lowers the Standard of Living–Due to the increasing amount of unemployment peoples' purchasing capacity falls. This reduces the general standard of living of the labour class. Those who are thrown out of employment cause a kind of burden to the other earning members of the family. It only creates poverty in the economy. A country where deflation exists most of the factors of production are wasted due to unexploitation.

4. Lowers the National Income–Gloom covers the economy during the times of deflation. Falling productive capacity, closure of many productive units, decrease in exports affects the national income in the economy. A country becomes economically weak during the period of deflation.

5. Disequilibrium–Deflation creates fluctuations in economy by creating a situation of disequilibrium in the economy. Supply is always greater than demand and it keeps on lowering the demand with its fall. This disequilibrium harms the economic structure of the economy. It distorts the development in all fields.

MEASURES TO CHECK DEFLATION

When we talk about the measure to check inflation that means to increase the money supply, to raise the money supply and activate the productive process. Following are the measure to check deflation.

(i) To Increase the Expenditure on Public Works–The government can raise its expenditure on public works like-spreading of rail, digging of cannels, dams and other undertakings of constructive works. It will give employment to large number of people at the same time more currency will come in circulation in the market in form of public expenditure. The people securing employment will also have some purchasing power which will increase the demand for commodities in the market.

(ii) To Induce Investment–Government must provide facilities for higher rate of investment in the economy. This will expand the industrial sector along with other sectors. It will further raise level of employment and purchasing power of the individuals. This can be done with the adoption of following techniques:–

(a) Lowering the Bank Rate–A low 'bank rate' will make the money cheap. More people will borrow from banks and thus credit will expand in the market.

(b) Suspension of Open Market Operations–Such method should be withdrawn and those who have deposited money should be returned by liquidating various credit papers issued by the central bank to overcome inflation.

(iii) To Raise Propensity to Consume–High rate of propensity to consume is necessary for a higher aggregate demand in the economy. Government must adopt healthy measure to raise the consumption function in the economy and to increase the demand.

An increase in demand will naturally push up the supply and provide momentum to hitherto decaying productive sectiors of the economy.

REFLATION

Inflation and reflation are the two terms whcih sometime resemble each other. The state of affair when deflation reaches to its extreme limit and prices fall down to extremely low limit and then the government resorts to inflation. In this situation efforts are made to increase money supply with a view to pushing the prices to the normal level.

According to **G.D.H. Cole**, "reflation may be defined as inflation deliberately undertaken to relieve a depression."

Reflation is a form of controlld "inflation. As observed by **Prof. Coulbornu**, "if there are unemployed men and capital goods and if profits are low, then higher price and income are essential., that's reflation, not inflation.

DISINFLATION

Disinflation is the situation under which the fall in prices is not accompained by a corresponding fall in the level of output, employment and income in the economy. As observed by **Prof Coulborn**, "...a lowring price, incomes and expenditure when they would be beneficial would be disinflation... no one wants deflation obviously, but things have got out of hand since the war, much money chasing too few goods, inflation and the cure is disinflation."

The period of the second world war and the post war witnessed a steep rise in prices all over the world. With a view to control the alarming situation of rising price the policy of distribution of essential goods was adopted so that money supply can be reduced to control inflation. The aforesaid situation is termed as disinflation.

Different between Inflation and Reflation

BASIS	INFLATIOIN	REFLATION
Cause	Inflation is caused by natural and voluntary causes on which the government has not control	Reflation is invariably adopted by the government as per a pre-conceived plan. It is always deliberate on the part of the government to relieve the situation of deflation.
Prices	During inflation prices rise very rapidly because production does not increase with the increase in price.	Price rise slowly and gradually under reflation because the pressure of price rise is effected by the increase in production.
Characteristics	Inflation is symptom of disease	Relatioin is a treatment of disease
Stage of Trade Cycle	It occurs in the boom stage of trade cycle or in other words, after the point of full employment.	It occurs in the recovery stage of trade cycle i.e., after the point of full employment is achieved.
Control	If inflation is not controlled, it may ruin the economy.	It brings about planned improvement in the already shattered economy.

Difference between Deflation and Disinflation

One of the common characteristics of deflation and disinflatin is that under both the situations money supply reduces and the price level goes down. Although the nature of both these situation is the same still that there are notable differences between these two situations as under :

BASIS OF DIFFERENCE	DEFLATION	DISINFLATION
1. Cause	It can be both man-made as well as natural.	It in always planned and is based on the government policy.
2. Results	Its end result emerges in the form of depression	In the situation of disinflation price level comes to normal conditions
3. Objective	It has no objective of its own	The objective of disinflation is to remove painful consequences of inflation
4. Price Level	In the situatin of deflation price level goes down. It goes below even the normal price level.	The situation of disinflation is created to bring down the price level to normal level.
5. Control	It is difficult to control	It can be controlled easily.
6. Effect on employment	It causes unemployment in the economy.	It helps in balancing the level of full-employment.
7. Nature	It is dangerous for the economy	It is beneficial for the economy though upto certain extent.

STAGFLATION

'Stagflation' is a novel situation. It is termed to a situation under which inflation of prices and stagflation of economic activity exist side by side. It is the situation in which the general priçe level tends to be high and inflationary pressures seem all round but inspite of that there occurs recessionary trend in certain industries particularly in construction industries.

According to *Keynes,* inflation starts as soon as the level of full employment in the economy is achieved. If the prices rises further and the inflation steps into hyper inflation. Its bad effects can easily be visualised. It is the situation under which the real income of the people begins to fall and they prefer to spend money rather than to save it for future. Therefore why they pull down the demand of some non-essential items. The demand under inflation goes up to certain extent and production starts falling and consequently, the production in some industries is either halted or reversed. Normally it happens in certain non-essential industries because inflation distorts the cost-price relationship and the people change their priorities. They prefer to spend first on necessities and then if purchasing power is left they buy other commodities.

INFLATION AND DEVALUATION IN INDIA

Price trends in India tell us about the inflationary problems in the country. In a developing economy like India, there has always been a tendency of rising prices. The rising prices (or inflation) may be good for some sections of the society particularly producers and businessmen. But certainly the rising prices are dangerous.

The objectives of monetary policy in India are to monetise the economy *i.e.,* to provide adequate money supply so that economic development may not suffer. In India, increasing investment in different sector of the economy has encouraged rise to inflationary pressure in the economy. If inflationary pressures in the economy go out beyond the control then it may be sufficient cause for ruination the economy. Thus it is clear that money supply should increase for the faster economic development but it should not increase at a rate that may generate inflationary pressure on the economy.

The Indian economy remained under inflationary pressures during five year plan as discussed below:

Inflationary pressures during 1951-1971

Among the various objectives of the *First plan,* the important declared objective of the plan was to combat inflationary pressures. Fortunately, the country succeeded in achieving this objective. The price situation was very favourable due to bumper crop. The favourable price movement of prices encouraged government to undertake more and more development work and greater degree of deficit financing. There was a gradual and steady price rise between 1955-56 and also 1960-61. During this period the general price level rose by 20 per cent.

The price position during the Third Five-Year Plan deteriorated badly. The main reason behind the scene was the Chinese invasion towards the end of 1962 and Indo-Pak conflict in 1965. The economy was under heavy strain of inflation as prices had gone up because of extensive hoarding and black marketing in foodgrains and other essential goods. Between 1961 and 1966, the economy of the country was on the brink of a galloping inflation. If we take example of price rise trend of some essential commodities then we find that during the aforesaid period the rise in the prices of food stuffs was over 40 per cent, in cereals it was over 45 per cent and in pulses it was 70 per cent. But the situation of inflationary rise in price was completely arrested in 1967-68 due to the bumper harvest. In 1968-69 pries even fell marginally by 1 per cent.

Inflation before and during Emergency

Even though the inflationary pressure on Indian economy has been steadily rising ever since economic planing was initiated in 1951, the upward movement of prices during the Fourth Plan (1969–74) was extremely significant. The price level was rather slow in the beginning but gathered momentum later on. Around 1973-74, the country faced the situation of double digit inflation. The main causes responsible for the inflation during this period were:

(a) Widespread failure of kharif crops in 1972-73

(b) Arrival of refugees from Bangla Desh.

(c) Indo-Pak war.

(d) Increase in money supply by 66.3 percent due to deficit financing.

(e) Increase in crude oil prices by OPEC countries in 1973.

There was a dramatic change in the inflationary pressure on Indian economy since September 1974 when the prices started falling. The steep decline in prices during this period was of considerable significance to the economy in the sense that it created an environment of stability and confidence.

The credit for checking the rise in inflation level was given to the declaration of emergency in June 1975.

Inflation During Janta Rule

A review of inflationary pressure on Indian economy during 1977-78 and 1978-79 bring out the fact that the Janta Government was indeed successful in holding the price line. In fact, the maintenance of price stability has been a positive achievement of the Government's efforts.

Inflation During the Eighties

The Congress (I) Government which came to power in January 1980 regarded inflation as its number one problem. The poor agricultural crop of 1979-80 and the consequent adverse effect on industrial production and hike in oil prices by 130 per cent in 1980 alone were responsible for boosting the price level.

Inflation Since 1990

The Wholesale Price Index (WPI) which had risen sharply in 1990-91 also continued thereafter. The average annual rate of inflation were 12.1 per cent and 13.6 per cent in 1990-91 and 1991-92 respectively. It was however restricted later on from August 1993. It started rising again because of heavy fiscal deficit. During 1994-95 and 1995-96 price situation remained under control. In April 1996, the rate of inflation was 4.5 per cent.

The annual rate of growth of price level in different plan period has been shown in the following table:

Table-1

Average Annual Growth of Prices

(in Percentages)

Plan	Rate of Growth %
First Plan (1951-56)	−3
Second Plan (1956-61)	6.2
Third Plan (1961-66)	5.7
Fourth Plan (1969-74)	8.9
Fifth Plan (1974-78)	6.3
Sixth Plan (1980-85)	9.3
Seventh Plan (1985-90)	6.9
Eighth Plan (1992-97)	9.0

DEVALUATION

Devaluation has been desfined as "the reduction of official rate at which one currency is exchanged for another. It can be more clearly explained as an act of reducing the value of a currency in terms of monetary metal or in terms of another currency.

Devaluation of Indian Rupee in India in 1966

The India rupee was first devaluated in 1949. The second devaluation was restorted to on June 6, 1966. This time Indian rupee was devalued to an extent of 36.6 per cent. In other way it can be explained as the foreign currency as compared to Indian rupee had been revalued by 57.5 per cent.

Main Reasons

The main reasons behind the devaluation of Indian rupee in 1966 were as follows:

(1) Continuous Price Rise– The prices in the Indian market were continuously rising and Government was unable to check them. As it was not possible to bring down the prices and Indian Government was compelled to devaluate the Indian rupee.

(2) Disastrous Export Policy– The contemporary Indian export policy was a complete failure. The Government of India has taken certain steps as an attempt to raise the exports but they were all proved in vain.

(3) Slump in Foreign Aid– Due to non-availability of much needed foreign aid, there was no option before the Government except to devalue the Indian rupee.

(4) Decline in Foreign Reserve– The rise of import in India as compared to the exports was also sufficient reason for fast decline in foreign exchange reserve. Hence, decline in foreign exchange reserve was another important reason for the devaluation of Indian rupee in 1966.

❑

9

Bank
Meaning & Functions

Bank is considered to be an ancient institution just like money. However, in ancient time the scope of world 'bank' was limited to the system of prescriber (*i.e.,* payment of an amount of money by draft) and prescriber (the demand of money). In ancient time it was only function of the banks to lend money and charge something for the same. The most accepted bank was known as the 'Bank of Venice', established in 1157.

A bank has been often described as an institution engaged in accepting of deposits and granting loans. It is the institution which deals in money and credit. It can also be described as an institution which borrows idle resources, makes fund available to . Those who need it and helps in the cheap remittance of money from one place to another. In the modern time the term 'Bank' is used in a wider term. Now it does not refer only to a particular place of lending and depositing money but it also act as an agent which looks after the various financial problems of its consumers.

Origin

There seem no uniformity amongst the economiost about the origin of the world 'Bank'. Accoring one galaxy of economists, the world 'Bank' has been derived from the German world 'BANC ' which mean Joint Stock of firm. There are some other persons holds the view that it has been derived from the Italiam word 'BANCO' which means a heap or mound. Infact at the time of establishment of Bank of venice in 1157, the German were influential and hence, perhaps the word '*BANC* or BANCO ' was used by Italians to denote the accumulation of securities with a Joint stock firm which later on with the passage of time came to be known as Bank'. The meaning of term 'Bank', as given in the dictionary is, 'a bench, office or institution for the keeping, lending and exchanging etc., of money; a money box for saving; a stock of money fund of capital; in games of hazard, the money, the proprietor or other, who plays against all.

In its simplest sense banks are institutions which deal in money. "Broadly speaking, bankers collect money from those who have it to spare or who are saving it out of their income and lend this money out against goods or securities to those who require it."

Definition

Bank is a comprehensive word. Various definitions have been given of the term Bank at various places and in various form. In order to understand the basic idea, few definition falls under different categories.are given hereunder to make the meaning of the term 'bank' more clear. Definitions of bank may be studied in dividing it in three form :

(I) Definition Given in Dictionary.

The Definition of the term Bank as given in English Dictionary are explained below :

According to *The Oxford English Dictionary,* "A bank is an establishment for custody of money received from or on behalf of its customers. Its essential duty is to pay their drafts on it. Its profits arises from the use of the money left unemployed by them."

Accorcding to *Webster's Dictionary,* "Bank is an institutions which trades in money, establishment for the deposit, custody and issue of money, as also for making loans and discounts and facilitating the transmission of remittances from one place to another."

(II) Views of Academicians

View expressed by academicians to define the term bank are discussed below :

According to *Prof. Kinley,* "A bank is an establishment which makes to individuals such advances of money or other means of payment as may be required and safely made; and to which individuals entrust money or means of payment when not required by them for use."

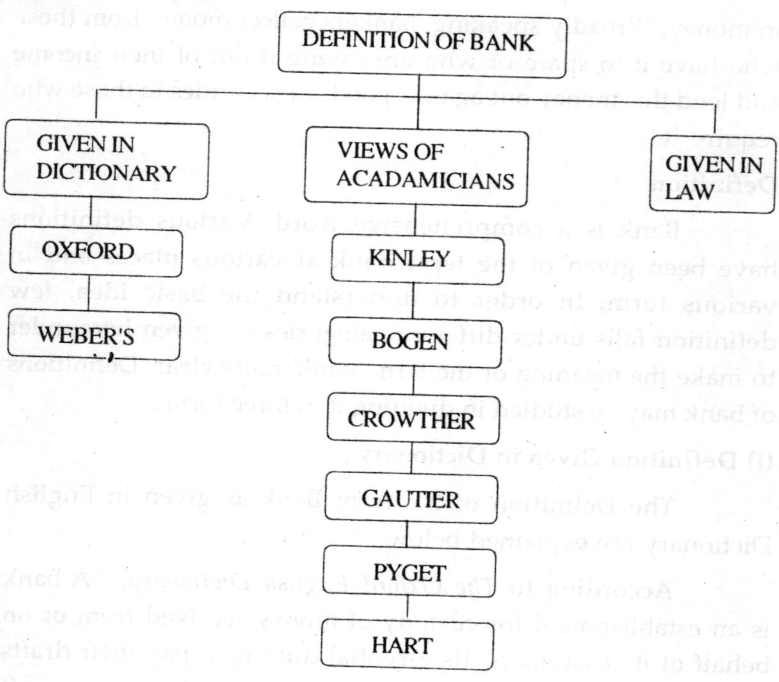

According to *Willis and Bogen*, "By banking in the most general sense is meant the business of receiving conserving and utilising the funds of the community or of any special section of it."

According to *Prof. Gautier*, "The word bank express the business which consists in effecting on account of other receipts and payments buying and selling either money or gold and silver or letters of exchange and drafts, public securities and shares in industrial enterprises in a word all the obligations whose creation resulted from the use of credit on the part of States and Societies and Individuals."

In the word of Prof. John Pyget's, "No one and no body corporate or otherwise can be a banker who does not (*i*) take deposit accounts, (*ii*) take current accounts (*iii*) issue and pay cheques drawn upon himself. (*iv*) collect cheques crossed and uncrossed for his customers and it might be said that even if all the above functions are performed by a person or body corporate, he or it may not be a banker or bank unless he fulfils the following conditions :(*i*) Banking is his or its knows occupatin, (*ii*) he or it must profess to be a banker or bank and the public take him or it as such, (*iii*) he or it has an intention of earning by so doing, (*iv*) this business is not subsidiary."

According to *Dr. H.L. Hart*, "A banker is one who, in the ordinary course of his business, honours cheques drawn upon him by persons from and for whom he recives money on current account."

According to *Findlay Shirras*, A banker or bank is "a person, firm or company having a place of business where credits are opened by deposits or collection of money or currency where money is advanced or loaned."

Crowther defines bank as an institution which "collects money from those who have it to spare or who are saving it out of their income, and lends this money out to those who require it."

Cairncroses defines, 'A bank is a financial intermediary, a dealer in loans and debt.

(III) Banking-Under Law

In law and Acts of different countries, the term bank has been used in different forms. Few examples of leading countries are discussed below :

The Banking Regulation Act defined institution engaged in "the accepting for the purpose of lending or investment, deposits of money from the public repayable on demand or

FUNCTIONS OF A MODERN BANK

Though borrowing and lending constitute the main functions of banking, yet they are not only functions of a commercial banks. Commercial banks are involved in diversified activities and performs varieties of function. The functions of a modern bank are classified under the following heads: otherwise and withdrawable by cheque, draft, order or otherwise."

(1) Accepting Deposits—The most important function of a commercial bank it to accept deposits from public. This is the primary function of a commercial bank. Bank receives the idle savings of people in the form of deposits and finance the temporary needs of commercial and industrial firms.

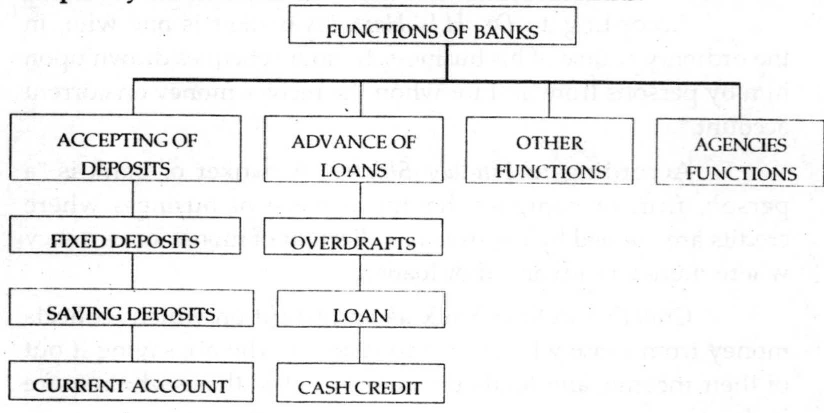

A commercial bank accept deposit from public on various account, important deposit account generally kept by bank are:–

(i) Saving Bank Deposits—This type of deposits suit to those who just want to keep their small savings in a bank and might need to withdraw them occasionally. One or two withdrawals upto a certain limit of total deposits are allowed in a week. The rate of interest allowed on saving bank deposits is less than that on fixed deposits. It is calculated on the minimum balance kept by the depositor during the month. The amount that the depositor has deposited is entered into the pass book. He is given pass book and a cheque book. Withdrawals are allowed by cheques and withdrawl form.

Cummulative Account Deposit or Recurring Deposit is a variant of the saving bank account. These account has been introduced by the bank to inculcate the regular savings . Bank offer comparatively higher rate of interest on the deposit in this account.

(ii) Current Deposits—This type of accounts are generally kept by businessmen and industrialists and those people who meet a large number of monetary transaction in their routine. These deposits are known as short term deposits or demand deposits. They are payable on demand without notice. Usually no interest is paid on these deposits because the bank cannot utilize these deposits and keep almost cent per cent reserve against them. On the other hand the bank charges a little commission for maintaining such accounts. This charge is known as 'incidental Charge' or 'Bank Charge'.

(iii) Fixed Deposits—These are also known as time deposit. In this account a fixed amount is deposited for a fixed period of time. Deposits are payable after the expiry of the stipulated period. Customers keep their money in fixed deposits with the bank in order to earn interest. The banks pay higher rate of interest on fixed deposits. The rates depend upon the length of the period and the amount deposited as well as the credit of the bank and the state of money market. The fixed deposits receipt is not a negotiable instrument. It can, however, be transferred by way of assignment to a third party.

Normally the withdrawals are not allowed from fixed deposits before the stipulated date. But some times, in order to oblige their customers, the banks allow them to withdraw their fixed deposits before its due date. In such circumstances customer can also get loan against the security of his fixed deposits.

(2) Advancing of Loans—The second main function of the commercial bank is to advance loans. Money is lent to businessmen and trade for short period only. These banks cannot lend money for long period because they must keep themselves ready to meet the short term deposits. The bank advances money in any one of the following forms:

(i) Overdrafts—Customers of good standings are allowed to overdraw from their current account. But they have to pay interest on the extra amount they have withdrawn. The banks allow 'overdrafts' to their customers just to provide temporary accommodation since the extra amount withdrawn is payable within a short period. The amount allowed in 'overdraft' varies from customer to customer depending on his financial position.

(ii) Loans—Loans are granted by the banks on securities which can be easily disposed off in the market, *e.g.*, Government securities or shares of approved concerns. When the bank has satisfied itself regarding the soundness of the party the loan is advanced. A borrow seldom wants the whole amount of his loan in cash. He opens the current account with the loan amount and thus a 'deposits is created' in the books of the name in the bank. The borrower gets a cheque book. He can draw cheques upon the bank upto the full amount of the loan, but interest is charged on the whole sum even though only a part is withdrawn.

(iii) Cash Credit—It is an arrangement by which a bank allows his customers to borrow money upto a certain limit against certain tangible securities as Government securities or shares of approved concerns etc. In this case interest is charged on the actual amount withdrawn by the customer and not on the limit allowed to him.

(iv) Discounting Bills—It is another important way of giving loans. The banks purchase bills and immediately pay cash for these bills after deducting the discount (interest). After the maturity of the bills, the banks get back its full value. Thus these bills are good liquid assets and moreover this investment is also very safe. The bills bear the security of both drawee as well as drawer; so that if one fails the bank can claim money from the other. Such advances are becoming very popular these days. It is mainly because the Central Bank gives rediscounting facilities at bank rate and the get discounts before hand.

(3) Agency Services—Modern Banks render service to the individual or to the business institutions as an agent. Banks usually charge little commission for doing these services. These services are as follows:

(i) A bank collects cheques, bills and promissory notes and receives their payments.

(ii) A bank collects dividend or interest on stock and shares. It also collect subscriptions and insurance premium.

(iii) A bank also buys and sells securities on behalf of its customers. It does not charge anything from the customers for this but gets some commission from the stock broker.

(iv) A bank acts as trustee or an executor on behalf of is customers in the administration of a will or of settlement.

(v) Lastly a bank helps in the transfer of funds from one bank or branch to another.

(4) Other Services—A modern bank now a days serves its customers in many other ways :

(i) A bank issues personal and commercial letters of credit. Through these letters of credit customers are able to benefit themselves out of the superior credit of the bank.

(ii) A bank also helps in the transaction of foreign exchange business.

(iii) A bank has 'safe deposit vaults'. It undertakes the safe custody of valuables and important documents. The bank acts as bailee of these goods or documents.

(iv) A few banks also supply trade informations and statistics. In advanced countries big banks keep separate information and statistical department. This department collects information regarding trade and business from both home and abroad and supplies them to their customers. A few banks also publish a monthly or fortnightly review which contains useful economic and financial information and statistics.

(v) A few banks also undertake to underwrite loans raised by Government, public or trading corporations.

(vi) A bank also supplies information about people and their general financial standing. This is a very valuable and reliable service to businessmen. It helps them to know about the general standing of the people with whom they have business transactions. The banks collect such information with great care and supply in utmost secrecy.

IMPORTANCE OF BANK

Bank is an important institution for society and economy. Their importance can explain as follows :

(1) Encourage Saving—Bank pays interest on the amount deposited in it. It create awareness of people towards savings. Hence banks play leading role in ecouraging savings. The nation is also bnefitted from it since people's savings are invested for nation's building.

(2) Helpful in Industrial and Economic Development—Bank proves equally helpful in development of industrial and economic development of the nation. Small savings obtained by banks from public are used for providing loans to industries and the Government.

(3) Facilitate Remittances—Bank plays important role in remittance safely and at the minimum cost. With the expansion of large banking network it is not costly and risky to send money from to any place of the world.

(4) Representative of Collection—Bank also plays role as reliable representative in collecting cheque, Bills of Exchange, amount of hundis on behalf of their esteemed customers. It saves their valuable time and avoid tension.

(5) Loan Facilities—Modern Business word more belief in running the business on credit. Bank helps, customer by providing loan facilities if required. Banks proved equally helpful in financing for imports and exports.

(6) Safety of Funds—Money deposited in Banks and other valuable assets kept in bank are fully safe. It is required no more to keep risk with anyone who realised importance of bank.

(7) No Need of Money Handling—It is no more required to physically handling money To avoid risk bank issue traveller cheque etc. and provides facility to pay anything through cheques.

(8) Saveing of Metallic Money—By proving facility of transfer of fund deposited in bank through cheque, it becomes possible for the central bank of the country to save costlier metal.

ROLE OF BANK IN ECONOMIC DEVELOPMENT

The commercial banks performs various important functions in the economic development of a country. Banks are significant in mobilisation of financial resources from non-productive to productive and constructive channels. It is not possible to think for development without appropriate network of commercial banks. The present rate of economic growth in the developed countries is sustained and enhanced wwith the help of the banks. It goes without saying that in the absence of sound commercial banking, developing countries cannot hope to join the rank of advanced countries. Banks accelerate the economic growth of a country in the following way:

(1) Capital Formation—This function of commercial bank is to accepts deposits. People deposits their savings in banks which later result in capital formation. The capital formation provides basis to the economic development of a country. Banks offer facilities for saving and thus encourage the habits of thrift in the community. They mobilise the idle capital of the nation and make it available for productive purposes. Thus realisation, mobilisation, chanelisation and utilisation of savings for productive purposes (i.e. capital formation) is made possible only with the help of commercial banks particularly in developing nations.

(2) Bank and Level of Economic Activity—The level of business activity, the mood of business community and expansion and contraction in business activities depend to a large extent upon the policies of banking institutions. Banks create credit on the basis of their primary deposits. Bank's deposits and credits have a great bearing on the rate of interest. When the commercial banks adopt a cheap and liberal credit policy, it proves to be an incentive for the investor class to expand the level of economic activities. Under conditions of unemployment bank credit will push up production in the country. On the other hand, a dear credit policy will mean higher rate of interest, discouragement of investment activities, fall in production, employment, income and ultimately fall in the level of economic activities.

(3) Provision of Finance and Credit—The other important functions of commercial bank is advancing loans. Nobody can self-sufficient in finance. Commercial banks provide finance and credit to trade and industry. By giving loans to trader and industrialists bank encourage them in running their business. In this regards their activities are not confined to domestic trade and commerce, but extend to foreign trade also.

(4) Distribution of Fudn Between Region —Banks also help in proper allocation of funds among different regions. Bank operate primarily for profit.

Introduction of branch banking system makes it possible for banks to choose different regions. Banks help in the transference of surplus funds from regions where they are not wanted so much to those regions where they can be more purposefully and efficiently employed Commercial banks help create the infrastructure essential for economic development by deploying credit to the priority sectors and neglected areas.

(5) Expansion of Markets—Commercial banks plays catalyst role in extending the size of market. The businessmen who are afraid of extending their field of operation in far off market due to paucity of fund and risks involved in such business operations are encouraged and supported by commercial banks in number of ways e.g. act as an intermediary, accepting bill of exchange, issuing of letter of credit etc.

(6) Allocation of Funds Between Regions—All regions of the country are nor equally developed. Certain regions are more developed than other. They have a surplus of funds. Banks collect them and transfer them to less developed areas. Banks can influence the direction of economic activity through rationale lending policy. By adopting appropriate lending policy banks help to create the infrastructure essential for economic development. In this way they bring about fair distribution of funds between different regions.

(7) Developing Entrepreneurs—Banks in India have also assumed the role of developing entrepreneurs. Bank help in the formation of new ventures and new ideas for entrepreneurs. Recently banks have entered in the field of promotion of new companies through the underwriting of shares, extending finance through purchase of capital goods. Banks also provide finance to sick industries for making them viable.

(8) Help to Consumer—Banks also provide loan for he consumer durables like T.V. fridge, motor car, scooters etc. There was a time when these things were out of the reach of the consumers to buy in lump sum. By this way, bank not only facilitate the consumers to repay the amount in instalment and improve their living standard but also help in creating demand of such consumer goods.

(9) Bank and Priority Sector—Commercial banks play a very singificant role in the development of the priority sectors, the growth of which is very vital for the economic development of the developing countries. Commercial banks, through a network of the branches throughout the country, relieve the small traders, small manufacturers, marginal and small farmers, artisans, small transport operators, exporters, etc. from the clutches of moneylen-ders and other traditional agencies. Commercial banks not only protect the weaker sections of the community from exploitation but also provide them credit facilities at concessional rates so that they can fully utilise their production potential and contribute to the development of the whole economy.

The commercial banks can rightly be crowned as "the nerve centre of all economic activity." A developed banking system is indispensable for the economic development of the country.

(10) Provide Elasticity to the Supply of Money—Banks create credit. Generally, banks create more credit than their deposit in order to efficiently meet the demand for money in the market. The credit can be contracted in the situation of low demand for money. The bank money has the capacity to adjust itself quickly in case of the fast expanding demand in the market. Thus the bank provide elasticity to the total supply of money in the market.

(11) Innovation—Innovation of the banking institution is landmark in the economic life of a country. It is the greatest event in the growth of economy which has continuously influenced the rate of economic development. In the early era of its beginning the functions of banks were confined to accepting deposits and advancing loans but with the passage of time their place and contribution has grown immensely.

In modern time Bank credit enables entrepreneurs to innovate and invest and thus uplift economic activity. In developing countries, where the entrepreneurs do not have wide scope and obvious economic significance. Bank loans enable the entrepreneurs to increase there productive capacity, to adopt new methods and ideas, and to improve working conditions, thereby raising output and the national income.

It is clear from the above explanation that Banks play a very special and dynamic role in the economic growth of every economy. Banks are an important constituent of the country's money market. Their lending and investment activities lead to changes in the quantity of money in circulation which in turn influence the nature and quality of production. Banks are the pivot of modern commerce. Industrial innovations become possible only through finance provided by banks. A study of economic development of developed countries shows that without the evolution of commercial banks, the industrial revolution would not have taken place in Europe. Thus, banks have come to occupy an important place in the life of a nation.

❑

10

Types of Banks

TYPES OF BANKS

In modern era banks provide a variety of services. Their customers come from almost all walks of the life. These days banks come across customers from a small business to a multi national corporation having its business activities all around the world. Banks also provide both short-term and long term credit. It has become obligatory for bank to satisfy the requirements of variety of customers belongs to variety of social group. All these have made banking business complex which requires specialised skills. As a result different types of banks have come into existence keeping in view specific requirements of the variety of customers. Keeping in view of their functions, banks can be classified into the following categories :

(1) Central Bank

(2) Commercial Bank

(3) Development Banks

(4) Co-operative Banks

(5) Social Banking

(6) Rural Banking

(7) Foreign Exchange Banks

(8) Savings Banks

(9) Export-Import Bank

(10) Indigenous Bankers

(11) Investment Banking.

(12) Merchant Banking

1. Central Banking

A central bank functions as the apex controlling institution in the banking and financial system of the country. It functions as controller of credit, banker's bank and also enjoy the monopoly of issuing currency on behalf of the government. The central bank has been established in almost all the countries of the world. A central bank is usually control and quite often owned, by the government of a country. The Reserve Bank of India is a such a bank in our country.

2. Commercial Banks

A commercial bank is an institution that operates for profit. It accepts deposits from the general public and extends loans to the households, the firms and the Government According to the Banking Regulation Act, 1949, the commercial banking consists in " the accepting, for the purpose of lending or investment, deposits of money from the public repayable on demand or otherwise, and withdrawable by cheque draft, order or otherwise."

Thus, the essential characteristics of commercial banking are as follows :

(i) acceptance of deposits from public;

(ii) for the purpose of lending or investment;

(iii) repayable on demand or lending or investment;

(iv) withdrawable by means of an instrument, whether a cheque or otherwise.

What distinguishes a commercial bank from other banking institutions is that it borrows and lends in the most general way without performing any specialised function. Another distinguish feature of commercial banks is that a large part of their deposits are demand deposits withdrawable and transferable by cheque.

3. Development Bank

A development bank is a hybrid institution which combines in itself the functions of a finance corporation and a development corporation. As financial corporation these banks act in providing medium-term assistance to business undertakings in the form of loans, underwriting and investment. They also act as catalytic agent in promoting balanced and viable development by assuming promotional role of discovering project ideas, undertaking feasibility studies, providing, technical, financial and managerial assistance for the implementation of project. In India Industrial Development Bank of India (IDBI) is the unique example of development bank.

Industrial Development Bank of India is the apex term lending institution in the country. It was established in 1964 . IDBI has been designated as the principal institution of the country for coordinating the working of the institutions engaged in financing, promoting or development of industry.

Functions. The IDBI performs the following function :

(i) refinancing loans given by various institutions working in the country.

(ii) short-term accommodation to the industrial units;

(iii) direct subscription to IFCI, SFCs, or any other notified financial institutions;

(iv) granting loans and advances, and underwriting the issue of shares or debentures of the individuals concerns;

(v) guaranteeing deferred payment;

(vi) arranging assistance for promotion, management or expansion of any industry; and

(vii) undertaking surveys for evaluation or dealing with marketing investment.

IDBI has been providing both direct and indirect assistance to the industries. The cumulative assistance (excluding guarantees) sanctioned and disbursed since inception of the IDBI up to end March 1996 aggregated Rs. 1,23,389 crores and Rs. 85,186 crores, respectively.

New initiatives have been taken by IDBI for increasing the pace of industrialisation of backward areas, particularly, the Non-Industry Districts (NIDs) liberalising terms of indirect assistance to small and medium scale units, encouraging modernisation through technological upgradation, rehabilitation of sick units and strengthening the institutional structure.

4. Co-operative Banks

The main business of co-operative banks is to provide finance to agriculture. They aim at developing a system of credit. Commercial bank have not been able to provide credit facilities to rural areas and therefore, the need of rural credit is fulfilled by the co-operative banks. Long-term loan is provided by land development banks, while short-term loans are provided by co-operative societies. Long-term loans are needed by the farmers for purchase of land or for permanent improvement on land, while short-term loans helps them in purchasing implements, fertilisers and seeds etc.

5. Social Banking

Social Banking could broadly be described as the extension of banking facilities to customer groups who would not be served by banks guided by commercial considerations alone. This objective and its pursuit manifests itself in diverse aspects of banks operations. There have been extension of banking facilities to rural areas even though the volume of business may not make such branches commercially profitable, extension of credit assistance to smaller borrowers in Priority Sectors, increasing the loans portfolio is sectors which have not had traditional support form commercial banking system, special treatment of weaker sections with reference to requirements of margins and security and interest so as to enable them to avail of bank's assistance and generally to pursue such measures as would enable banking services to encompass all sections of society . Several innovations are stated to have been introduced by the State Bank of India to bring banking within the reach of common man.

6. Rural Banking

A set of financial institution engaged in financing of rural sector is termed as 'Rural Banking. The policies of financing of these banks have been designed in such a way so that these institution can play catalyst role in the process of rural development. Regional Rural Bank is unique example of such type of Bank. Regional Rural Bank in India was first established on October 2, 1975, the date of birth of Mahatma Gandhi . The Regional Rural Bank have been set-up with a view to developing the rural economy by providing for the purpose of development of agriculture, trade, commerce industry and other productive activities in the rural areas, credit and other facilities, particularly to the small and marginal farmers, agricultural labourers, artisans and small entrepreneurs, and for matters connected therewith and incidental thereto."

7. Foreign Exchange Banks

These banks finance mostly to the foreign trade of a country. Their main function is to discount, accept and collect foreign bills of exchange. They also buy and sell foreign currencies and help businessmen to convert their money into any foreign currency they need. Though they accept deposits and undertake normally banking business, their main business is confined to the financing of export and import trade. Over a dozen foreign exchange banks branches are working in India have their head offices in foreign countries. In addition to this many Indian banks are also doing exchange business.

8. Saving Banks

These banks perform the useful services of collecting small savings. Commercial banks also run 'saving bank' to mobilise the savings of men of small means. The idea of saving bank is to encourage thrift and discourage hoarding. Different countries have different types of savings bank viz., Mutual or Trustee Savings Bank, Post Office Saving Bank, Commercial Saving Banks etc. Out of all these, commercial saving banks are most popular because of larger branch, net work and better facilities to the depositors.

9. Export-Import Bank

These banks have been established for the purpose of financing foreign trade. They concentrate their working on medium and long-term financing. Normally Exim bank help in encouraging exports of engineering and capital goods from the country. The Export -Import Bank of India (Exim Bank) was established on January 1, 1982 as a statutory corporation wholly owned by the Central Government . It took over the export finance function of the IDBI and began functioning on March, 1,1982.

Functions : The Exim Bank performs the following functions relating to export finance ;

(i) to provide financial assistance to exporters and importers;

(ii) to act as a principal financial institutions for coordinating the working of other institutions engaged in the field of financing international trade;

(iii) to undertake limited development and merchant banking activities in relation to export oriented industries.

(iv) refinance of loans and advances granted by banks and other notified financial institutions for the purposes of exports and imports.

(v) to provide investment finance to Indian companies towards their equity participation in joint ventures established abroad.

Since March 1982, the Exim Bank has been serving as the focal point for grant of package clearance to proposals submitted to the Working Groups by the exporters of capital goods and engineering goods involving deferred payment terms and those undertaking turnkey projects and construction contracts abroad.

Exim Bank has been participating in multilateral funded projects undertaken by Indian exporters. It has also set up an '*Export Development Fund*' which is utilised to finance those projects for which the existing banking and other financial institutions are not likely to grant such loans and advances or to enter into any such arrangements in the ordinary course of business. Exim Bank also provides financial assistance to Indian Exporters through lines of credit, relenting facility, export bills rediscounting, overseas investments, finance and assistance to hundred per cent export units.

10. Indigenous Bankers

Indigenous bankers have an important place in the rural economy of the country. Indigenous bankers are those persons and firms which accept the deposits, provide loans and deal in *deshi hundis*. According to the Central Banking Enquiry Committee, "indigenous bankers are defined as all bankers other than the Imperial Bank of India, Exchange Banks, the Joint Stock Banks and Co-operative Societies, and the expression includes any individual or private firm receiving deposits and dealing in hundis or lending money. Those who do not receive deposits fall under other indigenous agencies, e.g., the village money -lenders. Indigenous bankers carry on business in a hereditary way. Some of them operate branches in several part of the country. The branches are managed by their agents known as munims who enjoy their full confidence.

These bankers are found everywhere in cities, towns, mandis and villages. They are known by various names, such as, mahajans, shroffs, etc. They have been functioning in this country from time immemorial.

Indigenous bankers differ from money-lenders. Money lenders simply lend money. They do not take deposits, nor do they undertake the financing of trade. But the indigenous bankers receive deposits in addition to money-lending and finance most of the inland trade and industry in the country.

11. Investment Banking

Investment Banks are those which assists business corporations and government bodies to raise funds for their long-term capital requirements through the sale of share, stocks and bonds. They purchase entire issue of new securities of the business corporations or of government bodies and re-issue them for public subscription at a higher price. Hence these banks operate as underwriter of the issue of securities.

12. Merchant Banking

The concept of Merchant Banking is a recent development in the history of Indian banking. The State Bank of India took the initiative to open a Merchant Banking Division in 1972. Later on Bank of Baroda, Indian Bank, Canara Bank, Punjab National Bank, etc.,. also set up separate subsidiaries to provide specialised merchant banking services to the corporate sector.

The following services are provided by the merchant banking division of banks :

(i) Arranging the underwriting of the proposed public issue of shares, debentures of the companies from banks/bankers.

(ii) Mobilising resources from the capital market for the corporate sector by managing the public issue of shares, debentures, bonds, etc.

(iii) Handling the amalgamation and merger proposals of the companies.

(iv) Syndication of rupee and foreign currency loans from the financial institutions and banks including cash subsidy from government.

(v) Acting as trustee on behalf of the debenture-holders to the issue of convertible or non convertible debentures by the corporate sector.

(vi) Assisting firms in establishing corporate venture in collaboration with foreign parties within the framework of government rules and regulations.

(vii) Advising Non-resident Indian investors to invest in Indian companies; arranging purchase and sale of shares/ debentures of listed Indian companies by Non-resident Indians.

(*viii*) Assisting companies in preparation of project profiles, feasibility studies, obtaining letter of intent/license, DGTD registration, seeking govern-ment approval for foreign collaboration, etc.

In brief, Merchant Banks perform a variety of functions such as acting as issue houses, acceptance houses, financial brokers, trustees, giving investment advice to individuals, managing trust funds etc.

The scope of merchant banking is very limited in India. The amount of funds raised by industry on the new issue market is small and gradually declining. There is, however, good scope for providing consultancy services to medium and small-scale industrial units. The Government is encouraging the merger of sick industrial units with the successful units. There is also wide scope for the setting up of joint ventures abroad.

TYPE OF BANKING SYSTEMS

The Banking System is based on the lines of specialisation now-a-days. In old days banks used to perform certain but limited functions by keeping a limited areas as their working field. Now almost in every country and everywhere banks are found functioning speedly. The banking system has gone under an instantaneous transformation during the modern times.

Following are the different kinds of banking system :

1. Unit Banking.
2. Branch Banking.
3. Chain Banking.
4. Group Banking.
5. Correspondent Banking.

1. Unit Banking

The system of 'Unit Banking ' first came into existence in U.S.A. This system of Banking received great encouragement throughout the country till the beginning of 20th century.

Meaning. : 'Unit Banking' means the operation of banking services through one office of a bank. It does not spread its offices all over the country. Every banking business is undertaken by an independent office 'correspondent bank' system. Under this system the deposit is made by the country bank with the City Banks and City Banks make their deposit with the Reserve City Banks. This system facilitates the banks in remitting the amount through the corresponding links.

Merits of Unit Banking System

(1) *Easy to Manage* : The managerial problems are not so irksome as what faced in the case of Branch Banking System. Having only one office this system can manage its offices with the help of efficient and highly technical personnels.

(2) *No Red-Tapism* : There are meager chance of red tapism in this system. Every member of the staff perform his duties under the direct control of the unit manager. There are remote chances to irregularities and incapabilities under this system Personnels are expected to perform their functions more efficiently instead of delaying or postponing it for some time.

(3) *Less Diversification of Attention* : Under unit banking system the operation area is quite limited . There is no chance of diversifying limited number of operations are required to performed. This enables the bank to pay more attention to the financial needs of its locality and to arrange for an efficient management to boost up economic development.

(4) *Quick Decision* : Under the Unit Banking System there is no higher authority as it is must in the case of Branch Banking System. The official can take decision on the spot.

They needs not to wait for the signal from the high command in helping the borrowers and businessmen in solving their various financial complexities.

(5) *No Hasty Transfer of Manager* : It is a pertinent characteristics of the Branch Banking System. Branch Manager are frequently transferred from one Branch to another Branch. No such problem arises in the Unit Banking System. Having a long term experience of the needs of the local people the unit manager is expected to be more sympathetic to the requirement of the local people.

(6) *No Disaster of Failure* : In case of the failure of a unit bank economy does not faces any kind of disastrous situation . Its impact on the economic structure of the country is very nominal.

(7) *Suitable to the Localised Markets* : It is generally held that due to the localisation of market unit banks are more suitable than the branch banking system. Unit banks are more capable of meeting the local needs.

(8) *Check on the formation of Monopolistic Banks* : Under Unit Banking System, the size of banks are generally small. There is absence of any big bank. Hence there is no possibility of the growth of monopolistic banks under this system.

Demerits of Unit Banking System.

There are merits of Unit Banking as discussed above yet there are certain demerits of this system of banking as mentioned below :

(1) *Limited Financial Resources* : Unit Banks have limited finance to meet the ever-expanding demand for credit. In case of heavy withdrawal and political insurgency this system may collapse, as it took place (during the period of world - wide depression) in U.S. A. in 1929.

(2) *Weak for Competition* : It is not easy for the unit banks to compete with other banks as their resources are limited. There is no chance of making their resources flexible. Because of the problem of 'cut-throat' competition they sometimes face failures.

(3) *No Diversification of Risk* : It becomes rather difficult for the unit banks to diversify risks. Their liquidity of assets is also of low degree. These all makes them basically weak. If a particular place suffers from business depression the banks suffer heavy financial losses which may results in the faliure of the bank.

(4) *Less Attraction to Better Staff* : Due to limited field of operation with less amount of money the unit banks may not be able to earn very high meager profit. It becomes difficult for them to attract better and experienced staff. They cannot afford to pay as the branch banks are capable in paying to their staff. If also prohibits the division of labour and specialisation.

(5) *Limited Contribution to the Development* : Operations of Unit Banks are confined to a particular area. Their contribution to the economic development and spreading the financial network is very small. They cannot pace with the fast expanding, huge amounts of demand of the economy.

(6) *Less Service and High Cost* : Unit banks are organised on the small basis. They suffer the loss of economies which is enhanced by the branch banking system. The per unit cost of service in the unit banking system comes to high. In lack of specialisation due to small scale organisation they serve a particular class at high prices.

(7) *Large Amount of Idle Reserve* : Under the unit system a bank has to keep large amount of idle reserve to meet the contingencies. Thus major part of the deposits remain unproductive whereas in the branch banking system it is not necessary to keep idle reserve because whenever the need arise a branch can take the help of some other branch.

(8) *No Remittance Facilities* : The provision of remittance facilities is very low in case of unit Banking System. Though there is correspondent link between the units and Reserve City Banks, yet it is not as flexible and efficient as the branch banking system. It also makes the movement of funds more expensive and inconvenient for the people.

(10) *Expensive Cheque Clearance* : Under the Unit Banking System the clearing of cheques are more expensive and difficult . It takes a longer time in comparison to the Branch Banking System.

(11) *Inequality of Interest Rates* : Interest rates are generally lower in industrially and commercially advanced areas but higher in the backward areas which hinders the development of backward and underdeveloped area of the country.

2. Branch Banking System

Meaning : In the branch banking system every bank operates through a large network of branches spread over the whole of the country. Branch Banking System is contrary to the Unit Banking System Commercial Banks open their branches in the every part of the economy and do all the work through them . Regional or Zonal officers are there to control the branches and these 'Regional or Zonal' offices are finally controlled by the apex body i.e., the Head Office. The Head Office under the Branch Banking system is considered as single unit. The banks huge financial resources enables it to carry on its activities through a large network of branches on a large scale all over the country. The bank branches are constitute only a part of the total network.

Branches perform all the banking activities as per directions and according to the policies of the apex body. The branch is headed by branch manager who is accountable to the Head Office. This system originated in its typical form in England was subsequently adopted by Canada, Australia, South Africa and India.

It is held as one of the most practical system of banking structure due to its following merits. The Branch Banking System has certainly an edge over the Unit Banking System.

Merits of Branch Banking System

Branch banking system enjoys following advantages :

(1) *Provision of Better Services* : Branch Banking System enables a branch to have comparatively a small number of customers as their number is quite large. So the number of customers per banking office is less. This facilitates the branches to provide better services. They are more efficient and specialised as they are organised on the large scale basis.

(2) *Maximum Use of Reserve* : Under the Branch Banking System; it is not obligatory for a branch to keep large amount of idle reserves to meet current requirement . They use their resources to a maximum level. In case, if they need any amount of cash of a sudden nature ; they can take the help of other branches who will certainly come to their ally's help.

(3) *Proper Staffing* : In branch banking system a large number of staff is required to undertake the work at all the branches. Thus the Bank can adopt its requirement and other personnel policies to get proper staff. They are in better position in allotting right place to right people. This increase the efficiency of the bank and also provides it stability due to a determined personnel policy.

(4) *Diversification of Risks* : It is possible in the branch banking system to diversify the industrial as well as geographical loan risks. If there is loss to a branch due to depression in the local industries ; other branches will compensate this loss. The chance of failure is also minimised in the branch banking system.

(5) *Remittance Facilities* : Branch system embodies very easy remittance system. It is easier as well cost saving for clients to transfer funds from one place to another because of large network of branches all over the country. Inter-branch

payments are easier than inter-bank payments. Facilities exist in a branch system to get a payment from any branch by depositing the credit instrument.

(6) *Easy Clearance of Cheques* : Cheques are easily cleared away in the branch banking system. Any cheque deposited in the branch is sent to the clearing house office, which does the rest of work in the most customary way. Thus it is easy to encash a cheque in the branch banking system without any complication.

(7) *Less Chances of Insolvency* : Solvency and stability is one of the greatest requirement of a sound banking system. In the branch banking system there is facility to every branch. If the reserve falls short the branch can have the money from the other branches of the same bank. Thus the question of insolvency which is pertinent in the *Unit Banking System* is minimised in the branch banking system.

(8) *Uniform Rate of Interest :* Interest rate is the determining factor of the investment structure in an economy . In the branch banking system; due to large amount of contribution in the monetary market; bank can maintain uniform rate of interest. This facilitate the investors and depositors both.

(9) *Mobilization of Money* : Under the branch system, money is quickly mobilised from one place to other place. Having branches at every place and branch can swiftly transfer an amount from one place to another. This reduce the danger of theft or loot.

(10) *Maximum Service at Low Cost* : Branch system enjoys the advantages of division of labour . This provides specialization of labour which is consequency reduces the per unit cost. Various branches render more specialised services at a comparatively low per unit cost than unit system of banking.

(11)*Proper Use of Capital* : If a branch of the bank has plenty of deposits but no opportunity for investments, it can transfer its surplus funds to other branches which can make profitable use of such funds for trade and industry.

(12) *Efficient Credit Control* : It is much easier to exercise control over credit under branch banking system . In this system the Central Bank of the country to have a effective control over currency and credit . The Central Bank required to deal only with a few large size banks controlling a large number of branches.

De-Merits of Branch System

(1) *Delay in Decisions* : Under the branch system the branch manager is under obligation to forward every application of loan to the head office to get latter's approval. It delays the decision and harms the borrowers because, " Time is one of the greatest factors in business. "

(2) *Frequent Transfer of Branch Managers* ; This is another drawback of branch system. Manager are subject to frequent transfers from one branch to other branch. Generally the new manager becomes sympathetic to the local demand of finance.

(3) *Faliure may cause a Havoc* : Failure of bank having several branches in the different parts of the territory may cause unrepairable damage to the economic arch of the nation. It may result even into faliure of currency; thus giving great setback to the development of the country.

(4) *Difficulty in Management* : Branch system implies the working of a large number of personnels in different branches of a bank. It becomes rather difficult to assert an effective management. Mismanagement on a large scale is imminent in the branch system. The expenditure on management goes up which ultimately reduces the profit.

(5) *Wastage* : Branch system heads towards cut-throat competitions . To meet the competition, banks spend a lot of money which leads so wastage.

(6) *Monopolistic Trends* : Under the branch system big banks tend to control the credit by spreading their branches. The power concentrates in the hands of a few people. It was the opinion of S.E. Thomas a well known economist that branch system gives stimulation to the Monopolistic Organisations.

Thus, from the above analysis we find that branch banking has certainly an edge over the unit banking. According to *Prof. Sayers, " A comparison between Unit Banking and Branch Banking is essentially a coınparison between small scale and large scale operations. "*

3. Chain Banking

Meaning : In order to remove deffects experienced under the system of unit banking, new form of banking organisations have been evolved. Chain banking is also a relative new form of banking organistion. Chain Banking is the system in which one or a number of persons hold stock ownership. In simple word it is a system in which the banks are controlled by one or more than one individual. This system grew in U.S.A. Where in 1925, thirty three chains were in existence which comprised nearly 933 banks. In the chain system there is no holding company to control the interest of the banks.

Advantages :

The major advantages of Chain Banking are described below :

(1) *Optimum Utilisation of Resources*: Under this system optimum utilisation financial and human resources is possible.

(2) *High Level of Earnings* : Efficient use of financial resources facilitate high level earnings to bank.

(3) *Economy in Administration and Operation*: Co-ordination in management makes it possible to obtained economy in administration and operation.

(4) *Diversification of Risks*: When there is any issue of risk is arise it is diversified amongst all the banks of Chain.

(5) *Centralised Control* : Though all the banks are independent in their day-to-day operation but are controlled by the central authority.

(6) *Unified Management* : It is possible under the chain banking to manage all the banks in a unified manner since all are managed and controlled by central management.

Disadvantages :

The major disadvantage of chain banking is that it becomes difficult to supervise all the banks since banks have been located at different places. These banks are owned by private ownership because of which the system also faces lack of efficiency. Further point of operation and control are for from each other so that bank may avoid policies and it also becomes difficult to control personnel. Following are the disadvantages of Chain Banking :

(1) *Lack of Flexibility* : These banks are operated on certain uniform principles and procedure set -out by controlling bank. Hence it becomes impossible to adopted flexibility in the working of different banks of chain.

(2) *Absence of Efficient Supervision* : Since different banks of the Chain are established geographically at different place, it becomes difficult to exercise efficient supervision on each of them.

(3) *Speculation* : There may be possibility of harm due to the existence of speculation.

(4) *Irregularities* : The different banks of Chain may commit irregularities in the absence of efficient supervision.

(5) *Danger* : There are possibilities of more cases of mal-administration and fraud etc. under such types of banking system.

The origin of chain system was to satisfy the capitalists, lust for power. This is not a healthy system to adopt as its motives are never sincere. It never serves the public.

4. Group Banking

Meaning : When two or more than two banks are controlled by a holding company which provides management for the banks and keeps a centralized control over all of them; it is called group banking. It does not affect the separate entity of the banks, but control lies in the hand of holding company.

The aim of establishing this system was to bring co-operation between banking corporations and industrial corporation. Because alongwith the banks; other business units were also to be under the control of the same holding company.

This system also originated in the United States of America in the early twentieth century i.e. between 1925 and 1929 . But during the Great Depression of 1929 several of these banking group failed and thereafter the importance of group banking declined.

Advantages of Group Banking System

1. *Separate Existence* : Separate personality of every bank. They can maintain their separate Directorates.
2. *Better Advice* : Better advice is given by the central office which devises various means to improve the technique of services to be rendered by a bank.
3. *Liquidity of Resources* : Less expenditure on publicity due to unified control.

4. *Standardization Accounts* :Standardization of Accoun-ting System, is adopted under Group Banking.
5. *Credit Facilities* : Provision of better credit facilities are available under this system of banking.
6. *Advertisement* : Economy in advertisement expenditure is also possible under Group Bankings. It is because the trust advertise Jointly for all the banks belongs to group.
7. *Economical Operation* : Economy in purchases and other operation is possible under Group Banking.
8. *Role as merchant Banker* : This system helps member banks to place their investments and banking business on a sound footing.
9. *Adequate Liquidity* : All the banks of the group are required to follow norms with regards to maintain liquidity . It is difficult for bank to avoid direction in this regard . Hence always there exists a proper level of liquidity.

Disadvantages of Group Banking

Following are disadvantages of Group Banking :

1. *Problem of Control* : Loose administration implies low level of official efficiency.
2. *Crisis* : One member bank's failure affects the other member bank.
3. *Corruption* : There are possibilities of shelter to corruption due to common purchasing agency.

5. Correspondent Banking

In order to remove inherent defects in Unit Banking System, banks are organised under a new system. Under this banking system banks working in surrounding roral areas opens their accounts in a large size bank operating in city. It facilitate transaction of money among correspondent bank easy. Beside the large size bank able to invest funds laying with small bank and can also provide financial assistance if so required. They can also provide advise to small sized banks. Hence through correspondent banking, various banking units are linked with each other. The system of correspondent banking was extensively used in USA.

Merits

The following are important merits of correspondent Banking :

(1) Freedom—Like unit banking, all banks of correspondent bank are independent in their working. Each bank enjoy freedom in managing their affairs. The correspondent bank mere provide advise.

(2) Relationship with Other Banks—Though each bank of correspondent banking is independent but each is linked like branch of correspondent bank. Hence each bank enjoy the benefits of Branch Banking.

(3) Maximum Use—Each unit of correspondent bank remits their extra funds to large size bank with whom they are linked so that the fund can be invested in huge side.

(4) Consultation—Correspondent bank provide advise to small bank on various economic issue. It helps them to improve their working and policy.

Demerits

Beside the aforesaid merits, the correspondent banking suffers following demerits :

(1) Limited Resources—Since size of each bank under the system is too small, their financial resources also found in small size. Due to this limitation, these bank find themselves unable in providing credit of large amount

(2) Pressure of Big Banks—Normally, there seem to be possibility that big bank pressurise small banks in one form or other. This tendency create obstacle in the working of small banks.

Which Banking is Better-Branch or Unit?

It is clear from the aforesaid explanation that normally or fundamentally there are only two type of banking system—Branch Banking and Unit Banking. The remaining three type of banking *i.e.*, chain, group and correspondent is just a reform in the banking system and normally these are not found in practice. After studying merits and demerits of both types of banking—Branch and Unit, it is not that easy to express as which system is better. Each one having their merits but at the same time demerits too

Unit Banking may suited best to American condition where because of availability of adequate capital and other resources and where per-capita income is high. Therefore why concept and popularity of correspondent Banking developed in U.S.A. However now economist does not found correspondent banking appropriate even in U.S.A. In U.S.A. too concept of branch banking getting currency importance as it proves most suitable in facing circumstances created by emergency of depression in comparison to unit banking. Hence it can be concluded that in comparison to unit banking and its reform like chain banking, group banking and correspondent banking, branch banking is most suitable.

CHARACTRISTICS OF A GOOD BANKING ORGANISATION

In business activities banking organisation plays important role. Keeping into consideration, it is necessary that banking should proves as sound organisation. There must be following charactristics in a good banking organisation :

(1) Fulfilment of Objective—The prime objective of banking institution is to safe invest hard earned saving of people so that production activities may not suffer. Banking organisation must be so sound which can discharge this responsibility successfully.

(2) Encouragement to Savings—A Sound banking structure must posses the quality of attracting savings from public. Bank should invest people's savings in profitable venture so that can earn more. Bank can attract more savings on higher interest. Bank organisation should be sound so that peoples have no hesitation in deposit their savings.

(3) Favourable to National Conditions—The best banking organisation is one which can function according to the need of nation and social circumstances. The bank organisation should select appropriate sector and extend credit for the development of nation.

(4) Credit Control—Banking system should work in well planned manner. How much credit should be extended to a particular sector? Is there not any problem of expansion or contraction of credit? There should be these qualities in a sound banking organisation.

WHICH SYSTEM IS MOST SUITABLE FOR INDIA

After studying the suitability of a particular type of banking system internationally it requires to be answer as which system is most suitable for India. After reaching on the decision on the basis of detailled discussion it is found that branch banking most suited to Indian condition. Merits and advantages of branch banking are self-explanatory. There are empharical evidances available in favour of suitability of branch banking. In 1929-30 at the time of great dipression in USA several unit banks have failled but on the other hand in UK branch banking successfully faced the situation. At the time Indo-Pak participation in 1947, Punjab National Bank faced crisis because it had no branch.

(5) Co-ordinating System—A best bank organisation is one which can establish co-rdination among all the banks working in the country. There should be no problem of over-banking or under-banking in the country.

(6) Uniformity in Policies—There must be uniformity in the policy decisions taken by various bank organisation. There should also be uniformity in decisions taken by one bank organisation on different occasions. These tendencies increases creditibility of bank.

(7) Effective Administration—Bank organisation runs administration of bank. The organisation should take decisions which can able to provide effective administration to bank. The organisation will be called bad if faill to provide effective administration.

❑

11

Credit Creation and Investment Management by Bank

Macleod observed Importance of Credit as "What the steam engine is in mechanism, what differential calculus in mathe-matics that is credit in commerce." According to Walter W. Haines importance of credit in trading is as wide as the importance of oxygen in the life. The economic structure get disturbed due to lack of credit facility.

Meaning of Credit

The word 'Credit' has been derived from the Latin word 'Credo' which means 'I believe' or 'I trust' which signifies a trust or confidence reposed in another person. The term credit thus means, resposing trust or confidence in somebody. In economics, it is interpreted to mean, in the same sense, trusting in the solvency of a person or making a payment to a person to receive it back after some time or lending of money and receiving of deposits etc. All this being possible because one enjoys the confidence of the other. with this background of the term some definitions of this technical term as we use it in economics are described below.

Definition of Credit

1. Prof. Cole—"Credit is purchasing power not derived from income but created by financial institutions either as on offset to idle income held by depositors in the bank or as a net addition to the total amount or purchasing power."

2. Prof. Gide—It is an exchange which is complete after the expiry of a certain period of time.

3. Prof. Kinley—"By credit, we mean the power which one person has to induce another to put economic goods at his disposal for a time on promise or future payment. Credit is thus an attribute or power of the borrower."

4. Prof. Thomas—"The term credit is now applied to that belief in a man's probability and solvency which will permit of his being entrusted with something of value belonging to another whether that something consists, of money, goods, services or even credit itself as and when one may entrust the use of his good name and reputation."

On the basis of above definitions it can be said that credit is a exchange function in which creditor give some goods or money to the debtor with a belief that after some time he will return it. In other words trust is the credit.

Charectristics of Credit

In extending credit to an individual or to a business enterprise there are some elements or characteristics of credit that are of prime importance. The following are the important characteristics or elements of credit :

(1) Confidence—The essential basis of extending credit is confidence. The person or authority must have confidence in the debtor.

(2) Capacity—There must be confidence in the borrower's capacity to pay. Creditor must satisfy himself with regards to paying capacity and ability of the debtor before extending credit. His reputation for ability based upon certain personal qualities, training and successful experience, gives reasonable assurance that he will in appropriate time acquire the means with which to repay the loan.

(3) Goodwill—Goodwill of debtor also matters in extending credit. If a person has a reputation of repaying his outstanding in time, he will be able to obtain credit without any difficulty.

(4) Security—Banks are main instrument of extending credit. Bank properly ensure before extending credit as whether the debtor has proper securities or not. The availability of credit to person depends on property and assets possesed by him. If the borrower is a successful businessman, he is usually in a position to borrow adequate credit.

(5) Size of Credit—Availability of credit is also depends on the amount of credit. Normally credit of small amount is easily available rather than credit of large amount.

(6) Period of Credit—Likewise Size, the period of credit in its availability also plays a significant role. Normally long term credit can not easily be obtained as more risk element is involved in its security and repayments

INSTRUMENT OF CREDIT

The term credit refers to instrument in the form of written document between the borrower and the lender which also contains the terms and conditions.According to these terms and conditions transaction has been negotiated between the two parties. The credit instruments are proves very helpful in the encouragement and the development of credit in its turn, helps in the promotion and development of trade and commerce. The unique feature of these credit instruments is that these are transferable with the change hand. There are several documents used as credit instruments andthe more important among them may be discussed as below :

1. *Cheque* : Use of cheque has become most popular now a days. A cheque is an order drawn by a depositor on his bank to pay a certain amount of money out of the money that he has deposited with a bank. In the words of *Hartley Withers*, A cheque is a bill of exchange payable on demand."

2.*Bill of Exchange* : It is also an instrument of credit , this instrument enable a seller of a commodity to issues an order to a buyer to make the payment either to him or to a person whose name and address is mentioned therein either on the sight of the bill or within a period of time specified therein. In the words of *S.E. Thomes*, it is "an instrument in writing, containing an unconditional order, signed by the maker, directing a certain person to pay a certain amount of money only to or to the order of a certain person or to the bearer of the instrument."

3. *Bank Draft* : A benk draft is another important instrument of credit used by a bank on either its branch or the head office to send money from one place to the other. Money sent through a bank draft, is cheaper, convenient and involves less risk.

Promissory Note : According to the Indian Negotiable Instruments Acts, ' A promissory note' is an instrument in writing containing an unconditional undertaking signed by the maker to pay a certain sum of money only to or the order of certain person or the bearer of the instrument.

Government Bonds : These days the government has resorted to large scale borrowing for her development expenditure . For that purpose , it issues a sort of certificate to the person who subscribes to these loans. Such *certificates* are called the government bonds. There are three methods of issuing them at a discount, or at par, or at a premium and they are payable at the end of a specified period. All these bonds carry a certain rate of interest. Some of them are, however, prize bonds and are income-tax free. These attractions are provided in order to attract more loans and encourage more savings. They are very helpful in developing credit in the country.

Treasury Bills : These bills are also issued by the government and have been so issued since long for the first time in 1970. They are issued in anticipation of the public revenues for the period of three months, six, nine or twelve months. These bills are also issued at a discount, but are repayable at par which means that the difference goes to the buyer of these bills or the investors as a sort of interest.

Traveller's Cheques : This is one of the recent additions in the field of credit instruments; a facility given to the people by the banks. It is a sort of letter of credit . It is cheque, but the value of the same is written there and to prevent any fraud, all the cheques are required to be signed by the traveller in the presence of the banking authorities and then on their authority , the money can be collected at the branches of the bank.

Significance of Credit : The credit system has become very important in modern economies. It appears impossible to carry on without the same. It is not wrong to call credit as the life-blood of business. The modern age can be rightly described as the credit age where all transactions are made through credit . The importance of credit is clear from the fact that now a cash transaction is looked upon as a sign of backwardness. All purposes , big or small, are made in the advanced countries through the instruments of credit. A person need to carry only a pen and a cheque book in his pocket and need high standard of honesty and morality-the very corner stone of the system of credit. The growing importance of the credit has been very well summed up by *Daniel Webster* in the following words : "Credit has done more –– a thousand times more —to enrich nations than all the mines of the world." It has excited labour, stimulated manufactures, pushed commerce on every sea and brought every nation, every kindgom and every small tribe among the races of men to be knwon to all the rest.

Advantages

The main advantage of credit may be put forth as below :

(1) Economic Medium of Exchange : Credit provides a very conveninent and economical medium of exchange. It makes useless all standard money made of precious metals which would involve a huge amoung of wear and tear and depreciation. In so doing, it asvoids all risk of carrying on person much precious metallic reserves.

(2) Elasticity of Monetary System : Credit system provides elasticity to the monetary system of a country because it can be conveniently expanded and contracted without much difficulty. The fiduciary issue system is based upon this principle, because more currency can be issued without providing for proportionate metallic reserves.

(3) Capital Formation : Credit helps in capital formation by making available huge funds, from those who cannot use the same to those who can use the same. This method not only gives returns to those hoarders whose fund would have remained idle, but enables those who do not have enough to use the same in a fruitful manner. It enables the employment of those factors of production which further stimulate spending and saving- the two important constituents of capital formation in a country. This also encourage employment by providing more and more of avenues.

(4) Increase Consumption : Credit increases consumption of all types of goods perishable and non-perishable. While doing so , it helps to stimulate large scale production which in its turn leads to lower costs of production. A reductin in costs of production results in rising standard of living because this helps to raise consumption.

(5) The system of credit promotes thrift among the people : As we have stated above encouraging capital formation in the economy it encourages thrift because the attraction of interest and dividends encourages more and more as savings.

(6) It also encourages output and employment in a country : Credit expansion can help an economy to get out of depression and its contraction can help ease boom conditions. This is how the banks do and are expected to do when they follow the respective instructions of the central bank of a country. Credit has been used as a good handle for fighting the evil effects of trade cycles.

(7) Development of Entrepreneurs: It is the present day credit which has helped the development of large scale enterprises and corporate business. Is has helped the different entrepreneurs to tide over difficult periods of financial crisis. It can help the ordinary consumer to meet his requirements even when he is not in a position to make the payment.

(8) Easy Payment: Through the various credit instruments like the drafts the traveller's cheques , the bills of exchange, it has enabled large amounts of money to be paid without much difficulty and botheration. Even the international payments have been facilitated very much.

(9) Supplement Credit : The manufacturer and the producer can supplement his credit facilities.

(10) Help to System Of Exchange : Besides ensuring this capital supply, it can also help a system of exchange e.g. credit system enables a debtor to use something which he does not own completely. In this way, the debtor is provided with control as distinct from ownership of certain goods and services.

Dangers of Credit :

Credit is a mixed blessing. It involves certain advantages , at the same time certain dangers too. Credit is that double edged weapon which can harm the user even. Credit is your servant as long as it is subordinate to you, but once you let it loose, it will be your master instead. It has , therefore, to be used very cautiously, lest it spoils all industry and enterprise. The following are the inherent dangers invol ed in it : —

(1) Encourage Weakness : Credit enables big entrepreneurs and business maganates continue to conceal their inherent weakness. Their own shortcomings are met by the borrowed capital. Even the losing and dwindling concerns continue with the help of borrowed capital in the hope that they will survive. There is nothing wrong so far as it goes. But what beyond this. If the business fails , it not only lends the borrowers in danger but also thousands of those people who advanced credit to such people.

(2) Dangerous Beyond Limit : A more serious situation arises when the credit in a country is expanded beyond certain limits and it results in over investment. It is such a situation which gives rise to the evil of inflation. This danger, has been emphasised by *Prof. Thomas* in his Elements of Economics, in the following words : "There is no automatic limit to the expansion of a credit system as there is to an expansion of a metallic circulation through the intervention of human element: the usual accompaniment of uncertainty and variableness is the chief source of danger in a credit organisation."

(3) Economic Crisis : There are several occsasions when credit has been direcly responsible for economic crisis. The banks expand credit byond certain limits and with a slight 'shake' up in the confidence of the people, they suffer from a run on banks and the consequent disaster.

(4) *Evils of Monopoly* : The system of credit has also resulted in the creation of monopolies and vested interests. The different organisations like the trusts and cartels have grown with the emergence of credit and they have worked to the detriment of both the consumers and the workers.

(5) *Encourage Wasteful Expenditure* : It also encourages wasteful and lavish expenditure not only by the individuals, but also by commercial institutions like banks and governments- the idea being that the money is not their own.

(6) *Encourage Inefficients* : Credit also encourages certain inefficient and worthless producers. They come into the market because they feel that they have nothing at stake and they have to play only with other's money. In this way , people who could not have come otherwise are allowed to play their business.

It is thus clear that the government or the central banking authorities must keep the credit within limit so that no evil is allowed to crop up in the economy.

CLASSIFICATION OF CREDIT

In modern transactions credit constitutes an important role. Credit transactions cover wide range of activities. These may be classified on the various basis depicted in the following diagram.

(1) According to Term

When the credit is extended on the pre-determined repayment period it is termed as term credit. On the basis of term the credit may be classified into following categories.

(i) Call Credit—Though it is not a routine category of credit but when the credit is sanctioned for a very short period is known as call credit. The aforesaid period may be either few hours, few days or few week. The amount sanctioned against call credit is also payable on demand.

(ii) Short-term credit—Credit for a period of 3 months to about 18 months is termed as short-term credit. Such credit are normally required for current production needs or for consumption needs or for carrying on marketing operations.

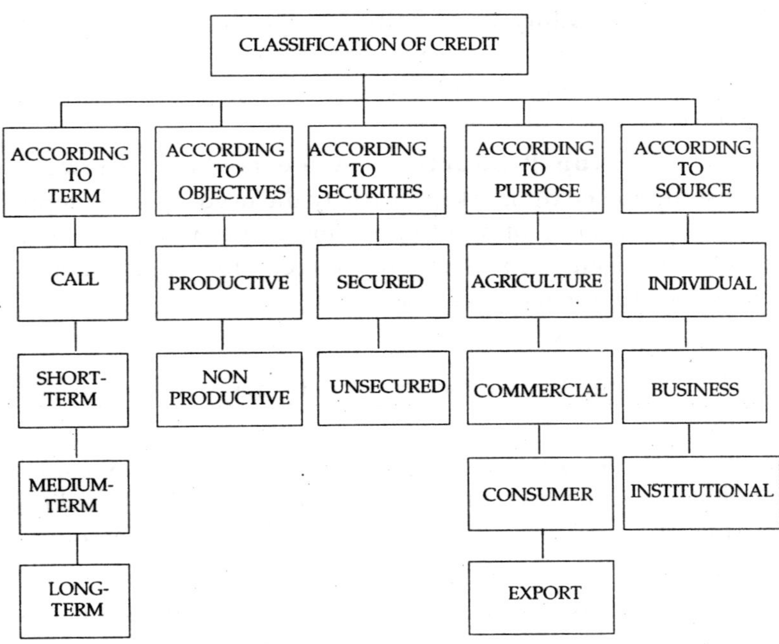

(iii) Medium-term Credit—Medium-term credit is given for a period ranging from 2 to 5 years. Such type of credit is generally sanctioned for capital investment such as purchase of machinery etc.

(iv) Long-term credit—Credit sanctioned for over 5 years comes under this Category. Such type of credit is given for purchase of new lands or for bringing some permanent improvement in business or for purchase of some costly machinery.

(2) According to Objective

Credit may be sanctioned for a variety of objectives. On this basis creditor and debtor mutually decide as for what purposes credit will be used. On this basis credit may be classified as follows:

(i) Productive Credit—The productive credit is the credit taken for the purpose of carrying on productive activities with a view to augmenting income. It may be needed to create some fixed assets in business.

(ii) Non-Productive Credit—Also knows as consumption credit is taken to satisfy the needs of consumption goods or services of a entrepreneur. There was a time when institutional suppliers used to refuse credit for consumption, but now the attitude has gone a sea change.

(3) According to Security

On the basis of security credit may be categorised as follow:

(I) Secured credit—Credit covered by some security is termed as secured credit. In the sanction of secured credit the value of security must be more than that of the amount of credit.

(ii) Unsecured credit—When credit is granted without any security is called as unsecured credit. This type of credit is granted just on the basis of trust.

(4) According to Purpose

According to purpose Credit may be classified as follows :

(I) Industrial Credit—The Credit provided for the purpose of industrial activity is known as industrial credit. Industrial credit is used for purchase of machinery, construction of industrial premises, fulfillment of working capital requirement and other financial requirements. This type of credit may be extended for short-term, medium term and long-term.

(ii) Agriculture credit—The credit provided for the purpose of agriculture is known as agriculture credit. Such type of credit is provided by cooperatives and regional rural banks for the purchase of seeds and equipment, land reform and transportation of farm produce etc.

(iii) Consumer Credit—In order to improve living conditions of masses, such type of credit is gaining more and more importance. Consumer may obtain credit from banks, financial institutions and financial companies for the purchase of consumer durables through hire-purchase agreement.

(iv) Export Credit—The credit provided for the purpose of export is known as export credit. The credit so obtained is utilised for the payment of import or for importable goods. The export credit is provided by commercial banks and specialised banks established for the purpose like Export Import bank.

(5) According to Source

On the basis of the source, the credit may be of three types as discussed follow:

(I) Institutional Credit—The credit extended by credit institutions is known as institutional credit.

(ii) Individual Credit—The credit provided by an individual to another individual for mutual help is known as individual credit. This type of credit is normally provided by relatives, friends and money lenders.

(iii) Business Credit—This type of Credit is provided for business purposes i.e. financing the manufacture and marketing of goods. The goods and services soldout by whole saler to consumer or retailer on credit is called as business credit.

CREATION OF CREDIT

One of the most important function of a commercial bank is, 'the creation of money or credit'. For this reason a bank is known as a factory of credit. A bank receives deposits from the public on the promise to pay them on their demand. Now the bank does not keep these deposits cent per cent with it. These deposits are lent out to business community for short periods. The bank keeps only a small proportion of cash reserves against these deposits in order to meet the demand of the depositors. The bank can do it only because it knows that all the depositors do not come to withdraw all the amount at once; some may withdraw while others may deposit. Thus on the basis of a small reserve, a bank can create a huge superstructure of credit. This is known as credit creation power of a bank.

Meaning of Credit Creation

Credit creation means the expansion of bank deposits through the process of more loans and advances by the bank.

For obtaining loan from a bank a person must furnish sufficient security to the satisfaction of a bank. Usually a bank accepts Govt. securities or securities of approved concerns. After this is done, the required loan is permitted to the borrower. But the borrower does not want to get the whole amount of his loan in cash. He prefers to deposit it in his current account with the bank. In case he has no account, he opens a new one and the borrowed money is deposited in it. It looks as if the borrower has deposited that sum. Thus a deposit is created in his name. He is given a cheque book with an authority to draw cheques on the bank upto the full amount of the loan. In this way a bank is able to lend money without losing cash. It is here that the bank has created credit.

Again the bank buys securities but does not pay cash. It pays the sellers of these securities with its own cheques. A Banker's cheque is not cash, it is simply a promise to pay cash. When this cheque is deposited in any bank, credit or deposit is created in favour of the seller of the securities.

So we conclude that the bank's loan creates deposit or it creates a credit for the borrower.

Process of Credit Creation

The process of creating credit is somewhat as follow : Suppose Rs. 1,000 has been deposited in a bank. The bank would not keep cent per cent cash with it. It would keep only a small proportion of this deposit to meet the demand of the depositor and the rest of the money will be available for loan. Bankers have learnt, by long experience that only a small percentage of cash reserve to the total liabilities is required.

In western countries like England and U.S.A., where banking habit of the people is developed the banks keep nearly 10 per cent to meet the demand of the depositors. In under-developed countries, however, banks keep even more than 20% cash reserve because the banking habits of the people have not been developed. Thus out of a deposit of Rs. 1,000, the bank will keep Rs. 100 in cash and Rs. 900 cash will be available to the bank to be used in any way the banks likes.

Now if the bank only lends this sum of Rs. 900 left with it in cash, it would not give it adequate resources for making loans or advances. The bank, therefore, takes to create credit. So the bank will create a fresh credit to the extent of Rs. 900 by keeping the remaining sum of Rs. 100 (i.e., 10% of Rs. 1000) in cash. This sum of Rs. 900 is created money or bank credit. In this way each time when a cash deposit is made, the bank creates money. As a matter of fact the banks are able to create money on the assumption that the people are not likely to withdraw (in a given period) in excess of 10 percent of their credit deposits (created money) also.

Let us explain the process of credit creation when there are many banks in existence. We make the following assumptions :

(1) There are a number of banks, X, Y, Z etc. with different deposit.

(2) Every bank has to keep 20% of cash reserves against its deposits.

(3) A new deposit of Rs. 1000 is made with bank X to start with.

After the fresh deposit of Rs. 1000 in the bank X, its balance sheet will be as follow :

BANK X

Liabilities		Assets	
New Deposit	Rs. 1,000	New Cash	Rs. 1,000
Total	Rs. 1,000		Rs. 1,000

Now the bank X, will keep 20% reserve in cash against its Rs. 1000 and the balance of Rs. 800 it will lend to some party say Mr. A. After the loan has been made, the balance sheet of the bank X, would be as follows :

BANK X

Liabilities		Assets	
Deposit	Rs. 1,000	Cash	Rs. 200
Total	Rs. 1,000	Loan to Mr. A	Rs. 800
		Total	Rs. 10,000

Now Mr. A pays off the amount of Rs. 800 to his creditor who may be assumed to deposit the same with his bank, say Bank Y. The balance sheet of the Bank Y will be as follows :

BANK Y

Liabilities		Assets	
New Deposit	Rs. 800	New Cash	Rs. 800
Total	Rs. 800		Rs. 800

Bank Y will find more cash with it. It will keep 20% (*i.e.*, Rs. 160) of the new cash received and the balance, i.e., Rs. 800 Rs.—160=Rs. 640 will be lent to Mr. B. This will change the balance sheet of the Bank Y as follows :

BANK Y

Liabilities		Assets	
Deposit	Rs. 800	Cash	Rs. 160
		Loan to Mr. C	Rs. 640
Total	Rs. 900		Rs. 800

Mr. B also pays off his creditor who deposits this amount in his bank, let us say Z. The balance sheet of the Bank Z will be as follows :

BANK Z

Liabilities		Assets	
New Deposit	Rs. 640	New Cash	Rs. 640
Total	Rs. 640		Rs. 640

Bank Z finds that its cash reserve has increased. It will keep 20% of Rs. 640 (i.e., Rs. 128) and the Balance of Rs. 512 will be lent to Mr. C. after the loan is made the balance sheet of the bank Z will be as follows :

BANK Z

Liabilities		Assets	
Deposit	Rs. 640	Cash	Rs. 128
		Loan to Mr. C	Rs. 512
Total	Rs. 640		Rs. 640

Likewise Mr. C will pay off his creditor who would deposit the money in another bank. Thus the process of deposit becoming loan or an advance or an investment goes on and on till the original deposit of Rs. 1000 is completely exhausted. We know that original deposit of Rs. 1000 becomes additional deposit of Rs. 800, 640, 512, 410, 328 etc. and if we add these deposit together the total would be equal to Rs. 5000. The total amount of deposit expansion would be reverse of the cash reserve ratio. Let us suppose if cash reserve ratio is 20% or 1/5, credit expansion would be 5/1 or 5 times the original deposit.

It must be remembered that it is not really necessary to assume that there are many banks, the process of credit creation will take place even if there is only one bank in a town.

It should be clearly noted that the 'Bank credit' i.e., money created by banks becomes part of the total amount of money in circulation. Thus it becomes necessary for the monetary authority to control the volume of Bank credit.

Limitation on Credit Creation by Banks

So far we have studied that banks are creators of credit. But they cannot create as much credit as they like. This power to create credit is subject to certain limitations which are given below:

(1) Cash Deposit—To begin with the power of a bank to create credit is limited by 'cash deposits'. Cash deposits are made by the people and depend upon the banking habit of the people and also on the total amount of currency in circulation. Other things remaining the same if the bank's cash deposits increase it would be able to create more credit and the reverse would happen when its 'cash deposits' decrease.

(2) Ratio of Reserve to Deposits—The second limitation is set by the 'safe cash ratio' of the bank. Cash reserve or safe cash ratio is the amount which the banks consider it safe to hold against their liabilities. The level of cash ratio or cash reserve depend upon the banking habit and confidence of the people. In more advanced countries like U.K. or U.S.A. banks consider 10% as safe cash ratio. Thus a bank can create $1000 against a cash deposit of $100 but in less developed countries like India where the people have not developed banking habits and confidence, banks have to keep more cash reserves and thus their power to create credit is less. In India, for example, people have less confidence in credit. They prefer cash transactions. So there are less number of bank accounts and less number of cheques etc, in circulation. Thus the banks will have to keep 20% cash reserves. Thus against a cash deposit of Rs. 100 a bank can credit upto the limit of Rs. 500 only.

(3) People's desire to Hold Cash—We have come to know that the power of credit creation of a bank depends upon the amount of cash with it. But the amount of cash with the banks depend upon the people's desire to hold cash with them. If at any time people's liquidity preference is increased, i.e., for any reason they decide to hold more cash with them (assuming the total supply of cash remaining constant), they would deposit less cash with the banks. Now since the banks are left with a smaller amount of cash, they will be able to create less money or credit. But if on the other hand, people decide to hold smaller cash with them, they deposit more cash with the banks. As a result of it banks will be able to create more credit.

(4) Business Conditions—The fourth limitation on bank's power to credit creation is set by business conditions prevailing in the country. During boom people demand more and more money from the banks as loans and advances for the purpose of investment and as such banks will be able to create large amounts of credit. But during depression the reverse will happen. People's demand for loans and advances will fall greatly, so there will be smaller credit creation by bank.

(5) Control by the Central Bank—The fifth limitation is set by the central banking authority in every country. Since the bank credit becomes part of the total amount of currency in circulation, it becomes necessary for Central Bank to control the volume of credit of these banks. The Central Bank has the power to fix minimum cash ratio which every commercial bank is required to keep in the Central Bank. When the Central Bank increases this minimum 'cash ratio' the cash reserves of these banks fall and their power to create credit is also reduced. The central Bank has the power to influence the volume of credit of commercial banks by direct methods as well.

INVESTMENT MANAGEMENT BY BANKS.

The Most important problem in banking administration is that of investment management which is also known as portfolio management. The banks investment is an arranged and digested scheme of its assets. It is difficult to suggest any universal policy of investment management as it depends on the nature of funds of the bank. For example if a bank can acquire funds of more or less permanent nature, it can acquire more profitable assets. If the fund acquired by the bank are subject to wide fluctuations, it is required by the bank to keep a large part of the fund in liquid form. The soundness of a bank is judged by the distribution of its funds on different types of assets. A good investment policy is one which brings maximum profits to shareholders and provides maximum security to the depositors.

It is difficult to lays down any uniform rule to determine investment management of a bank. The investment policy of a bank is greatly influenced by the local conditions in which the bank operates. The nature and availability of funds differ widely from region to region within the same country. For example, the problems faced by banks in rural areas are materially different from those of the problems faced by the banks in urban areas. The main occupation of people in rural area is agriculture. Therefore the demand in rural areas for loan is usually less liquid and less diversified. These differences influence to the investment policy of the bank.

Apart from the local condition, there are some important principles which a banker keep in to consideration while formulating its investment policy. These are the guiding principles of the investment policy of a Commercial bank described as follows:

(1) Liquidity—It refers to the capacity of the bank to pay cash in exchange of the deposits. The bank accepts several types of deposits and large part of these deposits is withdrawable on demand. Hence according to this principle the bank must keep a sufficient degree of liquidity in its assets.

(2) Profitability—The bank by nature is a business institutions. Therefore, its most important objective is to earn as much profit as possible. The bank must formulate its investment policy so wisely which may provide sufficient income from its assets. The bank will then only be able to meet all its expenses and pay a fair percentage of dividends to the shareholders.

(3) Security—The other important principle of bank investment policy is safety and security. The bank should never overlook the principle of utmost safety in investment of funds entrusted to them by their valuable depositors. It is a very important principle in comparison to above two principles as bank deals in other people's money. The survival of bank depends on the confidence of people. The bank should earn profit as much as possible with a view to satisfy the shareholders. But it cannot afford to sacrifice the principle of safety and security of its investment

All the guiding principles of bank investment policy are equally important. No one is less or more important. The bank cannot afford to sacrifice one in favour of the other. The banker must strike a balance between liquidity, profitability and safety and security. All banks should formulate their investment policy. But the formulation of good investment policy is an art which require wide knowledge.

4. Productivity—Commercial banks are profit earning institutions. Therefore it is necessary for them to plan their investment in such a way to as to secure an adequate and permanent income because the important source of earning of banks is its earning form investment. It should be keep in mind by the banker that profitability should not be at the cost of liquidity and safety. With a view to earn the maximum profits out of its investments, a bank should use its resources at the optimum level.

(5) Stability—The bank must invest its surplus funds only in those securities whose prices in the market tends not to fluctuate frequently and widely. It is because the bank may have to suffer heavy losses in case the prices of such securities suddenly fall in the market.

(6) Diversification—The bank should keep into consideration the issue of diversification of risk while making investment. The bank must see that a significant part of its investible funds are not invested in a particular type of security. Likewise bank should not advance only to a particular type of business enterprise. The bank should plan its investment and lending policies in such away so that it can invest the funds at minimum risks. Therefore it is worthwhile for the bank not to concentrate on a particular type of security or business. Instead, it should diversify its investments in variety of securities and business to avoid risks.

❑

12

Central Banking

Central banking is of recent origin. There had been no clearly defined concept of central banking anywhere in the world prior to the commencement of the twentieth century. But, today there is no country in the world which does not have a central bank.

A central bank functions as a top controlling bank for all other banks of the country. It is the bank which also acts as the leader of the money market. A central bank is an institution which is charged with the responsibilities of management of currency system and carrying out the monetary policy of government. As a top controlling bank, it supervises, regulates and controls the functions of commercial banks and all other financial institutions. It functions as controller of credit, banker's bank and enjoys the monopoly of issuing currency notes on behalf of the government. In our country the Reserve bank of India enjoys these privileges.

Definition

It is difficult to give a brief and accurate definition of central bank in precise words. The definition of central bank is derived from the functions performed by it. The functions of a central bank have grown considerably with the passage of time. Further these functions have varied from country to country. Despite of all these difficulties, efforts have been made to define central bank. Many writers have attempted to define a central bank by laying emphasis on any of the function performed by the central bank.

Hawtrey pointed out that the essential function of a central bank is to act as the lender of last resort.

Veera Smith holds the view that, "the primary definition of central banking may be as a banking system in which a single bank has either a complete or residuary monopoly in note issue".

M. H. Dekock also define a central bank by including all the important function entrusted to it. Dekock's definition appears to be better than any of the other definitions. The only criticism against his definition is that it is too long.

According to *Dekock,* "a central bank is a bank which constitutes the apex of the monetary and banking structure of its country and which performs, as best as it can in the national economic interest".

A careful study of the above definitions of Central Bank shows that in these definition emphasis has been laid down one aspect or the other. While Smith considered note issue as the primary function, others accorded importance to credit control, lender of the last resort and maintenance of stability of credit and control etc. as the important functions of the Central Bank. The definition of Dekock, however seems to be more comprehensive.

We may conclude the definition of a central bank as "a central bank is one which acts as a banker to the government and has the monopoly of note is use, operates the currency and credit system of the country and does not perform the routine commercial banking functions."

Role in Economic Development

The central bank is as apex banking institution plays an important role in the economic development of a country. In almost all the countries of the world, central banks have been called upon to provide financial resources to carry out the developmental activities of the state. The role of central bank is to perform in economic development in much larger form in developing countries as compared to developed countries.

Developed Economies

(1) Maintaining stability—The central bank in any country is fully charged with the responsibility of maintaining the stability of internal and external economy of the country.

(2) Control of economy—In all types of economies, irrespective of their level of economic development and ideology, a central bank is delegated with all such functions as entrusted to it in order to control of the economy.

Developing Economies

As far as the role of central banks in developing economies is concerned they have much more important role to perform in economic development of respective countries. In a developing economy, the central bank is to shoulder additional responsibility of acting as an agent of growth. It participates directly or indirectly in building-up of growth-creating sectors in the economy. For this purpose, over and above the functions stated above, the central bank has to play additional role as mentioned below :

(1) Control of bank system—One of the important responsibility entrusted to central banks in developing countries is to build-up a sound, effective and adequate system of commercial banking keeping in view the needs of industry, trade, commerce, agriculture and other sectors of the economy. The prior permission is required for the establishment, expansion, amalgamation branch expansion etc. Apart from this the central bank also regulate the working of the commercial banks and thus provides conducive network of banking structure which plays catalyst role in economic development.

(2) Promotional function—The central bank directly contribute in the promotion of banking in the country. The central bank also helps in establishing industrial banks, agricultural bank and co-operative credit societies. The central bank can also induce banks and other financial institutions by providing more and more medium and long term loans by giving them re-discounting facilities.

(3) Proper credit facilities for economy—The central bank also undertakes the responsibility to improve currency and credit system of the country. The establishment of more and more financial institutions will provide larger and cheap credit and divert voluntary savings into productive savings or into productive channels.

(4) Price stability—Control of money and credit is the most important function of the central bank in a developing economy. The object of credit control is to secure price stability. It is the prime responsibility of the central bank to control inflationary pressures arising in the process of economic development.

(5) Developmental Functions—The central bank in a developing economy encourages economic development by promoting and developing various developmental banks engaged in providing long-term finances to various sectors of the economy.

(6) Debt management—The central bank undertakes the responsibility of selling and buying of government bonds and makes timely changes in the structure and composition of public debt. Thus debt management by central bank helps in accelerating the rate of economic development.

FUNCTIONS OF CENTRAL BANK

Different authors have defined a central bank differently. In their definition, authors have laid emphasis on any one or more functions performed by the central bank. Keeping in view the difference of opinion *Dekock* observed, "In practice, it is difficult to single out any particular function of the central bank in order of their importance. Since they are interrelated and complementary. A true central bank should always be ready to perform any of the functions enumerated above, if the condition and circumstances in the area of operation render it necessary or desirable for it to do so. The guiding principle for a central bank, whatever function or group of functions it performs at any particular moment, is that it should act only in the public interest and without regard to profit as a primary consideration.

According to *R. S. Sayers*, "The business of the central bank, as distinguished from a commercial bank, is to control the Commercial Banks in such a way as to promote the general monetary policy of the state. There are three fundamental points implicit in this, *first*, a central bank does not, as a commercial bank does, exist to make maximum profits for its owners; *second*, it must have some means of controlling the commercial banks; and *third*, it is subordinate to the state.

The main functions of a central bank are discussed in the following heads :

(1) Right of note issue—One of the most important function of a central bank is the issue of currency note. In almost every country the central bank has been given the sole right of note issue. The central bank is entrusted with the responsibility in order to ensure uniformity in the currency and to secure control over currency. Moreover, it becomes easier for the government to supervise and to control note issue. As pointed by Dekock, "The privilege of note issue was almost every where associated with the origin and development of central bank. Infact, until the beginning of the twentieth century they were generally known as bank of issue".

In issuing notes, the central bank is governed by certain rules as laid down by law. It must keep reserves of gold, silver and good securities in fixed proportion to inspire confidence in the people in the paper currency. For example, in India notes are issued under the proportional reserve system by the Reserve Bank of India. Since Oct. 1957 it is required to keep minimum reserve of Rs. 200 crores of which Rs. 115 crores must be in gold.

(2) Agent and financial Adviser to the Government— As a Government bank the central bank renders all those services to the Government which other banks render to their customers. The central bank maintains the accounts of Government. In keeping the banking accounts of the government, the central bank performs the same functions as the ordinary commercial bank performs for its customer. It makes collections, disbursements and remittances on behalf of the Government. It provides short period loans to meet the current requirements of the government. It also manages long term finance of the government by sale of securities. As an agent to the government it buys and sells the foreign currencies.

The central bank also acts as the financial adviser to the government. In this capacity it guides the Government in securing the best possible terms in respect of Treasury Bill and securities. It also renders expert advice on financial problems to the various organs of the Government.

(3) Banker's Bank—It is also charged with the responsibility of securing orderly development of banking in the country. In every country the central bank is empowered to supervise the working of the member banks. For this reason the central bank can impose certain obligations on the member banks and thus keep a control on them. These conditions are imposed on the member banks in order to ensure sound banking system. The commercial banks recognise the supremacy of the central bank and accept it as their friend, philosopher and guide.

(4) Lender of last Resort—The central bank acts as the lender of last resort. In this capacity it is the responsibility of the central bank to provide directly or indirectly financial accommodation to the member banks in the time of need. When the central bank performs this function it is known as 'lender of last resort.' The arrangement regarding financial accommodation differs from country to country. The central bank plays its role as lender of last resort by assuming responsibility to meet all reasonable demand of commercial banks and directly or indirectly provide accommodation to member banks by rediscounting their first class bills of exchange or by advancing funds to them on the basis of short term securities. Thus the member banks can increase their cash reserves at the shortest possible notice and can make their position more liquid. Hence central bank is the ultimate source from which credit is obtained whenever a crisis or a panic develops into a run on the banks.

An important point to note here is that the Central Bank acts as the guardian of the member banks and the rest of the money market. It does not come in competition with other banks. According to *Howtrey*, The essential duty of the central bank as the lender of last resorts to make good shortage of cash among the competitive banks".

(5) Control of Credit—The control of credit is the most important of all the functions rendered by the central bank. The object of credit control is to secure price stability. The central bank controls the volume of credit in three ways by varying the reserve ratios of member banks; by raising or lowering the bank rate; and by resorting to open market operation.

The power of the central bank to alter the total amount of money in circulation through the mechanism of credit control. With large cash reserves, member banks can not lend more and *vice versa*. Whenever the central bank desires to effect a change in volume of credit, it can do so by changing the cash reserve of the banks–if it increases the cash reserve ratio, the banks' power to create credit is decreased and *vice versa*. Thus the total amount of money in circulation has a relationship with the creation of credit.

Again when the central bank finds the money market tight and wants to create 'easy money' conditions it purchases securities and provides funds into the market. A sale of securities by the central bank works in the opposite direction and removes surplus money from the market.

(6) Custodian of Cash Reserve of Commercial Banks— The Central Bank of the country acts as a banker's bank and in this capacity has to hold the cash reserves of commercial and other banks and acts as a sort of guardian to them. Thus the central bank acts as the conductor and leader of the banking system of a country. It acts as a friend, philosopher and guide of commercial banks. In the words of Crowther, "The Central Bank stands to the member banks in exactly the same relation as the member banks themselves to the public." To safeguard the interest of the depositors as also to look after the economic interests of the nation, these reserves are to be maintained by the Central Bank to use them in the times of financial stringencies. The Commercial Banks, thus are under an obligation to keep a certain percentage of their deposits with the Central Bank. The centralisation of cash reserves in the Central Bank is a source of great strength to the banking system of any country. Centralised cash reserves can at least serve as the basis of large and more elastic credit structure than if the same amount were scattered among the individual banks. Although the percentage differs from country to country, every one has got the practice.

(7) Custodian of Reserves of International Currency— The central bank also acts as a custodian of the country's reserve of international currency. Thus the central bank is charged with responsibility of meeting at any time an adverse balance of payments and maintaining the external value of home currency stable. The greatest factor which has necessitated the governments to control the foreign exchange through the central banks is the maintenance of the stable value of the international currency in the international market.

(8) Clearing House Function—Clearing house functions refers to the settlement of differences between commercial banks regarding their mutual transactions. It is a widely accepted function to be performed by the central bank. The central bank acts as the clearing house for settling the accounts of commercial banks. The settlements of these accounts are effected by drawing cheques upon the central bank. The commercial banks are able to adjust their obligations to each other by merely having their reserve balance debited or credited as the case may be.

It is a periodical work which is done either daily or periodical once in every week. This function enable the central bank in calculating the total amount of liquidity held by the people at the time of clearing. It also reveals the nature of transactions going on in the credit market.

CREDIT CONTROL BY CENTRAL BANK

Objective of Credit Control

The main objectives of credit control are as follows :—

(1) Exchange Rate Stability : The traditional obejctive of credit control was that of keeping exchange rate stable. As *Dr. De Kock* pointed out, the main reason for the general policy of stable exchange rate prior to 1931 was the universal belief at the time that exchange stability was of great importance for the maintenance of international confidence and for the conduct of international trade on the largest scale through which the maximum economic welfare of the world could be attained.

(2) Stabilization of the General Price Level : In recent years greater prominence is assigned to this objective of credit control. *Cassel* and *Keynes* regarded price stabilization as the ultimate goal of credit control. Stabilization of the general price level was though essential for the smooth working of the economy and for national economic welfare. A change in the price level causes wide disturbances in the economic relationships between creditor and debtor, producer and consumer, employer and employee etc. within a country as well as between countries . Price stabilization would eliminate such disturbances and maladjustments followed by elimination of trade cycles.

However, there are some writers who opine that though the attainment of these two objectives is highly desirable from the point of view of national economic welfare, maximum benefit can be attained by means of relative economic stabilization through a cheap money policy even at the cost of pricde fluctuations and exchange rates instability.

(3) Stabilization of the Money Market : Some economists stress that the credit control policy should aim at the stabilization of the money market. For this it should offset seasonal variations in the demand for funds and provide credit in times of crisis . Credit control should be such that demand and supply should be adjusted in all times. However, this objective has not been recognised because it is incompatible with the goal of stabilizing the other phases of economic activity.

(4) Elimination of Business cycles : It is pointed out by some writers that though the objectives of exchange stability and price stability are desirable in themselves yet they should be subservient to the objective of ironing out of the business fluctuations. It is held that business cycle is not caused merely by price movements and as such aim of the Central Bank should be to eliminate fluctuations in business activity rather than maintaining price stability.

(5) Full Employment : However of late, the emphasis has shifted from mere economic stability to full employment. The severity of great depression served as an eye-opener to the evils of unemployment. It was felt by all that the unemployment is socially dangerous morally indefensible and economically wasteful. Consequently full employment come to be regarded as the most important objective of credit control.

(6) Promoting Economic Growth : It has been now widely regarded that credit control should be conducive to economnic development. It should promote and maintain a high level of employment and income. As *Dr. De Kock* observes, " The most recent tendency in official monetary circiles is to combine the objective of international exchange stability with that of promoting and maintaining high levels of employment and real income."

Thus, now monetary policy has been coming more and more into its own as the promotion of income development is developing as an objective of credit policy of the central bank.

The central bank as the central monetary authority posesses greater responsibility to prevent both too much and too little credit creation by the commercial banks . The Central Bank should have aim at adjustment of the volume of credit to the volume of business. The central bank can control credit quantitatively as well as qualitatively. By exercising quantitative methods the central bank can control the total volume of credit outstnading in the market. The qualitative methods of credit control helps the central bank to controls the uses to which credit may be put.

Quantitative Credit Control—The Central bank controls the credit quantitatively through the mechanism of the following methods :

1. The Bank Rate—The bank rate or the discount rate is the rate at which the Central Bank of a country discounts the bill or gives advances to commercial banks. Bank Rate is differ from the interest rate which the commercial banks charge on advances given to their customers. The Bank Rate operates on credit through its relation with the interest rate. In every country, commercial banks borrow money from the Central Bank. On such borrowings they have to pay interest at the rate decided by it. When this discount rate is increased, the borrowings from the Central Bank become costly. To compensate this, the commercial banks will increase interest rate which they charge from their customers. Besides an increase in the Bank Rate causes an all round increase in the interest rates. The net result of such increase reflects in the form costlier of credit. This may discourage people in borrowings from the commercial banks. To the extent it happens, the supply of credit is restricted . An increase in the Bank Rate causes a fall in the price of stocks and bonds. The decisions to invest and to spend are, thus affected by the changes in the discount rate. An increase in it causes a contraction in credit. It creates impression among the peoples that the economy is passing through inflationary pressures.

Thus an increase in the Bank Rate reflects the tight credit policy which the Central Bank decides to follow.

It is a situation under which there seems shortage of money in the country. Hence the Bank Rate has to be lowerred. Such a step would mean easy credit, more borrowings, more investment and the withering away of monetary stringency. An announcement of reduction in the Bank Rate serves to ease the market . Business and investment activities get encouraged with the reduction in Bank Rate.

Diagram

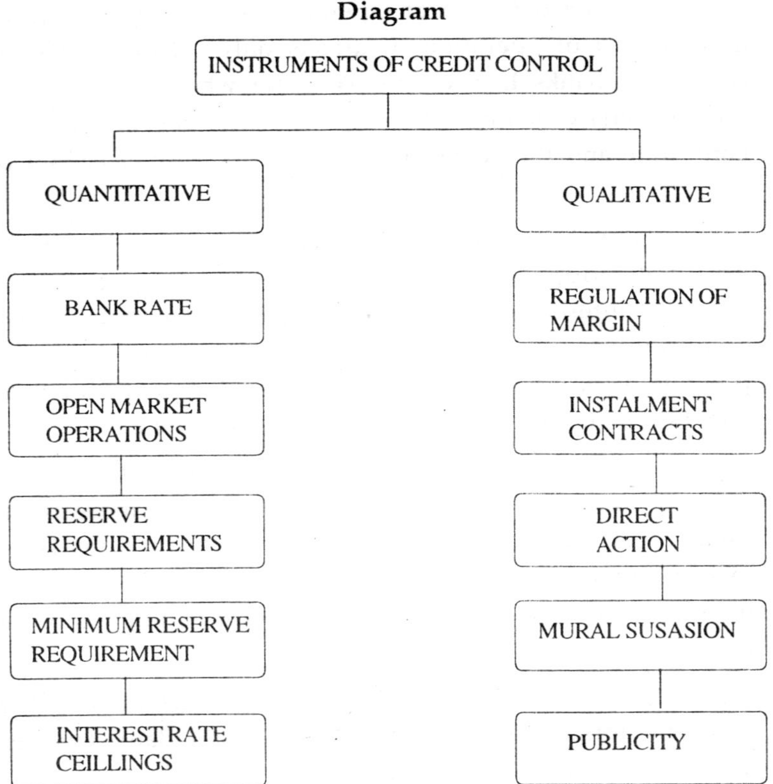

Limitations :

(1) Attitude of Commercial Banks—It will work only when commercial banks borrow from the Central Bank. The Central Bank can only decide the Bank Rate. It can announce the Bank Rate but cannot force the banks to borrow. All that it can do is to wait for banks to come to it. If they do not come, the Bank Rate will not work.

(2) Gap Between Discount and Interest Rate—If the gap between the interest rate and the discount rate is already sizeable, a mild increase in the latter will not cause any readjustment of the former.

(3) Limited Area of Operation—The Bank Rate has a limited area of operation. It affects only credit created by commercial banks. In a country like India, where there is such a great diversity of interest rates, with vast gap between the Bank Rate and the actual interest rate, the former cannot be operative.

(4) Subservient to Fiscal Policy—An increase in the Bank Rate adds to the interest liabilities of the government. Rates of interest on public loans have also to be raised accordingly. In a country where the government has a programme of large scale borrowing from the public the Bank Rate policy becomes subservient to the fiscal policy.

2.Open Market Operations : The Banks Rate policy is not as effective as open market operations. At intervals the Central Bank purchases or sells securities in the open market. It thereby pumps more money into the banking system or drains the same out of it. It is a continuous, never-ending job of the Central Bank.

Open market operations work in both directions. When there are inflationary condition the Central Bank will sell government bonds and will thus collect money by the system. Bonds are purchased either by banks or by individuals. It is immaterial who purchases the bonds. In fact, Bonds are sold in the market. What will be impact this transaction. The buyer will most likely pay for the bonds by cheque to the Central Bank . The Central Bank will present this cheque for payment to the commercial bank concerned . The commercial bank will lose an equivalent amount to the Central Bank. Its assets and liabilities will be cut down. This is the first effect of the sale of securities by the Central Bank. But later on since this amount was the basis of multiple credit for the commercial bank, there will be a large decline in credit. Sale of securities by the Central Bank thus restricts credit supply.

Purchase of securities will depicts the opposite effect. If there exists deflationary conditions, the Central Bank will buy securities in the open market. It will pump more money into the economy. This money will flow into the coffers of the commercial banks which the commercial bank will use for further multiple expansion . Credit will increase and with this, economic activities will look up.

Open market operations have one great advantage. Here the initiative is with the Central Bank. It is not to wait for the commercial banks to come to purchase . It can sell or buy its securities in the open market. Despite of all as mentioned above open market operation has its own limitations as described below :

(1) Utilisation of Cash : When a Central Bank sells securities the market to absorb any surplus cash reserves of banks, the banks may easily replenish their reserves by borrowing from the Central Bank. When the Central Bank purchases securities from the market, member banks will no doubt receive extra cash. But they may utilise the cash to repay their debts to the Central Bank. Under the circumstances their reserves may not increase.

(2) Increase in Reserve : When the Central Bank is trying to increase the cash resources of bank by purchasing securities, the public may withdraw cash from banks in panic with a view to hoarding. In that case, the reserves of banks may not increase.

(3) No Increase in Loan : Even if the Central Bank suceeds in increasing the cash reserves of banks, that does not mean that their loans will also increse. In the first place, bank may simply pile up more cash reserve to strengthen their position in the face of an emergency. In that case there will be no increase in loans.

(4) Unwillingness for Loan : Even if Banks are willing to lend, businessmen may be unwilling to take loans. Banks may place plenty of water before the public horse, but the horse cannot be forced to drink if it is afraid of loss through drinking water *i.e.* the horse it is not thirsty. This may happen when confidence is lacking in the acute phase of a depression. During such a period an expansion of bank loans and investment will not be easy of achievement.

Relation between Bank Rate and Open Market Policy— It is obvious that the use of the bank rate and open market operations cannot be separated from each other. Each by itself may not be as effective as is desirable. For example, a high bank rate may not always result in a contraction of credit. Other joint stocks may be in possession of surplus funds which they would go on lending at low rates, even if the bank rate is fixed up. The bank rate thus becomes ineffective instrument of credit control . Under such circumstances, the Central Bank will sell some securities in the market and absorb in the surplus funds of banks. The latter will then be forced to follow the lead of the Central Bank and Curtail their loans . Similarly, the market policy, if it is not followed up by appropriate changes in the .bank rate, may not always be effective. It can be explained with an example. Suppose in order to control credit the Central Bank sells securities, but has not raised its rate of discount. Since the bank rate is low, members banks may then replenish their reserves by discoanting these securities with the Central Bank . The policy of credit restriction will be unsuccessful. But if the bank rate is also simultaneously put up, other banks will find it unprofitable to rediscount the securities. They would call in their loans. Hence each of the two weapons may not always be successful, if it is not backed up by the other.

3. *Changing Reserve Requirements* : The Central Bank either by contracts or by law, has the power to raise or lower the required legal reserve ratio, and the commercial banks must observe this reserve ratio. If the Central Bank wants to make the credit tight, it can raise the required reserve ratio. Suppose the Central Bank raises the reserve requirement from 2% to, say 4% the banks sustain their earlier deposits, will have to pass on more cash to the Central Bank. Alternatively they will have to reduce their deposits.

If the Central Bank wants to ease the credit conditions, it can do the reverse. It can cut down the legal reserve ratio. Suppose, for example, the Central Bank decides to bring down the reserve ratio from 4% to 2% . This will release money for commercial banks which they can use for creating fresh credit.

Increase in reserve ratio, thus tightens the credit while reduction in the same bases it. It is a powerful tool, but it is used sparingly. It can be used more often, but the authorities find easy to do the same thing with the open market operations. Further in countries like India banks have excess reserves with them. In such a case, increase in the reserve ratio may not be as effective as otherwise.

4. *Minimum Secondary Reserve Requirements* : These reserves are over and above the minimum cash reserves to which reference has been made above. The idea underlying the scheme is to further restrict the power of the commercial banks to expand credit by limiting their capacity to convert government securities and surplus cash assets into business loans. This method has been extensively used by several countries of the world and it has certainly limited the power of the banks to expand credit and to use *De-Kock's* words, "It can be made to play a valuable part in any positive disinflationary monetary policy under conditions of exceptional inflationary pressures caused by war, rearmament or abnormal circumstances.

5. Interest Rate Ceilings : The Central Bank can also give instructions to the commercial bank regarding the maximum rate of interest on time deposits. Such interest rate ceilings will reduce the competition among banks. When interest rates are permitted to raise, deposits and credit will increase. On the other hand, when low ceiling is placed on interest rates, deposits with banks will be discouraged.

Qualitative Credit Control .

The Central Bank controls the credit qualitatively through the mechanism of the following methods :

(1) Regulation of Margin Requirements : It refers to the power of Central Bank for the imposition of changes in margin requirements on security loans. 'Margin means the difference between market price of securities and the amount of credit borrowed against them. Businessmen and speculators get credit by pledging securities to the banks. The banks do not advance loans equal to the value of the securities but less then its value. For example, a commercial bank lends Rs. 8,000 against security worth Rs. 10,000, the margin is 2000 or 20% . The Central Bank can increase this margin requirement to 40% or 50% or even to 100%. The higher the margin requirement, the lower the loan one can get on a security of certain value. The lower the margin requirement, the larger the loan one can get on a security of certain value. The Central Bank may totally stop the advancing of loans against any particular type of security e.g. wheat, rice or cotton. The idea behind such excercise is to reduce hoarding with the help of bank credit.

(2) Instalment Contracts : The Central Bank may also use the power to exercise control over instalment contracts. In the developed economies of the West, people purchase and consume things on instalment basis. They have to pay a part of the price in the beginning and the rest in easy instalments. In all this process the commercial banker come to the help of the

traders. The Central Bank can instruct the commercial banks and also the traders to change the conditions of instalment. The Central Bank can discourage purchases by making these scheme stricts and at the same time it can encourage by making them liberal .

(3) Direct Action : The Central Bank normally use this weapon in case all the other weapon proves ineffective . It implies coercive measures like refusal on the part of the Central Bank rediscount for banks whose credit is not in accordance with the wishes of the Central Bank.

(4) Moral Suasion : The Central Bank of a country in addition to the above legal powers can also make a request to the commercial banks to follow the rules of the economy and to help it in maintaining price stability. For example, the Central Bank can instruct commercial banks not to increase their advances beyond the last year's ceilings. Though the request has no legal binding the commercial banks may respect it or not. Sometimes bankers are called for mutual discussions during which appeal to the community spirit is made. The commercial banks may, or may not accept the appeal , but they do not want to gain the displeasure of the Central Bank and, therefore, co-operate with it.

(5) Publicity : This device of publicity means issuing of weekly statistics, periodical reviews of the money market conditions public finance, trade and industry and the issue of weekly statement of assets and liabilities in the form of balance sheet, etc. According to *Burgess* "The information supplied by such publications is as effective as any specification taken by the Central Bank.... It may well prove in the long run, as important a factor making for financial stability as discount or open market policy." The German and Swedish Central Banks have frequently made use of this method.

Difficulties of Credit Control

It has been discussed above the methods normally exercised by the Central Bank to control the money market .Though each of these methods plays their role in control of credit but beyond certain limit they proves subject to serious limitations. Following are the main difficulties in the way effective implementation of credit control measures by the Central Bank:—

(1) Inadequacy—Bank credit is not the only form of credit. Inaddition there is commercial credit like book credit, bills exchange and promissory notes which are not discounted by banks. Difficulties arises here that over these means of credit, the Central Bank has liberal or limited control. They possesses much purchasing power as any other form of credit.

(2) Lack of Relationship—All banks of the country do not have direct relation with the Central Bank. In India the indigenous bankers are still beyond the influence of the Reserve Bank of India.

(3) Co-operation of Commercial Bank—Commercial bank may not always co-operate with the Central Bank even they are member of Centrol Bank.

(4) Non-Banking Institutions—There are non-banking elements in the financial structure of a country. Among these are the various circumstances that affect the temper of the business community. These are beyond the scope of central banking action.

(5) Users of Credit—The Central Bank cannot control the ultimate use to which credit may be put. Strictly, commercial loans for example, may be used for speculative purposes.

This however does not mean that any attempt to control credit on the part of the Central Bank is bound to fail. It depends on variety of factors which proves useful in controlling credit. Thus effectiveness of credit control measureses depends upon how the same has been used.

❑

13

Reserve Bank of India

Origin

The need of a Central Bank in India was felt for a very long time because the control of currency by the Government and the credit by the Imperial Bank of India could not have satisfactory results. The Hilton Young Commission recommended to establish a Central Bank in India. But due to disagreement between the Assembly and the then government, the proposal was dropped in 1927.

A committee known as Central Banking Enquiry Committee was established to review the need of establishment of Central Bank in India in 1931. The committee strongly recommended that the establishment was, *"to be of supreme importance from the point of view of the development of Banking facilities in India; and of her economic development generally, that a central or Reserve Bank shall be created at the earliest possible date."*

The Legislative Assembly again reviewed the recommendation of the committee and realised the need to establish a Central Bank, which was passed in 1935. On the recommendation of the Legislative Assembly the Reserve Bank of India started its work from 1st April 1935.

Aim and Objects

The Reserve Bank of India Act, in its preamble embodies the objectives of the creation of the R.B.I. According to it the aim of the Ban k is :

"To regulate the issue of bank notes and the keeping of reserve with a view to securing monetary stability in India and generally to operate the currency and credit system of the country to its advantage."

At the same time pressing the necessity to establish a central bank, Hilton Young Commission stressed, the need for eradication of weakness lying in the times before the establishment of the Reserve Bank of India. Following are the important aims and objectives behind the establishment of Reserve Bank of India :

(1) Abolished Weak Currency System—Before the Reserve Bank was established, the two systems of currency and credit were being managed by two separate agencies. The currency was regulated by the Government, while the Imperial Bank regulated the credit. The Hilton Young Commission found that separation of these functions was defective from the point of view of economic development of the country and it pointed out "the inherent weakness of a system in which the control of currency and credit is in the hands of two distinct authorities, whose policies may be widely divergent and in which the currency and banking services are controlled and managed separately from one another." Therefore, with the object of putting an end to such a weak system and to vest the two 'reins' of currency and credit in a single authority, the Reserve Bank was established.

(2) Maintain the Value of Rupee Stable—The establishment of the Reserve Bank was also thought to be necessary to maintain the value of rupee stable. After its establishment, the Reserve Bank has assumed the function of *controller of currency* to secure monetary stability in the country.

(3) Pursue an Appropriate Credit Policy—The Reserve Bank has also been given the power to pursue an appropriate credit policy. The Reserve Bank can control the credit created by the banks in the country by its bank rate policy and other weapons which it has been vested by virtue of various statutes, particularly the Reserve Bank of India Act, 1934 and the Banking Regulation Act, 1949.

(4) To Act as Banker's Bank—It is the bankers' bank and it has control over the cash reserves of the commercial banks.

(5) Control Banking System—The Reserve Bank has also been given the power to issue licences to the banking companies in the country. It can inspect the books of accounts of the banking companies and issue them appropriate directions. Thus, it is an important object of the Reserve Bank to control the banking system in the country.

(6) Leadership in Money Market—Another important objective of the establishment to the Reserve Bank was to remove structural instability of the banking system and to provide leadership to the money market.

ORGANISATION OF THE RESERVE BANK

The Reserve Bank was originally organised as a shareholders' bank with a paid up share capital of Rs. 5 crores divided into 5 lakh shares of Rs. 100 each. Out of this, shares of the nominal value of Rs. 2,30,000 were allotted to the Central Government for disposal at par to the Directors of the Central Board of the Bank seeking to obtain the minimum share qualification. The remaining share capital was owned by the private individuals. However, the control of the policy of the Reserve Bank remained with the Government. The Government was empowered to supersede the Central Board of Directors of the Reserv Bank if the Board failed to discharge faithfully the obligations cast upon it by the Reserve Bank of India Act.

The Reserve Bank was nationalised with the passing of the Reserve Bank of India (Transfer to Public Ownership) Act in 1948. In terms of this Act, the entire share capital of the Bank was acquired by the Central Government and with effect from 1st January, 1949, the Reserve Bank started functioning as a state-owned and state-controlled institution. The private shareholders were paid compensation at the rate of Rs. 118 and 10 annas for every share of Rs. 100.

The nationalisation of the Reserve Bank was in tune with the contemporary world-wide tendency towards state ownership of central banks. The object of its nationalisation was stated "to implement the Government's policy that the Bank should function as state-owned institution and to meet the general desire that control of the Government over the Bank's activities should be extended to ensure greater co-ordination in the monetary economic and financial policies." An important impact of nationalisation of the Reserve Bank was the ruling out of any possible disharmony in the policy laid down by the Central Government and the monetary policy pursued by the Reserve Bank. This also facilitated the Central Government to confer wide powers on the Reserve Bank under the Banking Regulation Act, 1949 to control and regulate the affairs of the commercial banks in the country.

The affairs of the Reserve Bank are controlled by the Central Board of Directors consisting of 20 members as given below :

1. One Governor and four Deputy Governors appointed by the Central Government for such period not exceeding five years as may be fixed by the Central Government at the time of their appointment.

2. Four Directors nominated by the Central Government, one from each of four Local Boards. The term of these directors is related to their membership of the Local Boards.

3. Ten other Directors nominated by the Central Government. These Directors hold office for 4 years and there is a provision in the Act for the retirement by rotation.

4. One Government official nominated by the Central Government.

The chairman of the Central Board of Directors is the Governor of the Reserve Bank. He is assisted by four Deputy Governors, each of which is responsible for certain specific operations of the Bank. Besides the Central Boards, there are Local Boards for four regional areas of the country with their headquarters at Bombay, Calcutta, Madras and New Delhi. Each Local Board consists of five members and all of them are appointed by the Central Government. They are appointed for a period of four years only. The functions of the Local Boards are mainly advisory in nature. They may advise the Central Board on such matters as are referred to them generally or specifically. They also perform such duties as may be delegated to them by the Central Board of Directors from time to time.

Departments of the Reserve Bank

The Reserve Bank of India performs it functions through the following departments :

1. Issue Department—The Issue Department is concerned with the issue of bank notes and their management and the carrying on of business incidental thereto. There are seven offices and branches of the Issue Department at Bangalore, Bombay, Calcutta, Kanpur, Madras, Nagpur and Delhi. Each branch is divided into (*i*) the Treasurer's Department, which is sub-divided into the Issue and Exchange Branches, and (*ii*) the Central Department, which is sub-divided into the Registration Branch, the Cancelled Note Verification Branch, the Cancelled Note Vaultt Branch, the Claims Branch, the Account Branch, the Records Brach, and the Internal Audit and Research Branch.

2. Banking Department—The Banking Department is concerned with the ordinary central banking functions. This department has its offices at Bangalore, Bombay, Kanpur, Madras, New Delhi and Nagpur. The banking department of each office is under the charge of a manager and is divided into the Deposit Accounts, the Securties Account, the Public Account and the Public Debts Account.

3. Exchange Control Department—This department was created during the Second World War. The functions of this department are to control foreign exchange transactions and to maintain a stable rate of exchange. Exchange control continued to be an important function during the postwar period. It is now governed by the Foreign Exchange Regulation Act of 1947, and the meassures announced by the Government from time to time under the Act. But all the exchange transactions are routed through the Exchange Control department.

4. Department of Banking Operation and Development—The Department of Banking Operations and Development was created in 1950 to extend banking facilities to semi-urban areas and to help in the solution of the problems of rural finance. One of the principal duties of the department has been to implement the recommendations of the *Purshottam Das Committee* on rural banking. The Central Board of the Reserve Bank approved the Committee's proporals for an extension of remittance facilities at reduced rates, for the removal of impediments in the way of expansion of commercial banks in rural areas, for the improvement of the machinery of rural finance both as regards the mobilisation of rural savings and the extension of rural credit, and for the development of warehousing.

The primary function of the Department of Banking Operations is the supervision of the banking system. Under the Banking Regulation Act and the Reserve Bank of India Act, the

Reserve Bank has been vested with wide powers of supervision and control over all the banks in the country. The former Act has made bank inspections a regular feature of its activities by instituting systematic periodical inspections of all types of banks. It is significant to point out that this department also performs the functions relating to the nationalised banks entrusted to the Reserve Bank by the Banking Companies (Acquisition and Transfer of Undertakings) Act, 1970.

5. **Industrial Finance Department**—Provision of industrial finance as well as the inspection and supervision of State Financial Corporations formed a part of the work of the Department of Banking Operations and Development. But in view of the increase in the volume of work, a new department called the 'Industrial Finance Department' was created in September, 1957. This department has been entrusted with all matters pertaining to industrial finance including the activities of State Financial Corporations.

6. **Research and Statistics Department**—This department studies the economic, financial and banking conditions in India and abroad. It acts an agency for the collection and dissemination of financial information and statistics. It publishes monthly statistical tables relating to banks in India and an annual report on currency and finance. It also submits to the Government an annual report on the Trends and the Progress of Banking in India.

The work of the Department of Research and Statistics has been divided into two departments, *viz* ; (*a*) Economic Department; and (*b*) Department of Statistics.

(*a*) *Economic Department*—This department consists of nine divisions, each under a Director of Research. Each division conducts research in the area allotted to it. The division s are :

(*i*) The Banking Division;

(*ii*) The Monetary Economic Division;

(*iii*) The Fiscal Analysis Division;

(*iv*) The Division of International Finance;

(*v*) The Division of Trade;

(*vi*) The Division of Rural Economics;

(*vii*) The Division of Rural Surveys;

(*viii*) The Division of Planning; and

(*ix*) The Division of Publications and Press Relations.

(*b*) *Department of Statistics*—The main function of this department is the collection and compilation of statistical data relating to the banking and fiscal sector of the economy. It is responsible for preparing for the Reserve Bank's publication the part containing current statistical information. It is also responsible for preparing index number series on (*i*) prices and yields of giltedged and industrial securities, and (*ii*) industrial profits and profitability.

(7) Legal Department—The main function of the Legal Department is advisory in nature. It tenders legal advice on the various matters referred to it by the other departments of the Bank. These references involve mainly an interpretation of the provisions of the Reserve Bank of India Act, the Banking Regulation Act, the Foreign Exchange Regulation Act, the Public Debt Act, the Industrial Disputes Act and various other statutes.

8. Department of Financial Companies—The Department of Non-Banking Companies was set up at Calcutta in March, 1966 to administer and control the deposits of non banking financial companies and to regulate their deposits and also their business. The main function of the department is to regulate the acceptance of deposits by non-banking companies. This department was renamed as Department of Financial Companies in June, 1983.

9. Department of Accounts and Expenditures—The department is mainly responsible for the maintenance and supervision of the Reserve Bank's accounts in the Issue and Banking Department and also the compilation of the weekly and annual accounts of these departments.

10. Department of Administration and Personnel—This department deals with general administration, training of staff and employer employee relations. It has many sections like the Requirement Section, the Training Section and the Organisation and Methods Division.

11. Inspection Department—This department carries out periodic internal inspections of the different offices and departments of the Reserve Bank and submits reports to the Department of Accounts and Expenditures on the general conduct of their work.

12. Secretary's Department—This department is broadly concerned with diverse matters affecting the policy of the Reserve Bank. It generally deals with policy matters relating to open market operations, floatation of Government loans and Treasury Bills and the Reserve Bank's dealings with international financial institutions.

Functions

The Reserve Bank of India, as the Central Bank of India perform the following functions:

(1) Regulation of Currency– The Reserve Bank of India enjoys the monopoly of note issue in the country. The bank has established a separate department in its organisation for the work of note-issue named as issuing department. The department has been entrusted with the responsibility of the issue of currency into circulation and its withdrawal from circulation.

In this matter it occupies a strategic role in controlling the economy of the country. All currency notes except the one rupee notes (which is issued by the Ministry of Finance) and the coins are issued by the Reserve Bank of India.

The Reserve Bank of India Act 1934 provided for the Proportional Reserve System for the issue of notes. The Act has been revised several times and under the latest revised arrangement the Reserve Bank of India is required to keep in reserve against the note issue Rs. 200 crores worth of gold coin, god bullion and foreign securities of which the value of gold coin and gold bullion must not be less then Rs. 115 crore.

(2) Control of Credit—Control of credit is the main functions of the Reserve Bank of India. The object of control is to secure price stability.

The Reserve Bank of India keeps a control over the credit through the operation of the following weapons:

(i) The Bank Rate Policy

(ii) The Open Market Operations

(iii) Variable Reserve Requirements

(iv) Rationing of Credit.

(v) Moral Suasion

(vi) Direct Action.

All these methods with which the central banks are generally armoured for the control of credit are discussed at length separately in this chapter.

As controller of credit and the apex institution in the banking system of the country, Reserve Bank of India exercise the power of supervision as well as control over other banks. The powers of supervision and control of the Reserve Bank have greatly increased since the passing of the Banking Companies Act 1949 and its subsequent amendments. Now the

Reserve Bank of India possesses wide power over the lending policies of the banks. The Reserve Bank of India has been vested with the power to influence the volume of credit created by banks in India.

(3) Banker's Bank– The Reserve Bank of India also acts as the banker to the banks. All the banks work under the control of Reserve Bank. As a banker's Bank, the Reserve Bank performs all those functions in the country which an ordinary bank performs for clients. The Reserve Bank of India being the banker of commercial banks accepts deposits from, advance loans to them, act as a clearing house for them and comes to their rescue whenever they realise any difficulty as the lender of last resort. It also advises them whenever required. It also keeps their balance and remits funds on their behalf. On the other hand the member banks are required to submit a report to the Reserve Bank about their business and activities from time to time. They have to submit full balance sheets to the Reserve Bank. The Reserve Bank formulates rules for these banks.

(4) Banker to the Government– The Reserve Bank of India also acts as the banker to the Central Government and all the State Governments. The Reserve Bank of India undertake the functions involve receipts and payments of money on behalf of the government. As banker to the central and state government, the Reserve Bank of India performs the ffunctions described on next page;

(a) *Manage Public Debts-* The bank Manages public debts and help in flotation of new loans etc.

(b) *Mantain Currency Chests-* In order to provide currency for the transactions of the government, the bank maintains currency chests at prescribed places.

(c) *Short-term Credit–* The Reserve Bank of India provides short-term credit to the government against securities.

(d) *Adviser to the Government–* It also acts as the adviser to the Government on banking and financial matter.

(5) Custodian of Foreign Exchange Reserves– As custodian of foreign exchange, the Reserve Bank of India maintains the external value of the rupee, manages exchange control and acts as the agent of the government in respect of India's membership of the I.M.F.

Promotional Functions

In addition to the traditional functions which are performed by the central bank, the Reserve Bank of India has been entrusted with the responsibilities of some promotional functions as mentioned below :

(1) Provision of Agriculture Credit– The bank played a predominant rule in the field of agriculture credit. In order to fulfil this responsibility, the bank set-up a separate Agricultural Credit Department. The department is entrusted with the business of financing of agriculture and to study the problem of rural credit. The bank also encouraged development of co-operative credit movement in the country. The other developments in the field initiated by or on the advice of the Reserve Bank of India mainly include the following:

(a) Nationalisation of Commercial Banks– With a view to promote institutional rural credit and mobilisation of rural resources, 20 major commercial banks were nationalised in two phase- July 1969 and April 1980.

(b) Regional Rural Bank– Regional Rural Banks were established on October 1975 to provide credit facilities to rural marginal farmers, agricultural labourers, rural artisans and other small entrepreneurs.

(c) Establishment of NABARD– One of the significant development in the field of promotion of agriculture credit by the Reserve Bank of India is the establishment of National Bank for Agricultural and Rural Development (NABARD).

(2) Industrial Finance– The Reserve Bank of India has no direct responsibility to finance but has helped a lot in setting up special financial institutions for financing industries. The Reserve Bank of India has undertaken this function for the speedy industrial development.

(3) Training Facilities in Banking– The Reserve Bank of India set-up first Banker's Training college in Bombay in 1954 for the training of the supervisory staffs of commercial banks. The bank set-up another training college in 1968 in Madras for the benefit of its own junior supervisory staff.

CREDIT CONTROL

As the responsibility of credit control assigned to the central bank of other country the Reserve Bank of India has also been entrusted with the responsibility of controlling the credit in the country. The methods which are generally followed by the Reserve Bank of India are as follows :

(1) The Policy of Bank Rate–By bank rate, we mean the percent at which the Central Bank of a country rediscount the bills of commercial bank in to order to make them available some liquid money. The Bank Rate has been defined in the Reserve Bank of India Act, *as the standard rate which it (the Bank) is prepared to buy or rediscount bills of exchange or other commercial papers eligible for purchase under this Act.* In other words, it is the rate at which the reserve Bank extends advances to the commercial banks. By using the instrument of Bank rate, the RBI influences the availability of credit and deposit mobilisations. As observed by *Pigou*, "it directly affects the quantity of credit and price level".

According to bank rate policy changes in the bank rate change the volume of credit in the country and tereby influence prices and costs. A high Bank Rate is intended to raise the cost of Reserve Bank accommodations to banks, which in turn raises their own lending rates to the borrowers. At high rate of interest, business borrowing declines and, thus, bank credit contracts.

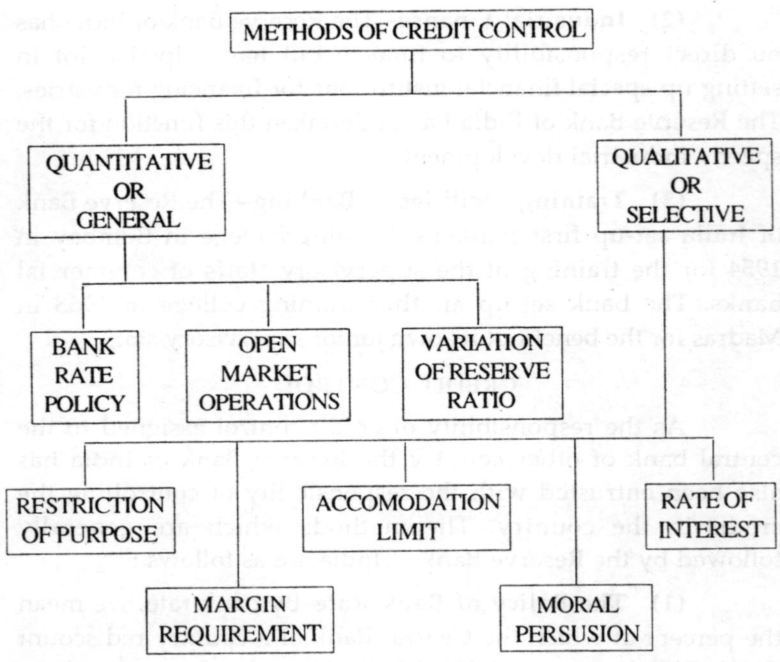

The Reserve Bank of India has not adequately used this instrument to control credit in the country. The first increase in the Bank rate took place in November 1951 when it was raised from 3 per cent to 3.5 per cent. The Reserve Bank has adopted the dear money policy, under which the Bank Rate has been adjusted upwards, except in the year 1968 when it was lowered from 6 per cent to 5 per cent. The current Bank Rate is 10.0 per cent with effect from June 26, 1997.

The Reserve Bank of India provides accommodation to commercial banks by way of rediscounting of eligible bills or as advance against approved securities. Banks cannot claim this facility as a matter of right. The availability of its accommodation facility is restricted by prescribing quotas and a system of deferential interest. In 1973 the Reserve bank also fixed the limits for the maximum amount that a bank can borrow from the Reserve Bank.

(2) Open Market Operations– Open market operations, as defined by the Reserve Bank of India Act, refer *"Broadly to the purchase and sales by the central bank of a variety of assets such as foreign exchange, gold, Government securities and even company shares."* In practice, however, they are confined to the purchase and sale of Government securities.

The Reserve Bank of India Act, 1934 confers upon the Reserve Bank the right to purchase or sell the Government securities. Originally, as provided in the RBI Act, there was a ceiling on the Reserve Bank's holdings of Government securities related to its capital reserves and deposit liabilities. However, since 1951, such restrictions have been withdrawn. Now, the Reserve Bank does not purchase these securities, instead the Bank provides temporary accommodation against collateral of Government securities.

The main objective of the open market operations is to assist the Government in their borrowing operations and to maintain orderly conditions in the *gilt-edged* market. Open market operations have also used to provide the seasonal finance to banks.

(3) Variable Reserve Requirements– Under Sections 42(1) of the Reserve Bank of India Act 1934, the scheduled banks are under an obligation to maintain with the Reserve Bank statutory cash reserves of 5 per cent of their demand liabilities and 2 per cent of their time liabilities. The Amendment Act of 1956 empowered the Bank to vary the minimum cash reserve between 5 and 20 per cent in respect of the demand liabilities and between 2 and 8 per cent in respect of time liabilities. In 1962, the reserve requirements were fixed at 15 per cent of the total demand and time liabilities of each bank.

The Reserve Bank, of late, has been frequently changing this reserve requirement. It was raised from 3 per cent to 5 per cent in June 1973 and to 7 per cent in Sept. 1973. Later, it was reduced to 4 per cent of the total deposit liabilities. It was again raised to 6 per cent in November 1976, and to 11.0 per cent w.e.f. the fortnight beginning July 30, 1988. In addition to this, banks had also to maintain incremental cash reserve ratio as 10.0 per cent their total liabilities after November 11, 1983. FCNR deposit liabilities are exempted from the 10% incremental CRR.

The average CRR reduced from 12.0 per cent to 11.5 per cent effective from fortnight of October 26, 1996 and further to 10.0 per cent w.e.f. Jan. 18, 1997. From the same fortnight CRR on FCNR (B) and NRNR deposits removed. CRR on outstanding NRE deposits was reduced to 10 per cent from 14 per cent with effect from the fortnight beginning January 6, 1996.

Under Section 24 of the Banking Regulation Act, 1949, all banks are required to maintain with themselves liquid assets of an amount equal to not less than 25 per cent of their demand and time liabilities in India. Higher liquidity ratio compels the banks to maintain a large portion of their resources in liquid assets. Another effect of the higher liquidity ratio is that the capacity of the banks to grant credit is reduced by the extent the liquidity is raised by the Reserve Bank. The Reserve Bank has raised the liquidity ratio a number of times in the recent past.

It has been raised to 35.5 per cent effective July 28, 1984 and to 36 per cent effective September 1, 1984. In recognition of the need to provide adequate resources for vital public sector investments in the Seventh Plan, the SLR was raised from 35 per cent with effect from July 6, 1985 and to 38.5 with effect from September 22, 1990. Following the recommendations of the Narasimham Committee, SLR for any increase in net DTL above the April 3, 1992 level was lowered at 30 per cent, however, the SLR on the outstanding net DTL as on April 3, 1992 would remain unchanged at 38.5 per cent.

With effect from October 16, 1993, the incremental SLR for the increase in domestic net demand and time liabilities (NDTL) of scheduled commercial banks (excluding RRBs) over the Sept. 17, 1993 level was brought down from 30 per cent to 25 per cent. The base on incremental NDTL for the purpose of maintaining SLR was further brought forward to September 30, 1994.

The SLR on the incremental deposits has now been brought down to 25 per cent.

This is being done with a view to force the banks to maintain a higher liquidity so as to reduce their capacity to grant loan and advances to business and industry and also to divert bank furnds for loans and advances to investment in approved securities.

(4) Selective Credit Control– The Selective credit controls are designed specially to curb excess flow of credit in selected areas without affecting other types of credit. The Reserve Bank of India has been given the power of instituting selective credit controls under the Banking Regulation Act, 1949. The Reserve Bank's directives may relate to any or all of the following :

(*a*) the *purpose* for which advances may or may not be made,

(*b*) the *margins* to be maintained in respect of secured advances,

(*c*) the *maximum amount* of advances to any company, firm, individual, etc.,

(*d*) the *maximum amount up to which guarantees* may be given by the banking company on behalf of any one company, firm, etc.,

(*e*) the *rate of interest* and other terms and conditions on which advances may be made by a commercial bank, and (*f*) prohibiting banks against entering into any particular transaction.

The Reserve Bank of India has been experimenting upon the selective credit controls since 1956 in respect of certain commodities which have been sensitive or in short supply. At present, selective credit controls are used against the following commodities
(*i*) foodgrains, (*ii*) cotton and kapas, (*iii*) oilseeds, (*iv*) vanaspatil, (*v*) sugar-khandsari, gur, and (*vi*) cotton textiles including yarn.

Certain policy changes have been made in the selective credit controls. These policy changes are in operation with effect from April 8, 1985 :

(*i*) *Levels of Credit.* For commodities where there is a stipulation on the level of credit based on certain base years, the new base period will uniformly be the three-year period-1980-81, 1981-82 and 1982-83. The bringing forward of the base would greatly reduce the burden on banks or monitoring credit utilisation.

(*ii*) *Minimum Margins.* The multiplicity of minimum margins prescribed for each broad commodity based on levels or stocks and geographical areas has been reduced in case of foodgrains, pulses, vegetable oils and vanaspati, cotton and kapas and sugar, gur and khandsari to provide some relief to the concerned sector.

(*iii*) *Exemption for Roller Flour Mills.* It was decided to totally exempt advances against wheat to roller flour mills from all the provisions of selective credit controls.

(*iv*) *Increase in Overall Exemption Limits for Advances.* Advances up to an aggregate limit of Rs. 5,000 per borrower against the stocks of commodities covered by selective credit controls has been raised to Rs. 25,000 per borrower.

Further, advances up to an aggregate limit of Rs. 50,000 per borrower will be exempted from selective credit controls against the present limit of Rs. 25,000 provided a borrower deals with only on bank.

The Reserve Bank of India has imposed fresh curbs on bank advances against oilseeds, vegetable oils, paddy, rice and cotton w.e.f. Oct. 1994 to discourage hoarding.

In the busy season credit policy for 1994-95, the Reserve Bank announced that the bank advances against paddy/rice to all borrowers will be exempted from all provisions of the selective controls, whereas the minimum margin on bank advances against cooton/kapas will be reduced across-the-board by 15 points.

In recent years, the policy of selective control has assumed greater importance. The unique feature of the policy is its flexibility. It is possible under the policy to withdrawn or re-impose restrictions on granting of credit according to circumstances. But on the whole, the policy of selective control is not successful in keeping down the prices of commodities over which it was applied.

(5) Moral Suasion— Sometime compulsion on member bank regarding credit control policy does not bring quick results. With a view to obtain results the Reserve Bank of India has started to exert moral influence over the lending policies of the members bank. But the success of moral suasion depend on willing and active co-operation of the commercial banks. The method of directing the commercial bank on the ground of morality to accept certain policies according to the time. The method is gaining importance under which it is expected that commercial bank will act according to the suggestions of the Reserve Bank. The Reserve Bank addresses the periodical letters to banks urging them to exercise control over credit in general, or advance against particular commodities or unsecured advances.

(6) Credit Rationing– The Reserve Bank of India also exercise control over credit through check the flow of credit flowing to unimportant channels. The shortage of capital and influx of credit to consumer purpose has been the cause of the formulating the policy of credit-rationing.

Under the system the bank has been made a policy to provide prepare to the long requirements of cottage and export-oriented industries. However at the same time interest of the import substitution is also to be safeguarded.

Evaluation of the Working

The Reserve Bank of India was established in 1935. Since the establishment of bank and during its working of more than 6 decades, efforts have been made by the bank to touch lives of peoples and the nation. No doubt bank achieved too much for what it established, but there are areas in which the bank could not achieved much headway. Below we discussed several achievement alongwith few failures of the Reserve Bank of India :

Achievements

1. *Flexible Monetary Policy* : The Reserve Bank of India since its inception adopted appropriate monetary policy most suitaed to the requirements of indian trade, commerce and agriculture. The monetary policy has been amended from time to time keeping in to the consideration to the need of various sector of economy.

2. *Success in Note-Issue :* Note-issue is one of the major functions of the Reserve Bank of India which has been performed by the Bank in most satisfactory manner.

3. *As Government Banker* : There has been continuous increase in the income of the Indian Government since the inception of the Bank. The Reserve Bank of India has always been successful in the role of Government banker. It has earned creditable reputation in the field of management of public debts and consolidation of Government reserves.

4. *As the Adviser of the Government* : The Reserve Bank of India has performed well in the capacity as the main adviser of the Government in monetary matters. The R.B.I. has always performed this work properly and has helped the Government to arrive at appropriate decision.

5. *Maintaining Stable Interest Rate* : The Reserve Bank of India has been successful in maintaining the stable rate of interest in the country. It has been achieved mainly by contracting and expanding the volume of credit according to the requirement of the Indian economy.

6. *Arrangement of Public debts* : The Reserve Bank of India has been successful as the government's bankers in arrangement of public debt. The Bank has successfully able to arrange considerable amount of public debts at low rate of interest.

The R.B.I. has protected the interest of government from bringing out of financial difficulties.

7. *Regulatory Control on the Indian Banking* : The Reserve Bank of India has contributed considerably in regulating the Indian banking companies. Under the Banking Regulation Act, the Reserve Bank of India has been vested with very wide powers and it has used them in right direction.

8. *Maintenance of Stable Exchange Rates* : Since twice has been the independence, the devaluation of Indian rupee but the fall in the exchange rate is much less than it was feared. The credit for this goes to the Reserve Bank. Through its relations with the International Monetary Fund, the Reserve Bank has been able to keep the external value of the Indian rupee stable to a sizeable extent.

9. *Contribution in the Field of Agricultural Finance* : The Reserve Bank of India has played a great role in the development of Indian agriculture. It has given sufficient financial assistance ,directly or indirectly, for agricultural

purposes and the Indian cultivators have been greately benifitted by obtaining financial assistance from the Reserve Bank of India.

10. Contribution to Industrial Finance : The Reserve Bank of India provided loans for the rapid development of Indian industries. In this way it has been responsible for the industrial development of the country. The bank has successfully discharged this responsibility.

Moreover the R.B.I. has rendered important financial and organisational assistance in the establishment of the Industrial Finance Corporation, State Finance Corporations and Industrial Development Bank of India. Thus it has removed a major lacuna in the Indian money market.

11. Research and Investigation : The Research and Investigation Department of the Reserve Bank has been successful in contributing to the research and investigation work in various directions includes mainly in the field of bank rate, money market etc.

12. Collection and Publication of Data : The Reserve Bank of India has been successfully played its role in collecting and publishing economic data. In spite of several difficulties in this field, the Bank has successfully discharge this responsibility.

13. Financing of Five-Year Plans : The Reserve Bank of India has helped in financing the Five-Year Plans. In doing so it has been helpful in development of activities related to agriculture and rural development. It is due to the successful working of the Reserve Bank of India that the Government has been able to resort to deficit financing without much troubles.

14. Development of Bill Market : The Reserve Bank of India, in the year 1952 made sincere efforts for the development of the bill market scheme in India. The contribution of Reserve Bank in this direction is really praiseworthy despite the fact there is still no true Bill Market in India.

15. *Facility to the Life Insurance Corporation* : The Reserve Bank has enabled to the smooth and proper working of the Life Insurance Corporation of India. The success of the Life Insurance corporation still to a significant extent depends upon R.B.I.

16. *Financial Assistance to the Banks* : The Reserve Bank to avert financial crises has advanced hug loans to the Indian Bank thereby saving them from failure.

17. *Clearing Arrangements* : It has simplified facilitated for the inter-bank transactions in the country. It has helped in popularise the use of cheques on large scale.

Failure of the Reserve Bank

Despite successes in many fields, the Reserve Bank has not been able to attain the expected success in regard to certain functions :

1. *No link with indigenous banking* : In India the indigenous banks even today play a prominent role. It was expected the Reserve Bank of India will play positive role in removing them from the scene. Contrary to expectation, the Reserve Bank has not been successful in establishing its contact with these indigenous bankers. It has failed miserably in exercising any control over the indigenous bankers, and still a large number of unauthorised banking sector operate outside the gambit of the Reserve Bank of India.

2. *Partial Solution of the Indian banking problem* : The Reserve Bank has been successful only in solving the problems of Indian Banking only upto limited extent. There are still many problems which requires immediate redressal. But the Reserve Bank of India never paid attention to these problems. The Bank has not yet been able to co-ordinate and integrate the banking system of the country in the most desirable way.

3. *Un-Controlled Inflation* : The internal value of the Indian rupee is continuously declining and the Reserve Bank failed in controlling the inflation. The prices of the commodities are touching and the Reserve Bank has been helpless in arresting price rise.

4. *Failed to develop a proper Bill Market* : The Reserve Bank has started a bill market scheme as early as in 1962 but even today there could not be developed a well equipped bill market in the country. There is great shortage of good and discountable bills of exchange in the country.

5. *Failure in the field of Agriculture Finance* : The Reserve Bank of India has contributed significantly in this field yet, there is much to be done. The problem of agricultural finance is still grave and in an agricultural country like India, the Reserve Bank can not disown its responsibility in providing sufficient finance to the agriculture.

6. *No uniformity in the Rates of Interest* : The rates of interest vary from time to time and place to place in the Indian Money Market. Some bankers provide loans on very high rate of interest, while other provides the loan at a low rate of interest. Big industrialists are able to secure loans at low rate of interest, while the poor people are given loans on much higher rates of interest.

❑

14

State Bank of India

Soon after independence a strong need was felt for carrying commercial banking to the rural areas. Imperial Bank of India which was the major commercial bank in the country was not in favour of this idea. Many people demanded its nationalisation to check concentration of economic power and to grant loans to the poor sections of the society who needed financial assistance the most.

All-India Rural Survey Committee recommended in 1954 for the "creation of one strong integrated State sponsored State partnered, commercial banking institution with an effective machinery of branch spread over the whole country, which, by further expansion (including further but minor amalgamation, where necessary) can be put in a position to take over cash work from non-banking treasuries and sub-treasuries, provide vastly extended remittance facilities for co-operative and other banks, and, generally, in their loan operations, in so far as they have a bearing on rural credit, follow a policy which, while not deviating from cannons of sound business, will be in effective consonance with national policies as expressed through the Central Government and the Reserver Bank...;" Thus one of the basic objectives of establishing such a bank was not only creating the machinery needed for financing the developmental activities but also for ensuring that the finance made available goes into the desired directions.

Imperial Bank of India was the biggest Commercial Bank in India during the period from 1921 to 1955. The bank having the largest amount of capital. The bank came into being in 1921 by virtue of amalgamation of the three Presidency Banks of Madras, Bombay and Calcutta. The functions of the banks were confined to discharge of general banking functions like (i) accepting deposits and (ii) granting loans and advances by keeping safe deposits. In addition to these general banking function, the bank was also entrusted with the responsibility of discharging function of central bank of the country.

In pursuance with the objective express by Central Government & Reserve Bank of India, the Imperial Bank of India was brought of this ownership from July 1, 1955 and was converted into the State Bank of India with the main objective of facilitating the extension of banking in the rural and semi-urban areas.

Nationalisation of Imperial Bank

The State Bank was established by the statutory amalgamation of the Imperial Bank. The State Bank of India Act was passed on May, 1955 and the State Bank of India came into existence on July 1, 1955. The reasons which promted the Governmnt to nationalise the Imperial Bank of India and create State Bank of India may be stated as follows:

(i) Diversion of profits to Government- The Imperial Bank earned huge profits partly because of enormous public confidence it commanded on account of its intimate association with the Government and partly because of the huge Government funds kept with it. Nationalisation was necessary to diver the profits of the bank arising from the Government funds into Government hands.

(ii) Discrimination in favour of foreigners.-The Imperial Bank was criticised on the ground that it was imperial in name, character and behaviour. The Bank was controlled mostly by foreigners and the important positions were held by the Britishers. The Bank discriminated between the Indian firms and the foreign firms and gave liberal facilities to the foreign firms. So it was argued that the foreigners should not be allowed to have control over the biggest commercial bank in the country.

(iii) Mobilisation of rural savings- After the Second World War, there was a significant redistribution of income in four of rural areas on account of the rise in the prices of agricultural products. It was realised that there was an urgent need to tap the rural savings for the rapid economic development of the country. This could be possible by nationalising the Imperial Bank so as to open branches in rural areas.

(iv) Provision of financial help to agriculture - The Rural Credit Survey Committee found that indigenous bankers and moneylenders supplied more than 90% of the credit required by farmers and other rural household and they charged very high rates of interest. Co-operative banks met only 3% of the requirements of the farmers. They were in need of urgent help from the Reserve Bank which could be channelised through the State Bank of India.

(v) Provision of financial help to small industries - Small industries were given greater importance in the Five Year Plans because they can generate more employment. But they were suffering from lack of necessary finance. Commercial banks were not granting loans to small industries since loans to small producers were considered risky. So the establishment of the State Bank was necessary to provide credit to small industrial units.

(vi) Effective control - The Imperial Bank of India occupied a unique position in the Indian money market. It acted as an unofficial leader on account of its large resources and prestige. Nationalisation was advocated on the ground that the monetary policy of the Reserve Bank would become really effective.

On account of the above reasons, the Imperial Bank of India was nationalised in 1955 and the State Bank of India was established by the statutory amalgamation of the Imperial Bank of India and the ten other state associated banks, viz, the Bank of Saurashtra, the Bank of Patiala, the Bank of Bikaner, the Bank of Jaipur, the Bank of Rajasthan, the Bank of Indore, the Bank of Mysore, the Hyderabad State Bank, the Bank of Baroda and the Travancore Bank. This was done in line with the opinion expressed by the Rural Banking Enquiry Committee that "if the banks could be integrated into one institution, and if that one institution could be aligned to national policies, then indeed that would be an extremely important and extremely desirable line of development." By 1959, eight banks in the erstwhile princely state were also brought under the control and full or near-full ownership of the State Bank of India. Ultimately creating seven bank as follows:

(i) State Bank of Bikaner & Jaipur.

(ii) State Bank of Hyderabad.

(iii) State Bank of Mysore.

(iv) State Bank of Patiala.

(v) State Bank of Saurashtra.

(vi) State Bank of Travancore.

(vii) State Bank of Indore.

Functions

Section 3 of the State Bank of India Act defines the functions of the State Bank. In addition to the functions of a commercial bank, the bank also act as an agent of the Reserve Bank of India and thus performs the following functions.

(1) Borrows Money - The Bank borrows money from the public by accepting deposits by way of current account deposits , fixed deposits and savings deposits.

(2) Lending - The second important function of the State Bank is lending. It lends money to merchants and manufacturers for short periods. It also lends to farmers and co-operative institutions. It lends mostly on the security of easily realisable commodities like rice, wheat , cotton, oil-seeds cloth, gold and government securities. The bank can lend against agricultural bills upto a maximum period of fifteen months and in case of other bills upto a maximum period of six months.

(3) Banker's Bank -- The State Bank of India acts as the banker's bank. In discharging this responsibility, the bank provides loans to commercial bank when required and also rediscount their bill. The State Bank of India also act as the clearing house of the commercial bank.

(4) Government's Bank – The State Bank of India also acts as the agent of the Reserve Bank of India. As an agent, the State Bank of India maintains the treasuries of the State Government. The Bank also manage the debts floated by State Governments.

(5) Remittance – The State Bank of India facilitate remittance of money from one place to another. It also helps in transfer of the funds of State and Central Government.

(6) Functions as Central Bank – The place where the Reserve Bank of India has not of its own branch. The State Bank of India performs the functions of a Central Bank.

(7) Subsidiary Functions - The State bank peroforms various subsidiary services also. It collects cheques, drafts, bill of exchange, dividends interest, salaries and pensions on behalf of its customers. It purchases and sells securities on behalf of its customer. It receives valuables and documents for safe custody and maintains safe deposit vaults.

Organisation and Management

The State Bank of India has an authorised capital of Rs. 20 crores divided into 20 lakh shares of Rs. 100 each and an issued and paid up share capital of Rs. 51.625 crores. The Reseve Bank of India is required to hold not less than 55% of the issued capital of the State Bank.

The State Bank of India took over the assets and liabilities of the Impercial Bank by paying compensation at Rs. 1.765.62 for each fully paid share of Rs. 500 and Rs. 431.77 for every partly paid share. Every shareholder was to receive each upto Rs. 10,000 and beyond that, the compensation was payable in the form of $3^1/_2$% government bonds. The shareholders were allowed the option to take State Bank shares for the compensation due to them. The shares of Rs. 100 were issued at Rs. 350 each.

The State Bank has its Central Office in Bombay. It has seven local head offices in Calcutta, Bombay, Madras, Delhi, Kanpur, Ahmedabad and Hyderabad. The management of the Bank is entrusted to the Central Board of Directors, which consists of:

1. A chairman and a vice-chairman to be appointed by the Central Government in consultation with the Reserve Bank of India.

2. Not more than two managing directors appointed by the Central Board with the approval of the Central Government;

3. Six directors to be elected in the prescribed manner by the shareholders other than the Reserve Bank;

4. Eight directors to be nominated by the Central Government in consultation with the Reserve Bank of India to represent territorial and economic interest in such a manner that not less than two of them have special knowledge of the working of cooperative institutions and of rural economy and the others have experience in commerce, industry, banking or finance;

5. One director to be nominated by the Central Government;

6. One director to be nominated by the Reserve Bank of India; and

7. Two directors to be appointed to represent the officers and staff of the Bank.

To keep the management free from politics, the Act stipulates that no member of Parliament or State legislatures shall be appointed as a director of the State Bank. The chairman and vice-chairman and the managing director shall hold officer for such terms not exceeding five years as the Central Government may fix when appointing them and shall be eligible for re-appointment. The directors elected by the shareholders and nominated by the Central Government will hold office for four years and are eligible for reelection or re-nominatiion. The other nominated directors shall hold office during the pleasure of the authority appointing them. There Hyderabad, kanpur, Madras and New Delhi to look after the management of the Bank in their respective areas. Each local board consists of the members of the Central Board in its area and directors, not exceeding four, elected by shareholders whose names appear in the branch register.

Role of State Bank of India

The State Bank of India is the biggest commercial bank in whole of Asia. It has a unique place in the Indian money market as it commands more than one-third of India's banking resources. It commands enormous public confidence because people feel that their money is safe if it is deposited in the State Bank. The State Bank of India has seven subsidiary banks: the State Bank of Mysore, the State Bank Patiala, the State Bank of Bikaner and Jaipur, the State Bank of Hyderabad, the State Bank of Travancore, the State Bank of Saurashtra and the State Bank of Indore.

The State Bank of India and its subsidiaries are known as 'State Bank Group'. The group has more than 15,000 branches throughout the country. More than three fourths of the branches are in semi-urban and rural areas. With the help of a big network of branches, it has been successful in mobilising the rural savings. The role of State Bank in the Indian economy is discussed below:

(1) Agricultura Finance - The State Bank of India has been granting loans directly and indirectly to farmers on a large scale. The objective of the Bank is to increase agricultural credit and not merely to substitute any existing institutional credit channel. The factors governing the eligibility of proposals for agricultural advances are primarly the progressiveness of the farmers and the economic viability of their schemes.

The State Bank introduced the Small Farmers Scheme' and the 'Farm Graduate Scheme in 1969 . The former is designed to help small farmers or group of farmers whose project is viable or can be rendered so, if necessary credit is made available to them. Farmers desirous of financial assistance are encouraged to form themselves into groups and when loans are granted to individuals, they are secured by the guarantee of all farmers in the group. The Farm Graduate Scheme seeks to extend credit to technically qualified personnel, particularly graduates in agriculture, dairy science, veterinary science and agricultural engineering who have wirtgwguke farn development projects but are unable to undertake them due to lack of resources Loans are ordinarily granted to land-holders and, in exceptional circumstances, for the purchase of land. The State Bank provides finance to agriculture indirectly also by rendering financial assistante to co-operative institutions and subscribing to the debentures of land development banks. The State Bank group has adopted more than 27,000 villages under "The Village Adoption Scheme.'

2. **Branch Expansion-** In keeping with the national policy of rapid geographical extension of banking services, the State Bank has been giving priority to opening of branches in unbanked and rural areas. The total number of branches of the State Bank of India at the end of March 1998 stood at 8,925 of which about $^{3}/_{4}$ th were in rural and semi-urban areas. The seven subsidiaries of the State Bank had 14,918 branch offices at the end of March 1998. At present the State Bank and its associate banks constitute the largest commercial banking network of its kind in the world.

3. **Assitance to Co-operative Banks** -The State Bank grants advances to co-operative banks against government securities at concessional rate of interest. It grants short term loans to State Co-operative Banks to enable them to provide finance to the societies affiliated to them. The State Bank also provides free remittance facilities to co-operative banks thrice a week. This enables co-operative banks to send funds from centres where there is less demand to centres where there is good demand. Besides, it collects cheques and bills on behalf of the co-operative banks at concessional rates.

4. Industrial Finance - The State Bank has re-oriented its loans and advances policy to increase the quantum of its finance to industry, without at the same time, affecting its financial assistance to agriculture. The bank gives special emphasis to basic industries and export based industries. It can grant medium term loans upto a maximum period of 7 years. It is also authorised to subscribe to the shares and debentures of companies.

The activities of the Bank are also directed to help small scale industries. Small scale industrial concerns which are on the approved list of government contractors and which supply goods to the Directorate of Supplies and Disposals, can get financial assistance by discounting the bills drawn on the Directorate for the goods supplied. Small scale industrial units can get medium term loans for purchasing machines and equipments.

5. Merchant Banking. The State Bank set up a Merchant Banking Division in 1972 to cater to the promotional needs of the corporate sector to encourage its fruitful development. The division gives advice on financial matters for new projects and helps in making technical feasibility studies. It also organises financial assistance of various types. Another distinctive feature of the working of the Merchant Bank Division of the Bank is that it also helps market. The Division has launched many issues and majority of these have been over-subscribed. It is a wholly owned subsidiary of State Bank of India. Its services include obtaining Government consents, feasibility studies, loan syndication, overseas credit, capital issue management and financial and corporate counselling.

6. Foreign Trade - The State Bank undertakes foreign exchange business. It purchases and sells foreign currencies. It has twenty five offices abroad besides worldwide system of correspondent banks. The number of foreign accounts with the

Bank and the Bank's accounts with the foreign banks have been increasing steadily. The Bank has made an all-round progress in its foreign exchange business. Its Rupee Travellers' cheques are also popular abroad.

In addition to the usual types of foreign exchange business, the Bank has been financing foreign trade arising from barter deals concluded by the Government and the State Trading Corporation. The Bank has special banking arrangement with overseas banks for handling business pertaining to Special Trade Agreement and other bilateral arrangements entrusted to it by the Government of India. The Bank initiated in 1963 a pilot scheme of export promotion to provide finance in foreign currency for the important of raw materials to be repaid out of the proceeds of exports of finished products. Now the Bank also provides medium term credit to exporters who offer deferred payments term to the foreign buyers for the purchase of engineering and capital goods made in India. Besides assisting the export of traditional goods and a wide range of capital goods the Bank makes special efforts to promote the export of high value turn key projects. The Bank also renders export assistance for setting up joint ventures abroad and for construction contracts.

7. **Overseas Operations.** The State Bank has opened its branches and representative offices in many countries. The Bank's New York, Colombo, Nassan, London, Male, Dacca, and Frankfurt branches, and representative offices in Beirut, Bahrain, Manila, Frankfurt, Tehran, Toronto and Moscow are playing an important role in popularising Indian rupee and in promotion of India's exports by providing credit facilities to exporters and the required information on trade and the standing of Indian exporters to the importers of goods from India. In addition, these offices help the non-resident Indians andpersons of Indian origin to effect remitances to India.

State Bank And Rural Credit

One of the chief objectives with which the State Bank was established, is to provide integrated credit to the rural sector. Soon after its establishment, a committee was appointed to decide the role the Bank should play in the matter of rural credit. The committee recommended that the Bank should provide rural credit through financing co-operative societies engaged in marketing, processing on industrial production. It is the only bank in the country with over 500 agricultural development branches devoted exclusively to agricultural development.

The State Bank's contribution to rural credit has been discussed below :

(i) General Assistance. The Bank has liberalised remittance facilities in the rural areas. It permits free remittance facilities thrice a week to the state and central co-operative banks. The Bank also grants short term credit facilities to the state and central co-operative banks against government securities at concessional rates ($^1/_2$% less than the rates charged from other customers). The Bank renders financial assistance to the Land Development Banks to enable them to provide long term credit for land improvement and development. It subscribes to the debentures floated by the Land Development Banks. It also grants loans to the farmers on the security of the debentures of the Land Development Banks.

(ii) Financing the Co-operative Societies. The State Bank provides finance to the co-operative marketing and processing societies in areas where they are unable to get adequate financial assistance from the co-operative banks. The Bank grants loans and advances to such societies against the pledge of produce and goods. Processing units like co-operative ginning factories and sugar factories can obtain financial help from the bank by pledging their products. This arrangement enables them to obtain better prices for their products.

(iii) Development of Warehouses. The Rural Credit Survey Committee stressed the need for providing storage facilities in villages by constructing a network of warehouses. This will enable the farmers to sell their produce when the prices in the market are high. The Bank finance to the cultivators against warehouse receipts can, to some extent, eliminate the middlemen between the cultivator and the consumer. The State Bank helps the development of warehouses by opening its branches in places where the Warehousing Corporation has constructed the godowns. It lends money to cultivators at concessional rates against warehouse receipts.

In addition to the indirect finance provided to the rural sector through co-operatives, the State Bank also undertakes direct financing of agriculture. It has introduced a scheme to advance credit to progressive farmers with adequate marketable surplus for all kinds of agricultural activities except the purchase of land. It advances money for purchase of inputs like seeds, fertilisers, agricultural machinery and implements, construction of farm structures and carrying out developments of land connected with water management such as levelling, boring of tube-wells, etc. It has also launched 'Green Card' scheme for providing crop loans to the farmers. The Bank is also providing finance to allied farming activities such as fruit cultivation, poultry farming and dairy farming.

The State Bank of India has also been operating the Village Adoption Scheme under which a branch adopts a few villages for intensive and integrated development. In these adopted villages all the farmers are expected to be financed by the Bank irrespective of ownership rights, size of holdings and the nature of crops. The last important step taken by the State Bank to strengthen rural credit is the sponsoring of Regional Rural Banks. It has sponsored 16 such banks. Apart from subscribing to the shared capital, the Bank has provided the regional rural banks with credit facilities at a concessional rate of interest of 9.5% per annum and has deputed its trained personnel to man some of the senior positions in the rural banks.

Evaluatiion of Performance

The State Bank of India is the leading public sector bank. The bank has been able to posted satisfactory overall performance during all the years since inception. The main objectives in nationalising the Imperial Bank of India was the setting up of a strong state-partnered commercial banking institution with an effective machinery composed of a larger network of branches over the whole country.

The State Bank of India and its associate bank as a group accounted for 34 per cent of aggregate banking business (aggregate of deposits and advances) conducted by the public sector banks and around 27 per cent of the aggregate business of the entire banking system. The importance of the bank can be judged with the help of the following parameters.

(1) Branch Network– The bank's endevouring to maintain the momentum of branch expansion taking a longer term perspective. The bank is also giving attention to the necessity of extending banking facilities to the rural areas. Amongst the public sector (as at the end of March 1997), the State Bank of India (SBI) group (SBI and its seven associates) is the biggest unit with 13,071 offices.

(2) Lending Operation– The net domestic credit of the Bank registered a substantial growth and has achieved a market share of 22.3% in the scheduled commercial bank credit. The State Bank of India (SBI) group (SBI and its seven associates) is the biggest unit amongst the public sector banks (as at the end of March 1997) with total advance of Rs. 83, 913.6 crores.

(3) Deposit Growth– The State Bank of India has maintained the higher deposit growth higher then that of the banking system as a whole. The bank's market share worked out to 20.5 per cent in the overall scheduled commercial bank business in India. Among the public sector bank, the State Bank of India (SBI) group (SBI and its seven associates) is the biggest unit with deposits aggregating Rs. 1,24,879.8 crore as at the end of March 1997.

(4) Assistance to Small Scale Industries– The State Bank Groups has been the most single source of institutional finance to small-scale industries in the country.

(5) International Operations– The bank hold the premier position in the foreign exchange business in India with a market share of about 40% inspite of increased competition from foreign banks and newly set-up private bank.

(6) Export Credit– The another noteworthy importance the bank has shown in the field of export credit. The bank presently representing a market share of 23% in overall export credit provided by all the scheduled commercial banks.

ACHIEVEMENTS OF THE STATE BANK OF INDIA

The State Bank of India has a novel and successful experience in the State-owned commercial banking with certain central banking functions. The domestic operations of the Bank were marked by higher deposit growth, restrained credit expansion, fulfilment of the stipulation in regard to advances to the priority sectors and increased involvement in community development. The important achievements of the Bank are summarised below:

(1) Development of Banking Infrastructure– The State Bank of India has successfully extended the banking facilities with a rapid speed. The total number of branches of the State Bank of India increased from 1557 in 1968 to 8,835 by end of March 1996.

Table 1

Branch Expansion by SBI

Year	1991-92	1994-95	1995-96	At the end of March 1998
No. ofBranches	–	8,797	8,835	8,925

The associates & subsidiaries of the State Bank of India have also maintained a rapid speed in their branch expansion network. Their total number of branches have increased from 837 in 1968 to 13,071 by the end of March 1997.

(2) Deposit Mobilisation– The domestic deposits of the Bank recorded a tremendous increase. The deposits of State Bank of India expanded from Rs. 1,011.5 crores in 1968 to Rs. 103,767 crores at March end 1997. Personal Banking Segment' deposits continued to be the largest source accounting for about 52 per cent of the Bank's deposit and registered 15.1 per cent growth during 1997. The bank's market share in scheduled commercial bank deposit worked out to 20 per cent in 1997.

Table 2

Deposit Mobilisation by SBI

Year	*1991-92*	*1992-93*	*1994-95*	*1995-96*	*1996-97*
Amount in Rs. Crores	4,907	55,146	8,0302	90,145	1,03,767

(3) Lending Operations– The net domestic credit of the bank registered a substantial growth of 18 per cent to 28 per cent and reached a level of Rs. 41,214 to Rs. 51,813 from March end 1995 to March end 1996 and to Rs. 55,023 in March 1997.

Table 3

Lending Operations of SBI

Year	*1991-92*	*1992-93*	*1994-95*	*1995-96*	*1996-97*
Amount in Rs. Crores	29845	38,300	42,214	51,813	55,023

(4) Industrial Finance– Industrial finance of the Bank accounts for around 63 per cent of the Bank's gross credit. There was an overall growth of 29 per cent in 1995-96, 23 per cent in 1994-95 in the outstanding industrial credit of the Bank against a decline of 2.1 per cent in 1993-94. Credit to all industry group registered positive growth.

The Bank's efforts in rehabilitating sick industrial undertakings also yielded good results.

(5) Priority Sector Lending– There has been phenomenal expansion of Bank finance to priority sector as explained in the following description.

Table 4

Priority Sector Lending

(Rs. in Crore)

Year	*Agriculture*	*Small Scale*	*Weaker Section*
1991-92	4,780	5,042	2,580
1992-93	5,235	5,069	–
1994-95	6,018	6,779	3,216
1995-96	6,749	7,790	3,886
1996-97	7,807	8,622	3,602
1997-98	8,794	10,014	3,711

(a) Agriculture- The Bank's assistance to agriculture and allied activities rose from Rs. 4345 crores in 1990-91 to Rs. 6,749 crores in 1995-96 and Rs. 7,806 in 1996-97. In financing to agriculture particular emphasis was laid on financing high-tech projects. The performance of Bank in recovery of agricultural advance has also been satisfactory which improved from 54.1% in June 1993 to 56.6% in June 1994 and to 60% in June 1996.

(b) Small Scale Industries and Small Business– Financial assistance to small scale industries rose from 6,779 crores in 1994-95 to Rs. 7,790 crore in 1995-96 and Rs. 8,622 in 1996-97. The Bank provide assistance through its Equity Fund Scheme, Entrepreneur Scheme, Differential Rate of Interest Scheme and Scheme for Urban Micro Enterprises.

(c) Assistance to the Weaker Sections– The Bank's assistance to the weaker sections of the society comprising of person belonging to SC/ST, small and marginal farmer, landless labourers and beneficiaries covered under the IRDP and DRI scheme has increase from Rs. 3,216 crores in 1994-95 to Rs. 3,886 crores in 1995-96.

(6) Sponsored Regional Rural Banks– The Bank has sponsored 30 RRBs in 14 States covering 76 districts with a network of 2,385 branches. Deposits and advances of these RRBs stood at Rs. 1,698 crores and Rs. 782 crores respectively in 1995-96.

(7) Community Service Banking– The Bank undertakes several banking and non-baking activities to serve the community at large, thereby meeting its social responsibility. These activities include financial assistance to women, physically handicapped person and victims of national calamities etc.

(8) The bank's International Operations- The State Bank of India hold the premier position in the foreign exchange business in India with a market share of about 40% in spite of increased competition from foreign banks and newly set-up private banks. The Bank has 50 offices overseas, spread over 34 countries.

(9) Bank's Overseas Operations– The Bank's foreign offices, which mainly cater to the needs of country's foreign currency resources to the Indian corporations have improve their performance. In spite of various adverse factors constricting the Bank's operations, overall performance of the Bank's foreign offices has been satisfactory. They continued to actively engaged in servicing India's foreign trade and to provide foreign currency resources to Indian enterprises. The Bank's overseas offices earned a net profit of Rs. 143.10 crores in 1996-97 recording an increase of about 55% over 1995-96.The business level of the Bank's foreign offices during 1995 and 1997 were as shown in Table 5.

Table 5

Overseas Operations of SBI

	31st March 1995		*31st March 1997*	
	Rs. in Crores	*$ in Million*	*Rs. in Crores*	*$ in Million*
1. Deposits	4,819.82	1530.10	6,933.83	1930.89
2. Advances	7,315.76	2322.46	7,210.19	2,007.85
3. Investments	874.27	277.55	1,115.13	310.54
4. Net Profit	-	-	143.58	39.48

(10) Export Credit - For promoting the country's exports, the Bank plays a key role by providing timely and adequate assistance to the exporter community. As in the last year, India's export growth remained sluggish during 1997-98. Consequently, the Bank's export credit at Rs. 7,151 crore reflected a modest increase of 14.8% over that in the previous year. As a proportion of the Net Bank Credit it stood at 10.25%

(11) Project Export Finance - Some of the major project exporters of the country are executing contracts overseas with the assistance of the Bank. The thrust of the Indian corporates is on infrastructure projects of less developed countries funded by the multilateral agencies. During the year the Bank supported 40 projects in 21 countries with an aggregate assistance of Rs. 4,662.19 crore.

(12) Shipping Finance - The Bank has been providing financial support to major private and public sector shipping companies for acquisition of ships mainly from abroad, and extending support to shipping companies for construction/ acquisition of ships from the Indian shipyards for coastal vessels. The additional exposure during the year was Rs. 229 crore, taking the total exposure to shipping industry to Rs. 935.01 crore.

(13) Export Promotion and Finance– The Bank has made commendable efforts for export promotion by providing promotional and developmental support to exporters, apart from providing conventional credit facilities. The total credit provided by the Bank has increased from Rs. 2,485 crores at the close of March 1992 to Rs. 6,311 crores at the end of March 1995.

(14) Project Uptech- The Project Uptech group was set-up by the Bank in 1988 to catalyse entrepreneurial thought and action, using specialist task forces positioned at selected industry clusters of small and medium enterprise. The group has successfully encouraged selected clients for improving their quality products and enhancing their competitiveness. Under the scheme, cash award is to be given by the Bank to the unit receive ISO certificate on their product.

(15) Customer Focus– The customer has been focal point of all operation of the Bank. It has been the constant endeavour of the Bank to identify the changing needs and preferences of existing as well as potential customers, design products which adequately meet these needs, package them and deliver at various points of sale. The quality of service at branches is evaluated on an ongoing basis and appropriate follow-up action is taken. Survey of customer satisfaction and preferences are conducted regularly by in-house teams as well as outside agencies. Grievance Redressal Cell at the Local Head Offices of the Bank ensures that customers' complaints are properly attended to. The Bank has identified 224 branches for developing into Model Branches. Of these, 52 have already achieved standards set in RBI guidelines.

(16) Branch Computerisation- The Bank's computerisation programme surged ahead during past few years. The computerised branches are well spread over the country and some of these branches are located in smaller industrial, commercial and tourist centres as well.

(17) State Bank Group- The State Bank Group comprises State Bank of India, seven Associate Banks, one fully-owned banking subsidiary, four non-banking subsidiaries/affiliates in India and seven subsidiaries and joint ventures abroad. During the year 1997, four of the Associate Banks, namely, State Bank of Bikaner and Jaipur, State Bank of Indore, State Bank of Mysore and State Bank of Travancore, augmented their capital base through rights issues. Capital funds were further augmented through sub-ordinated debt in four of the seven Associate Banks, namely, State Bank of Bikaner and Jaipur, State Bank of Hyderabad; State Bank of Saurashtra and State Bank of Travancore.

Table-6

SBI & Associate Banks Performance

(At the end of March 1997)

Name of the Bank	*Number of Branches*	*Deposits*	*Advances*	*Total Investments*	*Net Profit*
State Bank of India*	8,836	1,03,767	55,023	45,712	1,329
Associate Banks	4,226	37,192	20,668	14,918	356
Group Total	13,062	1,40,959	75,691	60,630	1,685

* *Domestic operations only*

Operations of Foreign Offices

Globally, the Bank's objective is to become a world class bank with excellence in India-related business. Keeping this in view, its foreign offices are mainly engaged in; (a) providing investment and trade advisory services, (b) providing project export finance under the aegis of multilateral funding agencies, (c) providing correspondent banking services to Indian banks, and (d) diversifying traditional business and ensuring increased customer satisfaction through technology upgradation. The Bank's plan for overseas expansion aims at establishing its presence at centres with potential for India related business. A Representative Office of the Bank was set up in Shanghai, China in August 1997. With this, the Bank's present network covers 52 offices spread over 33 countries.

Table-7

Assets/ Liabilities of Foreign Offices(At end-March 1998)

(excluding Subsidiaries and Joint Ventures)

	Rs. Crore	US $ million
Resources		
Deposits	6,490.28	1,643.109
Other Funds	3,575.77	905.259
Borrowings	22,407.66	5,672.824
Total	**32,473.71**	**8,221.192**
Deployment		
Cash & balance with banks	220.92	55.930
Investments & Placements	21,542.38	5,453.767
Advances (Net)	10,182.00	2,577.721
Other Assets	528.41	133.774
Total	**32,473.71**	**8,221.192**

Computerization of the Bank's branches continued at a rapid pace. At the end of the year 1997-98, the Bank had fully computerized 1,211 branches, which included 1,009 urban and metropolitan branches out of 2,350 such branches of the Bank. The computerized branches accounted for 36 per cent of the Bank's deposits, 58 per cent of advances and 72 per cent of forex turnover at end- March 1998.

The new economic environment has thrown several challenges before the Bank. Considerable progress has been achieved during recent year. The State Bank of India always determined its objective to become a world class bank with achieving excellence in India. The aforesaid evaluation of Bank's performance depicts that State Bank of India has been successful in achieving this objective upto a great extent. The Bank is fully committed to a healthy banking structure in the country that can able to fullfil the need of every segment of economy.

❑

15
Recent Trends in Indian Banking

COMPOSITION OF BANKING SYSTEM IN INDIA

The system of commercial banking in India at the end of January 1998 consisted of 338 scheduled bank (including foreign banks) and 1 non-scheduled banks. Over the period from march 1990 to march 1997 the number of scheduled bank increased by 23 and non-scheduled banks declined from 4 to 1 . Of the scheduled banks, 223 are in public sector and which account for about 80 per cent of the deposits of all scheduled banks. In the public sector banking system there are also 196 Regional Rural Banks. The remaining 27 banks (New Bank of India since merged with Punjab national Bank in September 1993) are in public sector. These public sector banks transact all types of commercial banking business. The State Bank of India (SBI) group (SBI and its 7 associates) is the biggest unit amongst the public sector banks.

RECENT TRENDS

These have been an unprecented growth and diversification of banking industry since the nationalisation of major commercial bank in India. The phenomenon has been so stupendous that it has no paralleled in the annals of banking anywhere in the world. During the last three decades since 1969, tremendous change have taken place under which banks have shed their traditional functions and have been innovating, improving and coming out with innovative and variety of services to cater to the emerging needs of their curstomers. The widening and deepening of the banking network transferred the fundamental character of class banking to mass banking. These trends include the following :

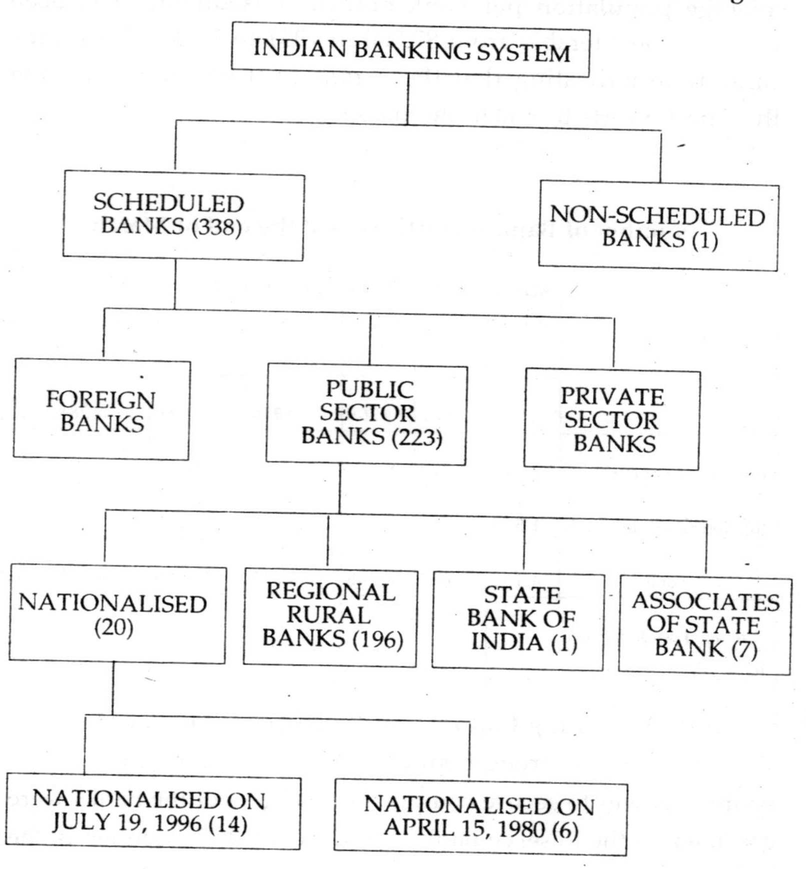

(1) Branch Expansion– A redeeming feature of he modern banking system in India is that despite the slump in number of banks, there has been a considerable rise in the number of baking branches. The number of bank branches in India, which stood at 4151 at the beginning of First Plan Period; rose progressively through the succeeding plan to reach 63,788 at the close of March 1998. Thus, there was a more than fifteen fold increase in the number of banking branches. The average population per bank branch consequently has been reduced considerably from 87,000 in 1951 to 11,000 during the same time indicating that the commercial banks are making their best efforts to reach the masses.

Table 1

Number of Banking Offices as at the end of March

	March 1957	*March 1961*	*March 1969*	*March 1970*	*Mach 1980*	*March 1988*	*As on 31 March 1998*
	1957	*1961*	*1969*	*1970*	*1980*	*1988*	*1998*
(a) Scheduled Banks	2,647	4,390	8,624	20,680	31,072	54,976	63,780
(b) Non Scheduled Bank	1,504	622	181	137	137	39	8
Total	4,151	5,012	9,005	20,817	31,209	50,015	63,788
Average Population Per Bank Office (in 000)	87	88	60	26	21	12	11

(2) Banking Liquidation, Amalgamation and Merger— With a view to strengthening the banking structure in the country power to secure compulsory mergers of the banks were confined on the Reserve Bank of India in 1960. Consequently the banking scene underwent a phenomenal change during the plan period. One of the most striking feature was the precipitate decline in number of commercial banks. There were, in all 566 commercial bank in 1951 which register a continuous fall during the planning period to reach an all time low number of 83 at the close of 1972. However the number of bank showed a rising tendency after 1972, and reached 297 at the end of March 1997 as exhibited in the following Table 2.

Table 2

Number of Banking Offices as at the end of March

	Dec. 1951	Dec. 1956	Dec. 1964	Dec. 1979	Dec. 1985	Dec. 1987	March 1997
(a) Scheduled Banks	92	89	71	131	264	275	295
out of which RRBs	–	–	–	56	183	196	196
(b) Non Scheduled Bank	474	334	210	7	4	4	2
Total	566	423	281	138	268	279	297

(3) Banks in Unbanked Areas– The opening of new branches by the Indian Banks have been so devised as to serve many hitherto unbanked centre so as to reduce regional disparities. During 27 years since 1969 (till March 1998) of the 62,881 office openedby Indian banks, out of which more than half were opened in unbanked centres. Such unbanked states are Assam, Bihar, J&K, M.P, Manipur, Meghalaya, Nagaland, Orissa, Tripura, U.P. and West Bengal account for the large part of these new offices openedas depicted in Table 3.

(4) Expansion of Banking in Rural Areas– The another most important trend of our banking system is the thrust of banking expansion in recent years has been mostly into rural areas. The branch expansion of Public Sector Banks and other Commercial Banks on march 31, 1998 shown in Table-4.

Table 3

Branches Open in Unbanked Centres

	States	June 1969		Deceember 1997	
		No. of Branches	%Share in Total	No. of Branches	%Share in Total
1.	Assam	74	0.89	830	1.84
2.	Bihar	273	3.30	3,076	6.85
3.	J & K	35	0.42	253	0.56
4.	Madhya Pradesh	343	4.15	2,845	6.34
5.	Manipur	2	0.02	56	0.12
6.	Meghalaya	7	0.08	127	0.28
7.	Nagaland	2	0.02	62	0.13
8.	Orissa	100	1.21	1,336	2.97
9.	Tripura	5	0.06	91	0.20
10.	Uttar Pradesh	747	9.04	5531	12.32
11.	West Bengal	504	6.10	3,376	7.52
	Total	2,092	27.27	10,334	39.13
	All India Total	6,262	100.00	44,869	44,869

Table 4

Branch Expansion in Rural Areas

As on 31st March 1998

Bank Group	*No. of Offices as on 313.98*	*Rural Branches as on 31.3.98*	*% age of col. (3) to col. (2)*
A. State Bank of india & Associates	13,063	5,507	42
B. Nationalised Bank	31,558	13,917	43.7
C. Regional Rural banks	14,432	12,307	85.3
Total of Public Sector Bank (A+B+C)	59,053	31,727	53.4
D. Other Indian Scheduled Commercial Banks	4,537	1,135	24.1
E. Foreign Banks	190	0	0
All Scheduled Bank	63,780	32,862	51.1
F. Non-scheduled Banks	8	3	33.3
All Commercial Banks	63,788	32,865	51.1

Source : The Economic Survey - 1998-99.

It is evident from Table 5 that the share of banking offices in rural areas in the total number of 8,262 branches at the end of June 1969 was 22.4 per cent has registered a continuous rising trend and has gone up to 56.1 per by the close of March 1994 but slightly declined at the close of March 1998 by 51.4 per cent.

Table 5

Expansion of Banks Branches in Rural Areas

Year	1969	1975	1980	1988	1995	1998
% Share to Total	22.4	36.3	42.1	56.0	56.1	51.1

This indicate that, until the nationalisation of major commercial banks in 1969, the commercial banks did not make any earnest attempt to make an impact on the rural scene.

(5) Branches in Foreign Countries—Recently Indian banks have opened branches in foreign countries. 98 branches, including off-shore branches and mobile agencies of 9 Indian commercial banks (which include 8 public sector banks and 1 Indian private sector bank) were operating in foreign countries as on June 30, 1996. These branches are spread over 26 countries and are located in major international centre. Besides, these branches, Indian commercial banking having 14 representative offices abroad.

These branches specialise in various areas of international banking including financial of foreign trade. They cater to the needs of Indian exporter and to that extent, they form an integral part of the domestic banking system.

(6) Deposits Mobilisation—There has been a spectacular growth of bank deposit, which swelled from Rs. 662 crores as on June 1951 to Rs. 6,56,119 crore by the close of September, 1998. The growth of deposits gathered appreciable momentum during the Third Five Year Plan, when the amount of deposits rose to almost double the figure of deposit mobilised during the Second Plan Period. In fact, there was more than twenty fold increase in bank deposits after nationalisation of banks. During the period of 1980-1997, commercial banks mobilised additional deposit of Rs. 4,88,816 crores.

As a result of increase in per capita income, massive bank branch expansion and rise in interest rates on deposit bank deposits now represent an important proportion of the national income as depicted in Table 6.

Table 6

Deposits of Scheduled Commercial Banks

(In Crores of Rs.)

	June 1951	*June 1956*	*June 1961*	*June 1969*	*June 1980*	*June 1987*	*March 1997*
Total Deposits	662	907	1,634	4,646	14,780	1,07,345	5,03,596
Ratio of Bank Deposits to National Income	6.6	8.0	11.4	15.3	29.3	35.5	50.09

Deposit mobilised by the banks are utilised (i) loans and advances to borrowers, (ii) investments in government securities and other approved securities and (iii) investment in mutual funds, leasing and other related activities.

(7) Increase in Investment—Commercial banks have been investing part of their deposits in government securities, bonds and debenture of government associated bodies in pursuance of liquidity requirements stipulated by the Reserve Bank of India. There has been a significant increase in the investment of bank in government and other approved securities from Rs. 1,04,516 crore in march 1993 to Rs. 1,58,890 crores in march 1997 inspite of substantial reduction in statutory requirements. Investments of funds by the scheduled commercial banks in such securities is now constitutes an important instrument of resource mobilisation for financing to plan programmes..

(a) Composition of Bank Deposits—The pattern of bank deposits during plan period and specially after nationalisation has undergone far-reaching changes. As may be noted from Table -7 that demand deposits (current deposits) accounted for the major portion of the total bank deposits till theend of Second Plan Period. In view of the comparatively larger increase in savings and fixed deposits during the Second Plan and onward, the proportion of time deposits rose from 43 per cent in 1956 to 82 per cent in 1987. Demand deposits lost its ground during all this time and dropped to an all-time low proportion of 16.2 percent in Jan. 1998.

Table 7

Composition of Bank Deposits

(In Percentage)

	June 1951	*June 1956*	*June 1961*	*June 1969*	*June 1987*	*Jan. 1998*
Demand Deposits	63.0	56.9	42.3	45.3	18.0	16.2
Time Deposits	37.0	43.1	57.7	54.7	82.0	83.8
Total	100.0	100.0	100.0	100.0	100.0	100.0

(b) Centre-wise Distribution of Deposits—A large portion of deposits of commercial banks has come from urban and metropolitan centres as may be lanced from Table 7. The table depict that metropolitan and urban centre together contributed over 58 per cent to the bank deposit. While the remaining 42 per cent were from rural and semi-urban areas.

Table 8

Centre-wise Distribution of Deposits of Scheduled Commercial Banks

Centre	*Percentage*
Rural	15.4
Semi-Urban	26.6
Urban	24.5
Metropolitan	33.5
Total	100.0

(8) Bank Credit—The total amount of bank loans and advances rose continuously between 1951 to 1998. The total amount of bank loans and advances aggregated Rs. 585 cores in 1951. During the period from 1951 to 1998, the amount of advances continued uninterruptedly and reached the level of Rs. 3,28,132 crores by the end of September 1998 as depicted in Table 9.

Table 9

Loans and Advances of Scheduled Banks

	June 1951	*June 1956*	*June 1961*	*June 1969*	*June 1979*	*June 1987*	*Jan. 1998*
Period Advance in Crores Rs.	595	770	1306	3,599	18,408	64,213	306,100

(9). Different Interest Rate Scheme—Under this scheme Banks charge nominal rate of interest of 4 per cent from low-income groups which cannot easily negotiate with bank but deserve financial assistance for productive activities. The outstanding advance under the scheme by the public sector banks at the end of March 1995 was Rs. 701.8 crores in 23 lakh borrowal accounts against Rs. 694 crores in 26.1 lakh borrowal accounts as at the end of March 1994.

(10). Lead Bank Scheme—The central idea behind the concept is to assign a particular area for operations to commercial banks depending on their area of operation pace-setters in providing banking facilities. The lead bank of a particular district has been entrusted the responsibility to assess the resources and potential for expansion of branches and diversification of credit facilities in the district allotted to them. The number of districts covered under the lead bank scheme were 504 at the close of June 1995. In these district the main function of lead bank is to establish co-ordination in deployment of credit.

(11). Regional Rural Banks (RRBs)—Regional Rural Bank, first established in the country on october 2, 1975 form an inttegral part of the rural financial architecture in India. It was a noval experiment in the series of rural credit institutions. Though these bank have proved as weak financial institution but in recent years some measures of reforms were introduced to improve their profitability, viability, competitiveness and efficiency besides recapitalisation of weak RRBs.

(12). Lending to Priority Sectors and Weaker Sections—An important feature of recent years is the large assistance extended by banks to the priority sectors and the weaker sections of the society. The assistance is rendered in two forms–liberal credit facilities and lending at concessional rate. The priority sector lending has been made available to agriculture, small-scale industries, road and water transport operators. Amount outstanding under priority sector lending of Public Sector Banks and private sector bank stood at Rs. 99,319 crores and Rs. 11,614 crores respectively till the close of March, 1998.

(13). Deposit Insurance—With a view a view to establish public confidence in Indian Banking, Deposit Insurance Corporation has started functioning in 1962. The corporation re-named as Deposit Insurance and Credit Guarantee Corporation. The limit of insurance cover per depositor for deposits in an insured bank has been fixed at Rs. 1,00,000. As at the end of June 1995, the deposit insurance covered 2064 banks.

(14). Para Banking Activities—The economic reform introduced in February 1994 allowed banks to introduced varieties of para banking activities. These activities mainly include leasing, hire purchase, factoring etc. The Reserve Bank of India advised Banks to select their certain branches to undertake these activities.

(15). Social Banking—Banks in India after nationalisation have taken the responsibility social banking alongwith commercial banking. Under the concept of social banking, banks are coming forward to help weaker section of society. In order to improving living standard of the poor banks are financing more and more to the small and marginal farmers, landers labourers, rural artisans, scheduled caste and scheduled tribes etc. Needless to pointout that it is recent diversion of banking policies which was earlier more concentrate towards big industrialists and upper class of the society.

(16). Improvement in the Standard of Banking Business—As a result of undertaking certain remedial measures by the Govt., unsound banking practice have gone to a great extent from banking operations. The chances of bank failure have now become very rare. Most of the banks are doing banking business according to the recognised banking practices and principles. These reserve are being properly built-up. Unsecured advances are being largely reduced and liquid assets are being considerably built-up.

(17). Varities of Attractive Scheme—Banks in modern era maintaining their social outlook up alongwith commercial outlook have introduced a number of varieties of attractive schemes in recent years. These includes mainly as Regional Loan Scheme, Credit Cards, Travelling Cheques, Investment Advisory Services, Travel Agency Work etc.

(18). Technology Banking—In recent years modernisation of banking operation through introduction of new technology and computerisation of bank accounts has assumed currency importance. in recent years efforts have been made to computerised more and more bank branches and installed Advance Ledger Posting Machine in order to obtain greater efficiency in banking operations.

(19). Opening of Private Sector Banks—The Reserve Bank of India, as an important segment of Banking Sector Reform in India, has recently permitted setting-up of private sector banks in the country. These banks will be governed by the provisions of the Banking Regulation Act 1949 with regards to their authorised, subscribed and paid-up capital. A few examples of bank opened under this category are UTI Bank, IDBI Bank Ltd., ICICI Banking Corporation Ltd., Global Trust Bank Ltd., HDFC Bank, The Times Bank Ltd., Bank of Punjab Ltd. etc.

(20). Development of New Specialised Financial Institutions—Commercial banks lend only short term advances. In order to lend long term loans to industries several specialised financial institutions have been established. Some of the important institutions established under this category are Industrial Development. Bank of India (IDBI), Industrial Finance Corporation (IFC), Industrial Credit and Investment Corporation, The Unit Trusts of India etc.

Indian banking system has made a creditable progress in recent years. But in spite of this impressive advancement there exist several serious defects in our banking structure and operations. An adequate and proper banking system cannot be said to have been yet developed in our country. There is no room of doubt that it will take some more years to attain the standards of adequacy and efficiency met within the other advanced countries.

16

Banking Regulation Act-1949

The Banking Regultion Act, 1949 came into effect from March16, 1949. Originally, the Act was named as Banking Companies Act, 1949 and had within its purview only comapnies transacting the business of banking. The name was subsequently changed to the Banking Regulation Act, 1949, and the co-operative sector was also brought under the ambit of this Act. Under this Act, the Reserve Bank of India has wide power to regulate and control the activities of banking institutions. Some of the important provisions of the Act are as follows:

(1) **Definition of Banking Business**– Under Section 5(b), banking means the accepting for the purpose of lending or investment of deposits of money from the public repayable on demand or otherwise.

In addition to the business of banking as also mentioned above, a banking company may engage itself in any one or more of the form of business. Such types of business referred to in section and example of which are given below:

(i) Carrying on and transacting of every kind of guarantee and indemnity business;

(ii) To act as agent for any other person or persons or any Government or local authority as case may be;

(iii) Undertaking and executing trusts;

(2) *Appointment of Managing Agent–* Section 10 of the Act provides that bank may not appoint any person as Managing agent. A person may not manage the affairs of a bank who is engaged in any other business or he is a director in any company which is not a subsidy of banking company. The person belongs to restricted category may appointed on the Board of Director for a tenure of not more than 3 months which can be extended for 9 month with the prior approval of the Reserve Bank of India. According to amendment made in 1959, if any person found guilty by avoiding the aforesaid law, he may be remove any time by the Reserve Bank of India. According to another amendment of 1963 such persons may be removed by just serving a notice in writing.

(3) *Paid-up Capital and Reserves–* With a view to ensure that no banking company commences or carries on business with a weak and valunerable capital structure , section 11 of the Act lays down the following minimum limits of paid-up capital and reserves to be complied with by a banking company wishes to commence or carry on business in India.

(a) *Indian Banks–* The obligation of keeping paid-up capital and reserve funds, Indian Bank has been fixed according to their area of business . In case of Indian banks, the following provisions have been laid down under the Act :

Types of Banking Company	Aggregate value of paid up capital and reserves Rs.
1.Banking Companies incorporated outside India	
(i) If it has a place of business in Bombay or Calcutta or both.	20,00,000
(ii) If it has places of business elsewhere,	15,00,000
2.Banking companies incorporated in India	
(i) If it has place of business in more than one State and none of them is situated in city of Bombay or Calcutta	5,00,000
(ii) If it has places of business in more than one State and any such place or places of business are in Bombay or Culcutta or both.	10,00,000
(iii) If it has all its places of business in one State none of which is situated in the city of Bombay or Calcutta —for the principal place of business	10,00,000
Plus	
(a) in respect of each of its other places of business situated in the same district plus	10,000
(b) in respect of each place of business situated elsewhere in the State otherwise than in the same district	25,000
Subject to an overall limit of	5,00,000
(iv) If it has one place of business and that also not in Bombay or Calcutta	50,000
(v) If it has all its places of business in one State one or more of which is or are situated in the city of Bombay or Calcutta	5,00,000
Plus	
in respect of each place of business situated outside the city of Bombay or Calcutta, as the case may be	25,000
Subject to an overall limit of	10,00,000

After an amendment in 1961 a banking company commencing business after the coming into force of the Banking companies (Amendment) Act , 1962, shall have a paid-up capital of not less than Rs. 5 lakh irrespective of the number of places of its business.

(b) *Foreign Bank* - In case of a Foreign bank (*i.e.*, banking companies incorporated outside India) , the aggregate value of its paid-up capital reserves shall as follows :

(i) Not less than Rs. 15 lakhs, and

(ii) If it has a place or place of business in the city of Bombay or Calcutta or both Rs. 20 lakh.

The banking company is required to deposit with the Reserve Bank either is cash or in the form of unencumbened approved securities or both an amount equal to the minimum amount specified above.

(4) *Restriction on Payment of Dividend*– According to Section 15 of the Indian Banking (Regulation) Act, no bank is allowed for payment of dividend until and unless all its capitalised expenses[1] have been completely written off. However, the Amendment Act 1959 allowed a banking company to pay dividend on its share without writing off some items.[2]

(5) *Prohibition of Common director*– Section 16 of the Act prevents a banking company to have a director who is a director of:

(i) Any other banking company; or

(ii) Companies which among themselves are entitled to exercise voting rights more than 20 per cent of the total voting rights of all the shareholder of the banking company. According to added Amended Act, 1968 [Sub-Section (3)], the aforesaid prohibition is not applicable in appointment of Director by the Reserve Bank.

(6) *Reserve Fund*– According to Section 17 of the Act, every banking company in corporated in India is required to (i) Create a Reserve Fund and (ii) Transfer to such fund , before any dividend is declared, a sum equal to not less 20 per cent of its net profit each year. The Central Government on the recommendation of the Reserve Bank may exempt any banking company from this requirement provided at the time of relaxing, the amount in the Reserve Fund together with the amount in the share premium account is not less than the paid-up capital of the banking company concerned.

Section 17(2) specified, if a banking company appropriate any sum or sums from the reserve fund or the share premium account, the fact must be communicated to the Reserve Bank of India within 21 day from the date of appropriation explaining the circumstances under which such an appropriation was made. However, in justified case, the Reserve Bank may condone delay if any, in reporting the said appropriation.

(7) *Cash Reserve*– As per the provision of section 18 of the Act, every banking company other than a scheduled bank must maintain in India, a Cash Reserve with itself or in a current account with the Reserve Bank of India or State Bank of India or any other bank notified by the Central Government in this regard, or partly in cash or partly in such account a sum equivalent to at least 3 per cent of the total of its time and demand liabilities in India.

The Banking Company must also submit to the Reserve Bank of India a return showing the amount so held on the Friday of each week of the preceding months before the 15th day of every month with particulars of the time and demand liabilities.

(8) *Restrictions on the Nature of Subsidiary*–

According to Section 19 of the Act, in order to prevent a banking company from carrying on trading activities indirectly by acquiring controlling interest, it is provided that no banking company can form a subsidiary company unless such subsidiary company is formed for one or more of the following purposes :

(i) the undertaking and executing of trusts,

(ii) the undertaking of the administration of estates as executor, trustee or otherwise,

(iii) the Providing of safe deposit vaults,

(iv) the carrying on of business of banking exclusively outside India with the prior permission of the Reserve Bank, and

(v) such other purposes as are incidental to the business of banking.

Except as aforesaid, banking company shall not hold shares in another company, whether as pledge , mortgage , or absolute owner of any amount exceeding 30% of the paid up share capital of that company or 30% of its own paid up share capital and reserve, whichever is less.

(9) *Restriction of Loan and Advances*– According to Section 20 of the Act, the following restrictions have been imposed in granting of loans and advances by banking company:

(a) A banking Company shall not grant any loans and advances on the security of its own shares.

(b) The loan and advances may not be granted to any individual in respect of whom any of its director is a partner or guarantor.

(c) The loan and advance may also not be granted to any company of which any of the director of the banking company is a director, manager, employee or guarantor or in which he hold substantial interest.

The Reserve Bank is empowered to exempt certain types of advances from applicatin of the above section. But while doing so, the Reserve Bank will take into consideration the nature of transaction, expected time and mode of repayment, the interest of depositors and other relevant factors.

Section 20-A restricts the power of the banking company to granting loans and advances. It is only after taking the prior approval of the Reserve Bank may give directions to the banking companies in respect of the following:

(a) the purpose for which advances may not be made;

(b) the margins to be maintained in respect of secured advances;

(c) the maximum amount of advances or other financial accommodation that a banking company can grant to any other company, firm or individual.

(d) the maximum amount up to which guarantee may be given by a banking on behalf of any one company, firm or individual; and

(e) the rate of interest and other terms and conditions upon which advances may be made and guarantees may be given.

(10) *Policy Regarding Loans and Advances*– The Section 21 of the Act empowered the Reserve Bank of India to control the advances by banking companies in the public interest or in the interest of the depositors or if necessitated by the banking policy. The Reserve bank of India in this regard may issue directions to any banking company either generally or particularly to any banking company or group of banking companies in connection with (a) purpose; (b) margins; (c) maximum amount, and (d) rate of interest for such advance.

(11) *Licensing to Banking Companies*– No company can carry on business of banking in India unless it holds a licence issued for this purpose by the Reserve Bank.

Before granting any licence under this section, the Reserve Bank may require to be satisfied by an inspection of the book of the company or otherwise that all or any of the following conditions are fulfilled , namely :-

(a) that the company is or will be in a position to pay its present or future depositors in full as their claims accrue ;

(b) that the affairs of the company are not being, or are not likely to be, conducted in a manner detrimental to the interests of its present or future depositors;

(c) in the case of a company incorporated outside India for the carrying on of banking business by such company in India will be in the public interest and that the Government or law of the country in which it is incorporated does not discriminate in any way against banking companies registered in India. Such a company must also comply with all the provisions of the Banking Regulation Act, 1949, applicable to banking companies incorporated outside India.

A Banking Company having applied for a licence , may carry on its business until in is served with a notice by the Reserve Bank that a licence cannot be granted to it.

Cancellation of the licence — The Reserve Bank may cancel a licence granted to a banking company —

(a) if the company ceases to carry on banking business in India; or

(b) if the company at any time fails to comply with any of the conditions imposed by the Reserve Bank.

(12) *Permission for Opening of New Branches*

Without obtaining prior approval of the Reserve Bank —

(a) no banking company shall open a new place of business in India or change otherwise than within the same city, town or village , the location of an existing place of business situated in India;

(b) no banking company incorporated in India shall open a new place of business outside India or change, otherwise than within the same city, town or village in any country or area outside India, location of an existing place of business situated in that country or area.

The permisssion of the Reserve Bank is not necessary where a banking company opens a temporary place of business for a period not exceeding one month, within a city, town or village or the environs thereof within which company has already a place of business , for the purpose of affording the banking facilities to the public on the occasion of an exhibition, conference of a mela or any other like occasion.

The Reserve Bank of India, before issuing the permission will satisfy itself regarding the following:

(i) Financial condition of banking company

(ii) The general character of its management;

(iii) The adequacy of the capital structure;

(iv) The capital structure and earning prospect of the banking company.

The Reserve Bank of India may grant permission subject to condition as it may think fit. The Reserve Bank of India at any time revoke the permission granted after affording reasonable opportunity to the banking company. Normally such happens when the banking company is not complying with the condition imposed in letter of granting permission.

(13) *Maintenance of Liquid Assets*– Under Section 24 of the Act, every banking company is required to maintain in India in cash gold or unencumbered approved securities, valued

at price not exceeding the current market price, an amount which shall not at the close of business on any day be less than 25 per cent of the total of its time and demand liabilities in India.

This is known as the Statutory Liquidity Ratio (SLR). This amount shall be in addition to the cash reserves maintained by the scheduled bank under section 42 of the Reserve Bank of India Act and by every other bank under section 18 of the Banking Regulation Act.

However, the following amounts may be included in calculating the aforesaid amounts and shall be deemed to be cash maintained in India:

(i) Any balances maintained by a scheduled bank with the Reserve Bank in excess of the balance required to be maintained by it under Section 42 (*i.e.,* cash reserves) of the Reserve Bank of India Act 1934.

(ii) Any cash or balance maintained in India by a banking company other than a scheduled bank in excess of the aggregate of the cash or balance or both required to be maintained under Section 18.

The balance mentioned in above (i) and (ii) will be kept by the concerned banking company with itself or in the current account with the Reserve Bank or the State Bank of India or with any other bank which may be notified in this behalf by the Central Government.

(14) *Maintenance of Assets in India*– According to Section 25 of the Act, the assets of every banking company in India at the close of business[3] shall not be less than seventy-five per cent of its demand and time liabilities. The provision has been incorporated in the Act to refrain the foreing banks from deploying outside India their deposit resources raised in India, thus, to safeguard the interest of the depositors in India.

Every banking shall within one month from the end of every quarter submit tot he Reserve Bank of India.

(15) *Final Accounts*– Certain provisions have been specified in the *Section 29, 30, 31, 32 and 33* with regards to final accounts and their audit.

According to *Section 29* of the Act, at the expiration of each calendar year, every banking company in India shall prepare with reference to that year a balance sheet and profit and loss account as on the last working day of the year in the forms set-out in the Third Schedule or as near there to as circumstances admit.

According to *Section 30,* the balance sheet and profit and loss account prepared in accordance within section 29 shall be audited by the auditor of companies.

According to Section 32, the profit and loss account and balance sheet together with the auditor's report shall be published in the prescribed manner. Three copies of the report shall be furnished as returns to the reserve bank of India within three months from the last day of the period to which they concerned.

According to *Section 33* of the Act, every banking company incorporated outside India is required to display in conspicuous place in its principal office and in every branch office in India a copy of its last audited balance sheet and profit and loss account prepared under Section 29.

(16)*Susmission of Return by Banks* -Sections 24(2) requires every banking company to furnish to Reserve Bank a monthly return of liquid assets and liabilities. Under Section25, every banking company is required to submit to the Reserve Bank a return within (one month from the end of every quarter showing that assets in India are not less than 75% of its demand and time liabilities in India. Section 27(1) requires every banking company to submit a monthly return of its assets and liabilities in India as at the close of business on the last Friday of every month. Section 26 requires every banking company to submit to the Reserve Bank at the end of each calender year a return of all accounts which have not been operated upon for 10 years. The Reserve Bank is authorised under Section 279(2) to call for any information relating to the business of affairs of the company. Section 28 of the Act empowers the Reserve Bank to publish any information obtained by it in such consolidated form as it thinks suitable.

(17) *Reserve Bank's Power of Audit and Inspection*– Under Section 35 of the Act, the Reserve Bank may, either at its own initiative or at the instance of Central Government, cause an inspection to be made by one or more of its officers of any banking company and its books and accounts. The director or officers of the banking company shall be under an obligation to produce to the inspecting team all the documents in his possession relating to the affiars and the account of the company, to find out whether or not the affairs of banking company are conducted in the interest of the depositors. On receipt of the inspection report received from the Reserve Bank, if the Central Government find it that the affairs of the banking company concerned are not being conducted in the best interest of the depositors, the Reserve Bank of India after giving opportunity to the banking company to explain its position. The Reserve Bank may -

(a) Prohibit the banking company from the receivig fresh deposits

(b) Apply to the High Court for winding-up business of the banking company concerned.

(18) *Management of Banking Companies* - The election of the Chairman of the Banking company must be to the satisfaction of the Reserve Bank. Section 35-B requires every banking company to take prior approval of the Reserve Bank

for the a ppointment of a Chairman, a Managing Directoror wholetime director. The Reserve Bank is also empowered under Section 36-AA to remove the top managerial personnel of the banking companies. The Reserve Bank may also appoint a suitable person in place of the person removed from office. Under Sections 36-AB, the Reserve Bank may appoint one or more persons to hold office as additional directors of a banking company.

(19) *Widning up of a Banking Company* - Under Section 37 (now Section 38), the Reserve Bank may make an application to the High Court for the winding up of the company. The Reserve Bank takes such step when it finds that the banking company has not complied with the different conditions laid down under theAct, and more particularly, conditions at which it was granted licence to carry on the banking business.

REFERENCE

1. These expenses include preliminary expenses, organisation expenses, share selling commission, brokerage, amount of losses incurred and other items of expenditure not represented by Tangible Assets.
2. Page 52.
3. Close of business denotes business on the last Friday of every quarter or if that Friday is a public holiday under the Negotiable Act, 1881, at the close of business on the preceding working day.

❑

17

The Reserve Bank of India Act-1949

The Reserve Bank of India is the Central Bank of India. The Reserve Bank of India was enacted on Feb. 16, 1934 to establish a central bank in the country (known as Reserve Bank of India) and to regulate its functioning. The Reserve Bank of India started its operations as a body corporate with effect from April 1,1935. It took over the management of currency from the Central Government and later assumed the role of Government 's banker, controller of credit and lender of the last resort as per provisions of the Reserve Bank of India Act.The Reserve Bank of India Act, 1934 as amended up-to-date has the following chapters:

The scheme of chapters of the RBI Act is as follows :

Chapter I	Preliminary (Section I and 2)
Chapter II	Incorporation, Capital, Management and Business (Section 3 to 19)
Chapter III	Central Banking Functions (Section 29 to 45)
Chapter IIIA	Collection and Furnishing of credit information (Sections 45A to 45Q)

Chapter IIIB	Provisions relating to non-banking institutions receiving deposits and financial institutions (Sections 45 H to 45Q)
Chapter IV	General Provisions (Sections 46 to 58 A)
Chapter V	Penalties (Sections 58 B to 58F)

Offices and Branches of RBI

The bank shall have offices in Bombay, Clacutta, Delhi and Madras. It may establish branches or agencies in any other place in India. It may also establish branches or agencies outside India with the prior permission of the Central Government (Sec. 6).

Management of RBI

The general superintendence and direction of the affairs and business of the bank shall vest in a Central Board of Directors who may exercise and do all acts and things which may be exercised or done by the Bank (Sec. 7)

The Central Board shall consist , of the following directors, namely :

(a) a Governor and not more than four Deputy Governors to be appointed by the Central Government :

(b) four directors to be nominated by the Central Government , one from each of the four local boards as constituted by Section 9;

(c) ten directors to be nominated by the Central Government ; and

(d) one Government official to be nominated by the Central Government.

The Governor and Deputy Governors shall devote their whole time to the affairs of the Reserve Bank (Sec. 8)

A local board shall be constituted for each of the four areas (i) The Western Area, (ii) The Eastern Area, (iii) The Northern Area, (iv) The Southern Area. Each Board shall consist of five members to be appointed by the Central Government. The members of the local board shall elect from amongst themselves one person to be the chairman of the Board (Sec. 9)

Business or Activities of RBI

Under Sec. 17 of the RBI Act, the Bank is authorised to carry on the following kinds of activities.

(1) the accepting of money on depsot without interest from and the collection of money for the Central Government, the State Governments local authorities , banks and other persons;

(2) the purchase, sale and rediscount of bills of exchange and promissory notes, drawn on and payable in India arising out of *bona fide* commercial or trade transactions or for the purpose of financing agricultural operations or marketing of crops, bearing two or more good signatures, one of which shall be that of a scheduled bank or a state co-operative bank or any financial institution, which is predominantly engaged in the acceptance of discountring of bills of exchange and promissory notes and which is approved by the Reserve Bank in this behalf;

(3) the purchase from and sale to scheduled banks of foreign exchange in amounts of not less than the equivalent of one lakh of rupees;

(4) the purchase, sale and rediscount of bills of exchange (including treasury bills)drawn in or on any place in any country outside India which is a member of the International Monetary Fund;

(5) the making to any scheduled bank or state co-operative bank, of loans and advances, against promissory notes of such bank, repayable on demand or on the expiry of fixed periods not exceeding one hundred and eighty days;

(6) the making of loans and advances to local authorities, scheduled banks, State Co-operative Banks, State Financial Corporations, Industrial Finance Corporation of India. Unit Trust of India Deposit Insurance and Credit Guarantee Corporation, Agricultural Refinance Corporation, Industrial Development Bank of India and any other financial institution notified by the Central Government in this behalf;

(7) the making to the Central Government and State governments advances repayable in each case not later than three months from the date of the making of the advance;

(8) the issue of demand drafts, telegraphic transfers and other kinds of remittances made payable at its own offices or agencies, the purchase of telegraphic transfers, and, making the issue and circulation of bank bills;

(9) the purchase and sale of securities of the Central Government or a State Government of any maturity or of such securities of a local authority as may be specified in this behalf by the Central Government on the recommendation of the Central Board;

(10) the purchase and sale of shares in, or the capital of the Agricultural Refinance Corporation , the Deposit Insurance and Credit Guarantee Corporation, the Industrial Development Bank, the State Bank, or any other bank or financial institution notified by the Central Government in this behalf;

(11) the keeping of deposits with the State Bank for such specific purposes as may be approved by the Central Government in this behalf;

(12) the custody of monies, securities and other articles of value and the collection of the proceeds, whether principal , interest or dividends of any such securities;

(13) the sale and realisation of all property, whether movable or immovable, which may in any way come into the possession of the Bank in satisfaction , or part satisfaction, of any its claims;

(14) the acting as agent for the Central Government or any State Government or any local authority for the Industrial Finance Corporation of India established under the Industrial Finance Corporatin Act, 1948 or any other body corporate which is established or constituted by or under any other law or the Government of any such country outside India or any such person or authority as may be approved in this behalf by the Central Government in the transaction of the following kinds of business namely :

- *(a)* the purchase, and sale of gold or silver or foreign exchange;
- *(b)* the purchase , sale, transfer and custody of bills of exchange, securities or shares in any company;
- *(c)* the collection of the proceeds, whether principal, interest or dividents of securities or shares;
- *(d)* the remittance of such proceeds at the risk of the principal , by bills of exchange payable either in India or elsewhere;
- *(e)* the management of public debt;
- *(f)* the issue and management bonds and debentures :

(15) the acting as agent for the Central Government :

(a) in guaranteeing the due performance by any small scale industrial concern approved by the Central Government, of its obligations to any bank or other financial institution in respect of loans and advances made, or other credit facilities provided, to it by such bank or other financial institution and the making as such agent of payment in connection with such guarnatee; and

(b) in administering any scheme for subsidising the rate of insterest of other charges in relation to any loans or advances made, or other credit facilities provided, by banks or other financial institutions for the purpose of financing or facilitating any export from India and the making as such agent of payments on behalf of the Central Government ;

(16) the purchase and sale of gold or silver coins and gold and silver bullion and foreign exchange;

(17) the purchase and sale of securities issued by the Government of any country outside India and expressed to be payable in a foreign currency, being in the case of purchase by the Bank, securities maturing within a period of ten years from the date of purchase;

(18) the opening of an account with or the making of an agency agreement with, and the acting as agent or correspondent of, a bank incorporated in any country outside India or the principal currency authority of any country under the law for the time being in force in that country or any international bank formed by such principal currency authority , and the investing of the funds of the bank in the shares and securities of any such international bank;

(19) participation in any arrangement for the clearing and settlement of any amounts due from, or to, any person or authority on account of the external trade of India with any other country or group of countries or of any remittances to, or from, the country or group of countries, including the advancing, or receiving, of any amount in any currency in connection therewith, and , for that purpose, becoming, with the approval of the Central Government , a member of any international or regional clearing union of central banks , monetary or other authorities or being associated with any such clearing arrangements, or becoming a member of any body or association formed by central banks, monetary or other similar authorities , or being associated with the same in any manner;

(20) the borrowing of money for a period not exceeding one month for the purpose of the business of the Bank and the giving of security for money so borrowed from any person outside India other than a bank which is the principal currency authority of any country under law for the time being in force in that country;

(21) the making and issue of bank notes subject to the provisions of this Act;

(22) the exercise of powers and functions and the performance of duties entrusted to the Bank under this Act or under any other law for the time being in force;

(23) the providing of facilities for training in banking and for the promotion of research, where, in the opinion of the Bank , such provision may facilitate the exercise by the Bank of its powers and functions , or the discharge of its duties;

(24) generally , the doing of all such matters and things as may be incidental to or consequential upon the exercise of its powers or the discharge of its duties under this Act.

RELATIONSHIP BETWEEN RESERVE BANK AND COMMERCIAL BANKS

The statutory basis of the relationship between the Reserve Bank of India and the commercial banks in the country is provided by the Reserve Bank of India Act, 1934 and the Banking Regulation Act, 1949. The former represents the Central Banking Legislation dealing mainly with the functions of the Reserve Bank of India, while the latter provides for statutory regulation of the commercial banks. In this Section, we shall deal with only those provisions of both Acts which are important for understanding the relationship between the Reserve Bank and the commercial banks.

The main provisions of the Reserve Bank of India Act which relate to commercial banks are those embodied in Section 17 which interalia indicates the types of papers eligible for obtaining accommodation there against from the Reserve Bank, Section 18 (Power of Emergency Advances) Section 42 (Cash Reserves of Scheduled Banks), and Chapter III (a) (Collection and Furnishing of Credit Information). In addition to these powers, the Reserve Bank has also got the power of supervision and control over commercial banks and control of credit. A brief discussion of various facets of the relationship between the Reserve Bank and commercial banks are discussed below :

(i) Authority of Supervision and Control Over Banks-The Reserve Bank has been conferred with powers by the Banking Regulation Act to supervise and control the affairs of the banking companies.

(i) *First* of all, no banking company can carry on banking business unless it holds a licence from the Reserve Bank of India. This power has been given by Section 22(1) of the Act. Prior permission of the Reserve Bank is also essential to open any branch office of a bank in the country.

(ii) Section 35 confers powers on the Reserve Bank to carry inspection of any bank , its books of accounts either on its own initiative or on the request of the Central Government.

(iii) Section 36 empowers the Reserve Bank to issue directions to a commercial bank in particular or to the entire banking industry in general. It may caution or prohibit the banks against entering into any particular transaction or class of transactions. The commercial banks are also required to submit a number of periodical returns and statements to the Reserve Bank.

In short Reserve Bank has been given wide power to exercise its supervisory and controlling authority over the commercial banks.

(ii) Control of Credit - Credit control is one of the important functions of the Reserve Bank. In order to perform this function, the Reserve Bank exercises its powers of control over the commercial banks. These powers have been given by the Reserve Bank of India Act, 1934 and the Banking Regulation Act, 1949 by virtue of which the Reserve Bank has been employing both the quantitative and selective techniques of credit control. The Reserve Bank can control credit in the following ways:

(a) by changing the statutory reserve maintained by the scheduled banks with the Reserve Bank under Section 42 of the Reserve Bank of India Act.

(b) by changing the bank rate and its policy of granting accommodation to commercial banks.

(c) by changing the statutory requirement regarding maintenance of liquid assets under Section 24 of the Banking Regulation Act.

(d) by issuing directives.

(e) by exercising moral influence over the banks.

(f) by Credit Authoriasation Scheme.

(iii) Banker 's Bank and Lender of the Last Resort - The Reserve Bank serves as the banker to the commercial banks, cooperative banks and exchange banks in the country. All these banks have their accounts with the Reserve Bank . The scheduled banks can borrow from the Reserve Bank on the basis of eligible securities; they can get the bills of exchange rediscounted. The Reserve Bank also acts as the clearing house of all the banks. It adjusts the credit and debit of the various banks by merely passing the book entries. It provides free remittance facilities to the banks. Thus, the Reserve Bank of India acts as the bankers' bank. it should also be noted that the Reserve Bank is the lender of the last resort as it grants short term loans to the scheduled banks against eligible securities in times of needs.

The powers of the Reserve Bank to grant loans and advances to scheduled banks and commercial banks are contained in Sections 17 and 18 of the Reserve Bank of India Act. According to these sections, the Reserve Bank can adopt the following ways to provide financial accommodation to the commercial banks:

(a) by rediscounting of bills.

(b) by sanctioning loans and advances.

(c) by sanctioning such advances in case of emergency.

REGULATION OF COMMERCIAL BANKS

Since the Reserve Bank of India acts as banker to the banks, it contains some sections which are directly concerned with the commercial banks. Under these sections, the Reserve Bank extends a large number of facilities provided to scheduled banks. The non-compliance of rules and regulations prescribed by the Reserve Bank under these sections can make a bank descheduled from the position of scheduled bank.

Scheduled Banks

As explained above in the Reserve Bank of India Act.Commercial banks are classified into two categories according to Section 42(6). These are (i) scheduled banks and (ii) non-scheduled banks. The need for introduction this classification was felt in order to establish relationship between Commercial Bank and the Reserve Bank. The names of scheduled banks have been included in the Second Schedule to the Reserve Bank of India Act.

Loans and Advances

Section 17 relates to the loans and advances by the Reserve Bank in general, and Section 18 to the emergency advances to various banks. This is so because the Reserve Bank acts as banker to the banks and lender of last resort. Advances can be granted by the Reserve Bank (i) by the purpose, sale and rediscounting of bills of exchange and promissory notes, and (ii) loans granted against specific securities bullion and certain other securities.

(a) Re-discounting of Bills : The following categories of bills are eligible for rediscounting with the Reserve Bank under Section 17)2:

(i) Commercial bills,

(ii) Bills for financing agricultural operations.

(iii) Bills for financing cottage and small industries.

(iv) Bills for holding and trading in Govt. Securities.

(v) Foreign bills.

The details of these bills are given towards the end of this chapter.

(b) Loans and Advances against Specific Securities.

(i) Under Section 17(4) the Reserve Bank grants loans and advances to State Co-operative Banks and scheduled banks against the following kinds of securities .

(ii) Advances against Govt. Securities : A large part of the advances by the Reserve Bank to scheduled banks and State Cooperative Banks is granted against Government securities under section 17 (4) (a0 of the Reserve Bank of India Act, 1934. The accommodation is wholly of a temporary nature as the maximum period for which such advances can be availed of is 90 days.

(iii) Advances against Bullion : Section 17(4) (b) authorises the Reserve Bank to grant advances against the security of gold or silver or documents of title to the same.

(iv) Rediscounting of Bills under Bill Market Scheme. Sec. 17(40 (c) provides for the making of advances against such bills of exchange and promissory notes as are eligible for purchase or rediscount by the bank and which are repayable on demand or on the expiry of a period not exceeding ninety days. Such bills or notes must be genuine trade bills or notes and guaranteed by the Government.

(v) Advances against Document of Title to Goods . Sec. 174(d) authorities the Reserve Bank to grant advances to scheduled banks and State Cooperative banks against their demand promissory notes supported by documents of title to goods.

In order to encourage exports, under Section 17(3) A—inserted in 1962—the Reserve Bank gives accommodation on easier terms to scheduled banks in connection with export finance provided by them. Under Section 3-B of the RBI (Amendment) Act, 1974, the Reserve Bank can give loans and advances to any scheduled bank or State co-operative bank for a period up to 180 days against the promissory notes of such a bank, provided that such a loan is required for *bonafide* commrcial transaction or financing agricultural operation or marketing of crops.

(c) Emergency Advances

Provision for emergency advances to commercial banks and state cooperative banks exists under Sec. 18 of the RBI Act. When in the opinion of the Reserve Bank, a special occasion has arisen making it necessary or expedient that action should be taken for the purpose of regulating credit in the interest of Indian trade, commerce, industry and agriculture, the Bank may, (notwithstanding any limitation contained in section 17) do any of the following.

(i) Purchase , sell or discount any bill of exchange or promissory note though such bill or promissory note is not eligible for purchase or discount by the Bank under that section; or

(ii) Purchase or sale of foreign exchange in amounts of not less than the equivalent of one lakh of rupees; or

(iii) Make loans or advances to -(a) a state co-operative bank; or (b) on the recommendation of a state co-operative bank, to a co-operative society registered within the area in which the state co-operative bank operates; or (c) any other person.

All such loans or bills should be repayable on demand or on the expiry of fixed periods not exceeding ninety days, on such terms and conditions as the Bank may consider to be sufficient.

Maintenance of Statutory Reserves

Under Sec. 42(i) every scheduled bank is required to maintain with the Reserve Bank an average daily balance. The amount of such balance shall not be less than 3% of the total of the demand and time liabilities in India of such bank as shown in the return filed by it with the Reserve Bank in the prescribed from [Sec. 42(2)].

The Reserve Bank has the power to increase the rate of cash reserves to be maintained by the scheduled banks with it by a notification in the Gazette of India. However , the rate shall in no case exceed 15% of the total of the demand and time liabilities.

Additional Cash Reserves. In addition to the above cash reserves, the Reserve Bank may direct every scheduled bank to maintain with it an additional cash reserve, with effect from a particular date as given in the notification . Such reserves shall be calculatd on the excess of the total of the demand and time liabilities as shown in the return on the specified date.

According to Sec. 42(2). , the return filed by the bank shall be signed by two officials and include the following particulars outstanding in the bank's books at the close of business on each Friday :

(a) the amount of its demand and time liabilities and the amount of its borrowing from banks in India, classifying them into demand and time liabilities.

(b) the total amount of legal tender notes and coins held by it in India.

(c) the balance held by it at the Reserve Bank of India.

(d) the balance held by it at other banks in current accounts and the money at call and short notice in India,

(e) the investments (at book value) in Central and State Government securities including treasury bills and treasury deposit receipts,

(f) the amount of advances in India,

(g) the inland bills purchased and discounted in India and foreign bills purchased and discounted.

Collection and Furnishing of Credit Information

Section 45A to 45G empower the Reserve Bank to collect credit information from banking companies and to furnish such information in a consolidated form to any banking company for the same alongwith the necessary fee. The term credit information relates to :

(i) The amounts and nature of loans and advances and other credit facilities granted by a banking company to any borrower or class of borrowers.

(ii) The nature of security taken from any borrower or class of borrowers for credit facilities granted to him or to such class.

(iii) The guarnatee furnished by a banking company for any of its customers or any class of its customers.

(iv) The means antecedents history of financial transactions and credit worthiness of any borrower or class of borrowers, and

(v) Any other information which the bank may consider to be relevant for the more orderly regulation of credit or credit policy..

The tern "banking company" includes for this purpose the scheduled and non-scheduled banks , the State Bank of India and its subsidiary banks, the nationalised banks and any other financial institution notified the Central Government.

Section 45 D enjoins upon the Reserve Bank to furnish to a banking company such credit information as may be specified in the application in connection with any financial arrangements entered into or proposed to be entered into with any person. The Reserve Bank is under statutory obligation to furnish such information in a consolidated form to any banking company applying for the same alongwith the prescribed fees not exceeding Rs. 25. The Reserve Bank shall furnish the credit information its possession, but it shall not disclose the names of the banking companies which supplied such information to the bank. At the same time the banking company shall have to treat such information as confidential and shall not publish or disclose except as specified in the Act.

There is a statutory protection to banks to freely exchange credit information mutually amongst themselves in accordance with the practice and usage customary among bankers or as permitted (or required) under any other law. If any person discloses any credit information, the disclosure of which is prohibited he shall be punishable with imprisonment upto 6 months or with fine upto Rs. 2,000 or with both.

Penalties

Sec . 58 B of the RBI Act contains the following provisions regarding penalieis :

(i) False Statement : Any body knowingly making a false statement in any application, declaration, return or statement, shall be punishable with imprisonment for a term which may extend to to 3 years and shall also be liable to fine.

(ii) Default in Furnishing Information : if any body fails to produce any book, account or other documents or to furnish any statement , information, particulars required to be produced to the Reserve Bank, he is punishable with fine which may extend to Rs. 2,000 in respect of each offence and if the default continues Rs. 100 for every subsequent day.

(iii) Divulging Credit Information : Any information the disclosure of which is prohibited and a person is traced disclosing the same, he shall be punishable with imprisonment for a term which may extend to six months or with fine which may extend to Rs. 1,000 or with both.

Offences by Companies

Where a person committeing a contravention or default referred to in section 58B is a company every person who, at the time the contravention or default was committed was in charge or, and was responsible to the company for the conduct of the business of the company, as well as the company, shall be deemed to be guilty of the contravention of default and shall be liable to be proceeded against and punished accordingly.

However, nothing contained in this sub-section shall render any such person liable to punishment if he proves that the contravention or default was committed without his knowledge or that he had exercised all due diligence to prevent the contravention or default. [Sec. 58(c)].

Notwithstanding anything contained in sub section (10 where an offence under this Act has been committed by a company and it is proved that the same was committed with the consent or connivance of or is attributable to any neglect on the part of any director, manager, secretary, other officer or employee of the company, such director, secretary, other officer or employee shall also be deemed to be guilty of the offence and shall be liable to be proceeded against and punished accordingly. [Sec. 58(c)].

Bills Eligible for Rediscounting

Under Sectin 17 (ii) of the Reserve Bank of India Act, the following securities are eligible for rediscounting :

(i) Commercial Bills : The Reserve Bank rediscounts commercial bills which are written and accepted against bona fide trade transactions. Such a bill must be drawn and payable i n India and mature within a period not less than 90 days and not more than 120 days. Another pre-condition for rediscounting is that the bill must bear good signatures of a minimum of two sureties out of which one should either be a scheduled commercial bank of scheduled state cooperative bank.

(ii) Bills for Financing Agricultural Operation : The Reserve Bank rediscounts those bills which are meant for financing of agricultural operations and the maturity period of which is not more than 5 months from the date of purchase or rediscount. Such a bill should be drawn and payable in India and bear at least two good signatures. One of the party signing the bill should be a scheduled commercial bank or a scheduled state cooperative.

(iii) Bills for Financing Cottage and Small Scale Industries: These bills must be drawn for production and marketing finance to cottage and small scale industries, approved by the Reserve Bank and must mature within 12 months. They should be drawn and payable in India and bear signatures of at least two parties including that of a State Cooperative Bank or State Financial Corporation. It is also essential that such bills should be guaranteed for payment by the concerned State Government.

(iv) Bills for Holding or Trade in Government Securities : Such bills should be payable in India within a maturity period of 90 days and should bear the signature of a scheduled commercial bank before they are actually rediscounted.

(v) Foreign Bills : Foreign bills can be rediscounted by the Reserve Bank if such bills are drawn and accepted against export transactions (export from India). Such bills must be drawn on any member country of the International Monetary Fund.

After the enactment of the Reserve Bank of India (Amendment) Act , 1974, the bills of exchange falling in categories (I), (II) and (III), above , and bearing the signature of any financial institution, which is predominantly engaged in the acceptance or discounting of bills of exchange and promissory notes and is approved by the Reserve Bank in this behalf , are also eligible for the purpose of re-discounting.

❑

18

Clearing House

Everyday, peoples deposit cheques drawn on different banks in their account in one bank or the other. These cheques are of different amounts and every bank may have to pay some money to some and to receive some money from the other banks. In the absence of well developed clearing house, whenever instrument deposited in the account opened with collecting banker, the collecting banker send the instrument through some messenger to paying banker. After receiving payment from the paying banker through the messenger the payment was made available by the collecting banker to the person concerned. Though the aforesaid practice was possible in the early age of development of banking when the number of banks were quite few. But with the passage of time and with the development of banking habits and consequent growth in number of banks, the above mentioned practice proved impracticable. It has become quite difficult for banks to sent the instrument for payment to other banks.

Meaning of Clearing House

The following definitions on Clearing House will make its meaning clear—

"A Clearing House is an institution where differences between the various banks are settled at end of each daily clearing by transfers between their respective account at the Central Bank"[1]

---

1. Spalding, W.F.

"A Clearing House is an institution where cheques drawn on Bank A and deposited in Bank B are offset against cheques drawn on Bank B and deposited on Bank A, and only the net difference remains to be settled in cash. Now these differences could be settled in currency, and in some countries they actually are settled by one bank handing over currency to another. But in most countries the banks settle these 'clearing differences' by drawing a cheque on the Central Bank, the banker's bank."[2]

In simple words, a Clearing House is an institution established by the commercial banks of a certain place to settle their counter claims of money. The device of a Clearing House System has been adopted with a view to economise the use of money required for settling the accounts of the various banks.

With a view to make payment possible in such cases and in order to save time and energy clerks from different banks started meeting on some common place. In beginning this practice was opposed by bank authorities but soon it has been realised that this method of disposal of work can be prove most important. Hence the practice should be adopted in planned way. The credit for developing this practice goes to a bank employee Mr. Irvin.

Under this method banks develop a routine organisational structure for clearing house which either by mutual payment or by adjusting the amount of instrument drawn on each other by making necessary adjustment entries by meeting at some common place.

Bankers' Clearing House

A clearing house is an organisation set up by the banks operating at a particular place, for facilitating settlement of their claims against each other. Such claims are represented by cheques, drafts and other instruments received by the banks

---

2. Crowther : An Outline of Money.

from their customers. Prior to the setting up of clearing houses the clerks of the banks used to go round the banks, handing over cheques and receiving payments, This was a risky process. Also, as the banking habit grew among the people, they started making more and more payment in the form of cheques. Therefore to the risk of carrying cheques from bank was added the difficulty of carrying large bundles of cheques. Development of the clearing house system has solved all these difficulties.

In England, a beginning in this direction was made in 1773 when a clearing house was started in a coffee house where clerks of the banks would meet to exchange cheques and reach a settlement. Today, this function is performed by the London Bankers' Clearing House were cheques are exchanged by the representatives of the banks so that each bank receives the cheques drawn on its branches. To settle differences in amounts, one bank pays another by drawing a cheque on its account at the Bank of England.

In India, the task of clearing was looked after initially by the Imperial Bank of India. With the setting up of the Reserve Bank of India, this task was shifted to the Reserve Bank. Now, the clearing house associations in different cities work under the control of the Reserve Bank of India or its representative, the State Bank of India. Let us see how cheques are cleared in clearing houses in India.

Each bank daily sends a clerk to the clearing house. When clerks of all banks have assembled, they exchange cheques amongst themselves so that each clerk ultimately receives all cheques drawn on his bank. The cheques delivered by a bank constitute its "outward clearing" while those received by it constitute its "inward clearing". After the process of exchanging has been completed, a bank has to pay or receive the net difference between its outward and inward clearings for the day. This settlement of the day's clearing is carried out through the accounts of the members with the Reserve Bank of India or its representative, the State Bank of India. At places where the Reserve Bank has an office, the clearing house at that place is managed by it; at other places the clearing houses are managed by the State Bank of India or its subsidiaries.

The clearing houses are autonomous bodies which frame their own rules and regulations regarding conditions of membership for banks, hours of working, arrangements for return of unpaid cheques, etc. The Reserve Bank provides assistance and guidance to them for framing these regulations.

Operation– Clearing house is normally operated by the Central Bank or representative commercial bank of the Central Bank. Generally branches of Central Bank not found at al the places. At those places where there is no branch of Central Bank, the function of clearing house is entrusted to bank whose branches are operated in all places of the country. But at those places where there are branch office central bank, the function of clearing house is performed by the branch office of the central bank. Those banks engaged in operation of clearing house is called as operative bank. The operative bank conduct the function of clearing house on pre-determined procedure. Normally clearing house is opened at the place where there are at least five branches of any bank are in operation.

The following illustration can be use to explain the operation of a Clearing House. Suppose there are three banks A, B and C and on a particular day these banks receive cheques on one another as follows—

Bank A receives cheques drawn on B and C of the value of Rs. 20,000 and Rs. 10,000 respectively; Bank B receive cheques drawn on A and C of the value of Rs. 10,000 and Rs. 30,000 respectively; and Bank C receives cheques drawn on A and B of the value of Rs. 30,000 and Rs. 20,000 respectively. For an easy understanding the claims of these banks on one another as follows—

	Rs.
Bank A receives cheuqes on B to the valueof	20,000
Bank A receives cheques on C to the value of	10,000
Total claim of A	30,000
Bank B receives cheques on A to the value of	10,000
Bank B receives cheques on C to the value of	30,000
Total calim of B	40,000
Bank C receive cheques on A to the value of	30,000
Bank C receives cheques on B to the value of	20,000
Total claim of C	50,000

The sum total of these cheques drawn on these different banks comes to Rs. 1,20,000. So Rs. 1,20,000 in cash are required if all these payments were to be made in cash. But in the Clearing House these 'clearing differences' would be settled by book entries and balance due from each of the other will be paid by cheques drawn on the Central Bank.

The credit and debit statements of these banks are given below—

Bank A has Rs. 30,000 in credit and Rs. 40,000 in debit

Thus there is debit balance of Rs. 10,000

Bank B has Rs. 50,000 in credit and Rs. 40,000 in debit

Thus there is no balance.

Bank C has Rs. 50,000 in credit and Rs. 40,000 in debit

Thus there is a credit balance of Rs. 10,000.

From the credit and debit statement of these three banks it is clear that the account of these banks would stand settled if Bank A pays Rs. 10,000 to Bank C.

Membership– The facility of clearing house are enjoyed by those banks who are member of it. It is obligatory for the bank intended to become member of the clearing house to maintain a bank account with the operated bank. In this account minimum fixed amount need to be deposited. On each working day at the end of clearing operation deposits and withdraws in this account are entered. In the case when clearing house is operated by representative bank of the Central Bank, the members banks are required to open their account in representative bank and representative bank into the central bank. The representative bank informs to central bank with regards to transactions performed each day on the basis of which entries are made in the account of "CLEARING BANK".

Working—The clearing house function is performed at some specified place where representatives of different banks dispose of their work. The representatives of different banks meet daily in Clearing House Office and settle their dues by the process of book entries. The banks settle these counter claims by drawing cheques on Central Bank. A committee is formed for the purpose. The higher authority of this committee work according to the instruction given by the Management Committee of the clearing house. The higher authority also sign on the statement of daily transactions.

For the function of learning, cheque related to different banks are divided in two parts–first internal clearing and second external clearing. Every representative from different banks in the clearing house during the clearing houses comes with cheques related to internal and external clearing. He classifies all the cheques with him drawn on different banks and determine the amount required to be received from different banks. A three column statement is prepared for the purpose in the first and second column of which amount and in the third name of concerned bank is mentioned.

Every representative from different banks deliver the bundle of cheques brought with him to the representative of the concerned bank and receive bundle of cheques concerned with his bank. At the end of clearing period daily balance of first and second column of representative table is tö be obtained. It shows credit and debt position of per bank per day. The account of a particular bank is debited or credited by co-ordinatory of clearing house. It will be appropriate here to mention that no cash payment is made to the representative bank but just an account entry is made in the book of clearing house and relevant information is furnished to the representative bank concerned.

Cheques received after **expirty** of time clearing hour of a particular day are not included in the clearing schedule. If the paying banker found the cheque correct for payment, the cheque is marked and preference is given to such cheques in clearing of next day.

It is the responsibility of paying banker to inform to the co-ordinator of the clearing house on the same day about the cheques dishonoured received for clearing so that it may be returned to the collecting banker.

Canara Bank

Clearing Memo

Date ....19.........

Sl. No.	Name of the clearing Member	Number of Cheques	Number of Cheques Delivered			Number of Cheques Received		
1.	Allahabad Bank							
2.	Bank of Baroda							
3.	Bank of India							
4.	The Bank of Rajasthan Ltd.							
5.	Bank of Maharashtra							
6.	UCO Bank							
7.	Central Bank of India							
8.	Dena Bank							
9.	Indian Bank							
10.	Indian Overseas Bank							
11.	Oriental Bank of Commerce							
12.	Punjab and Sindh Bank							
13.	Punjab National Bank							
14.	Rajasthan State Cooperative Bank							
15.	State Bank of India							
16.	State Bank of Bikaner and Jaipur							
17.	Syndicate Bank							
18.	Vijay Bank							
19.	Union Bank of India							
	Total Difference							
	Grand Total							

Balance To Received Rs. ....
To Pay Rs. ....

For Canara Bank

Clearing clerk Confirmed by me Clearing Superintendent

Despatched at A.M./P.M. ....

Canara Bank

Clearing House Register

Sl. No.	For Credit of	Cheque On	Amount		Voucher Total	Initial	Remarks	Initial for Remarks
			Rs.	P.				

The banks. are not the member of the clearing house sent the following format—

The Federal Bank Ltd.

Local Collection Schedule

To,

The Manager

____

____

Forwarded herewith under noted cheque etc. for payment by cheuqe/cash through our representative.

L.C. No.	No. of Cheques etc.	Amount		Remarks
		Rs.	P.	

Sd/-

Manager

ADVANTAGES OR IMPORTANCE OF CLEARING HOUSE

The importance of a Clearing House System lies in the fact that it economises the use of money required for settling the counter claims of the various banks. From the above illustration it is clear that an account of Rs. 1,20,000 is cleared only by a payment of Rs. 10,000 only by the Bank A to the Bank C. Even this amount is paid through a cheque drawn on the Central Bank.

The following are the advantages of clearing house arrangement—

1. As stated earlier, initially the clerks of different banks used to carry cheques in bundles and visit each bank personally for settlement of accounts. This system was highly inconvenient as well as risky. Development of clearing houses has saved all this trouble.

2. Since accounts are settled daily in a clearing house, businessmen can receive cash quickly. This helps in speeding up business transactions.

3. The system of mutual settlements reduces the pressure on the cash banlances of the banks. They are able to transact their business on the basis of smaller cash reserves.

(i) No money is required for payment.

(ii) Smooth and quick payment amongst banks.

(iii) The habit of use of cheque and their popularing gaining currency importance.

(iv) As the work of payment of different bank completed at one place, it facilitate savings of time, energy and expenditure.

(v) Avoid risk of carrying cash from one place to another as the process of payment is completed just by entries made in the books.

(vi) Quick receipt of payment by the person concerned.

(vii) It encourages mutual understanding amongst banks.

(viii) It has developed efficiency of bank.

(ix) In the presence of mutual understanding undesirable competition can easily be controlled.

(x) Banks need not required to keep huge amount in cash.

CLEARING HOUSES IN INDIA

The credit for established of clearing house in India goes to the establishment of Imperial Bank in 1920. With the passage of time and with the increase of banking habits. The need for development clearing house was realised and accordingly clearing houses have been established in Bombay, Calcutta and Madras. Before the establishment of the Reserve bank of India in 1935, these clearing house were managed and controlled by the Imperial Bank. But now clearing houses are managed by the Reserve Bank of India. At present functions of clearing house are performed by the Reserve Bank of India and the State Bank of India. At the places where there is office of the Reserve Bank, the function of clearing house is performed by the Reserve Bank, at other places this function is performed by the State Bank of India. All the places in India where there are more than five branches of various banks, clearing houses have been established.

In India, clearing houses are working as an independent unit. All the scheduled commercial bank are provided membership of clearing house. Before providing membership to any bank, a detailed study of economic status the bank interested in getting membership is completed.

As it has been already made clear that for the smooth functioning of clearing house, executive committee is constituted. This committee is represented by members from the State Bank of India and the representatives of member banks.

lakh in respect of commercial banks. In the case of SCBs/RRBs and SCARDBs, the interest rate on refinance is fixed by NABARD.

Functions of NABARD

The National Bank for Agriculture and Rural Development (NABARD) an apex development bank for promotion of agriculture, small scale industries, cottage and village industries, handicrafts and other rural crafts and other allied economic activities in rural areas, has been making considerable efforts in the field of rural credit securing prosperity of rural areas in the country. NABARD as an apex institution of the rural credit structure will perform the following functions :

(i) Serve as an apex refinancing agency for institutions providing investment and production credit for promoting various development activities in the rural areas.

(ii) Take measure towards institution building for improving absorptive capacity to credit delivery system including monitoring, formulation of rehabilitation schemes, restructuring of credit institutions, training of personnel, etc.

(iii) It will provide by way of refinance, credit for the promotion of the rural agriculture, small-scale industries units, cottage and village industries, handicrafts, and other allied economic activities in rural areas.

(iv) It will grant loans and advances to State Government for eriods not exceeding 20 years to enable them to subscribe directly or indirectly to the share capital of co-operative credit societies.

(v) NABARD shall be responsible for the development, policy planning, operational matters, coordination, monitoring, research, training, consultancy, etc., relating to rureal credit.

19

Investment Banking

The team investment banking has come into common use only within recent years. It is now employed to designate a distinct work or branch of banking, which is characterized primarily by the fact that it is concerned with long-term credits.

The old generic term of "banking", on the one hand, has been broadened considerably to permit this inclusion, and, on the other hand, the concept has been more sharply limited and defined through division into the two branches of commercial and investment banking, the one devoted to short-term financing, and the other to the financing of long-term or capital requirements. The development of this distinction has assumed greater importance during the past few years, and has brought with it sharp differences of opinion as to the proper limitations of each, and the suitable relationship between commercial and investment banking.

In its most primitive form, the bank merely receives and safeguards the funds of the individuals. In earlier days, this type of banking was well illustrated by the operations of the gold smith bankers of England, who in the seventeenth century were the chief custodians of the public's money in that country. In the present time, this type of banking is still carried on by safe-deposit companies which are formed by banks to rent space in safe-keeping vaults to individuals and corporations.

A step forward in the evolution of banking occurred when the bankers lent out at interest the funds which they received from the public. They added a vital feature to the banking process-the study and analysis of credit for the purpose of assuring the safety of the loan. The *Lombard bankers* in Italy and the *German bankers* in the Rhine cities carried on lending operations, with both their own money and that of depositors, even in the Middle Ages. The bank thus became an intermediary between the owners of capital who could not themselves use it productively and those who wished to utilize this capital in one form or another.

Scope & Structure of Investment Banking

General usage would hardly sanction any single clear-cut and definite distinction between commercial and investment banking. The factor which is most frequently used in making rough practical distinctions between the two is that of the commercial banking involving short-terms advances to borrowers, while investment banking involves long-term advances which generally are represented by negotiable securities. But, as will be seen below, other factors, which as the purpose of the loan, the character of the institution making it, etc., are also frequently to be considered in making a full distinction between these two concepts as they are customarily employed in current usage.

Although there is no intrinsic reason why this must necessarily be the case, commercial banking institutions operate in the main through the system of deposit and discount, while investment banking is carried on through the purchase of security issues and their subsequent sale, at a profit, to investors. Exceptions may be noted. Commercial paper may be bought and sold like securities; and commercial banks, after making short-term loans, may rediscount such paper with a Federal Reserve Bank. On the other hand, the savings bank, an investment banking institution, receives deposits in much the same way as to commercial banks, but uses the proceeds to buy securities in the capital market and make mortgage loans. Further-more, investment houses have been known to keep short-term securities purchased from issuing governments and corporations until their maturity, instead of selling them to others. Hence, from the point of view of method of operation, only rough and approximate distinctions can be made.

Types of Investment Banking Institutions

There are a number of different types of institutions performing their own particular functions in the capital market. The investment house will first be considered, for, as the security middleman, it is the core of the investment banking system. Taken together, these organizations originate new security issues through purchasing them from governments and corporations that seek to raise funds in the capital market. After the investment house, we shall consider the brokers and the stock exchanges, which furnish a market for these securities after they have been issued.

After these two broad classes of investment banking institutions, consideration will be given to two other major groups of organizations which devote themselves to purchasing investment securities for others.

First, there are the specialized in vesting institutions, such as the savings bank, investment trust, trust company, and mortgage bank.

Secondly, there are institutions which are formed primarily for some other purpose, but which incidentally carry on large-scale security-buying operations because of the vast funds they accumulate in the course of their other activities. The insurance companies, commercial banks, elemosynary institutions and large business corporations all fall within this class.

This institutional framework of the capital market is out-lined in Fig. 1 which seeks to summarize briefly the position of the various types of institutions which have been developed to facilitate the investment of the savings of the public in the securities of governments and corporations that turn to the capital market for funds.[1]

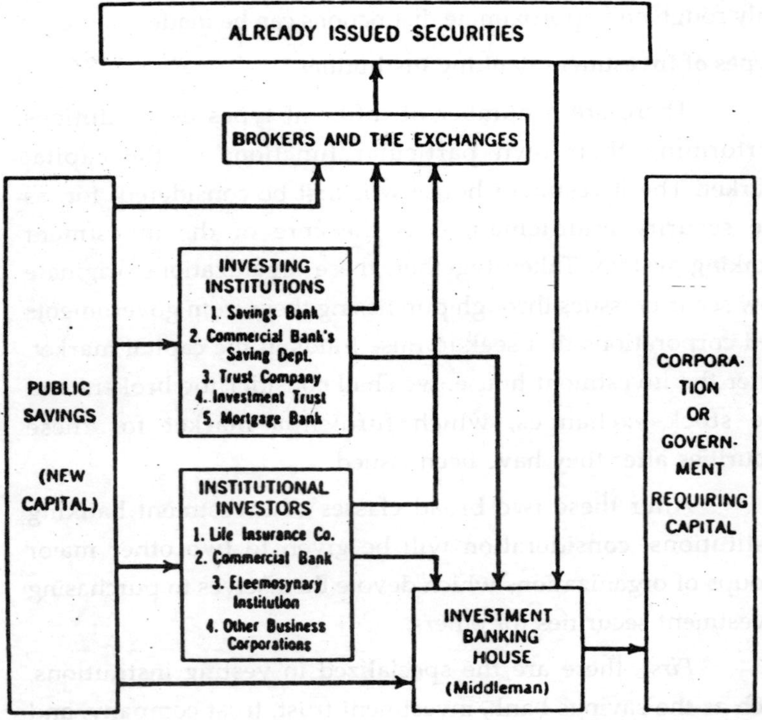

Fig. 1. Structure of Investment Banking

Indian Investment Banking System

India inherited an under-developed economy and the under-developed capital market from the British rulers. In the immediate post independence period things did not improve fast because of the unchanged economic environment. Concentration of money power, managerial skills and entrepreneurship, all rested with the handful of managing agency houses which wanted to move with gains and individual achievements creating acute dearth of long-term capital for industrial ventures. The various reasons for this dearth were noted *viz.*

(a) *lack of new investment:* tax evaded income held in cash and mostly used for speculation in the bullion and commodity market.

(b) impact of socio-economic and political reforms curtailed the investible funds because of drastic cut in privy purses of erstwhile rulers and princes, zamindari abolition curtailed income of zamindars who used to invest their surplus money in investment channels,

(c) lower savings and meager saving capacity dominated the economic scene. The unequal distribution of sources of income and wealth caused continuting existence of vicious circle of poverty in the country, and

(d) post-independence flight of foreign capital and evil effects of the country's partition created wide gaps in resources particularly availability of monetary resources.

A network of planned economic development was taken up by the Government duly supported by legislative and other measures. Growth of capital market was considered as one of the key areas for accelerating the pace of economic development by mobilising savings of the household and business sector into investible channels in industry and trade. Efforts to boost the capital market were supplemented through legislative measures, policy frame-work and institutional support. Drastic amendments were made in the legislative framework regulating the growth of business enterprise *viz.* Companies Act, Capital Issues (Control) Act, Banking Companies Act, etc. The managing agency system was sought to be abolished from the horizon of corporate management vide

Companies Act, 1956, to do away with the stumbling blocks it had created in the development of a free capital market in India.

To improve investment climate in the country and boost capital market activity Industrial Finance Corporation of India (IFCI) was established at national level under the IFC Act, 1948 to provide long and medium term finance to the industrial enterprises and give underwriting coverage to new issues. At State levels, State Financial Corporations (SFCs) were also established onwards 1951 under State Financial Corporation Act, 1950 with a view to provide financial assistance to industry.

These efforts were not enough to accelerate the pace of Industrial development in the country in a planned way as envisaged in the five years plans. In the report of the committee on finance for the Private Sector, Bombay 1954 highlighting the difficulties of the Industrial sector, it was observed that "it has been the experience of industries in general that it is more difficult to raise such capital in India than in more industrialised countries of the West".[2]

R.C. Mehta in his book on Capital Market for Planned Growth of the Country has explored the reasons for the inability of capital market to shelter new issues as "lack of issue houses, investment trusts or investments companies" like those in "UK and USA" which have the role to play for arranging equity finance for the corporate sector industries. Thus, the absence of merchant bankers to attend to the issue house activity was felt at every stage and a search for the lie institutions at Government level was continuously persuade.[3]

The Government anxiety to improve capital market in the country so as to make financial facilities easily and more readily available is reflected in the network of financial and investment institutions established over the years to achieve this objective. These institutions emerged one by one to meet the specific need felt at times as precisely narrated in the following paragraphs.

The Industrial Credit and Investment Corporation of India (ICICI) was set up in 1955, with the support of Indian and Foreign financial institutions and bankers under the Companies Act with a view to facilitate the foreign participation in terms of funds as well as technical knowhow in the development of industry in India. It is a non-Government organisation and aimed to provide developmental finance to industrial concerns inter alia, covering medium and long-term lending, investment in equity by way of direct subscription, underwriting of shares and debentures, etc.

Life Insurance Corporation of India (LIC) was established in 1956 under Life Insurance Corporation Act, 1956 as a result of nationalisation of Life Insurance business in the country which gave boost to investment climate and added improvement in the capital market.

The Refinance Corporation for Industry Ltd. (RCI) was set up in 1958 by Reserve Bank of India (RBI) with a view to enable banks to make medium and long term finance available to industries.

Industrial Development Bank of India (IDBI) was set up in 1964 by RBI under Industrial Development Bank Act, 1963 as an apex financial institution for providing term finance to industry and co-ordinate the activities of other financial institutions to make finance readily available to industries. Activities of RCI were taken over by IDBI.

Unit Trust of India (UTI) was established in 1964 under Unit Trust of India Act, 1963 to mobilise the savings in the corporate securities. The main objective of the UTI remains to encourage savings and investment and participation in the income, profits and gains accruing to the corporation from the acquisition, holding, management and disposal of securities.

More financial and investment institutions emerged with specialised purposes both at national as well as state levels *viz.*, National Industrial Development Corporation (NIDC) in 1965, State Industrial Development Corporation (SIDC), State Industrial and Investment Corporations (SIIC) in 1966 and onwards over the years, Industrial Reconstruction Corporation of India (IRCI) etc. IRCI was, subsequently, converted into Industrial Reconstruction Bank of India (IRBI). The basic objective of these institutions remained to fillip to industrial climate and provide infrastructural and financial backup to industry and support the investment climate in the country.

General Insurance Corporation of India (GIC) is another important investment institution besides the above mentioned institutions that provides full participation in capital market in the country. GIC emerged as a result of nationalisation of General Insurance business in India in 1972 and functions with its four subsidiaries. GIC along with its subsidiaries provides financial assistance to the industrial sector in addition to insurance business by way of under-writing of new issues of companies, granting term loans, subscribing to equity shares as well as debentures.

Nationalisation of commercial banks from time to time have also helped in spreading the network of financial institutions and investment organisations to meet varied demands for capital of the growing industrial sector and the corporate enterprises.

Thus, all the above institutions *viz.* IFCI, IDBI, ICICI, SFCs, IRBI, LIC UTI, GIC, NIDC, SIDCs, SIICs, provide a net work of financial assistance to industry and activise the capital market.

The participation of these institutions in capital market has been growing ever since their respective emergence. For example, during 1950s, only IFCI, ICICI and LIC were in existence and these institutions had participated to the extent possible in the capital market activity.

With a view to boost capital market for long-term and medium-term finance for industrial development, these institutions had taken up underwriting the capital issues of corporate units in mid 1950 along with the stock brokers and dealers. "Of the total amount of Rs. 14.4 core underwritten in 1962 about one half was underwritten by financial institutions *viz.* LIC 22%, bank 18%, ICICI 7% and IFCI 4% whereas the balance 50% was underwritten by brokers and the investment companies. Stock brokers had switched over to act as principal brokers or managing brokers for the public issues of reputed companies. These brokers were able to manage the public issues quite satisfactorily.[4]

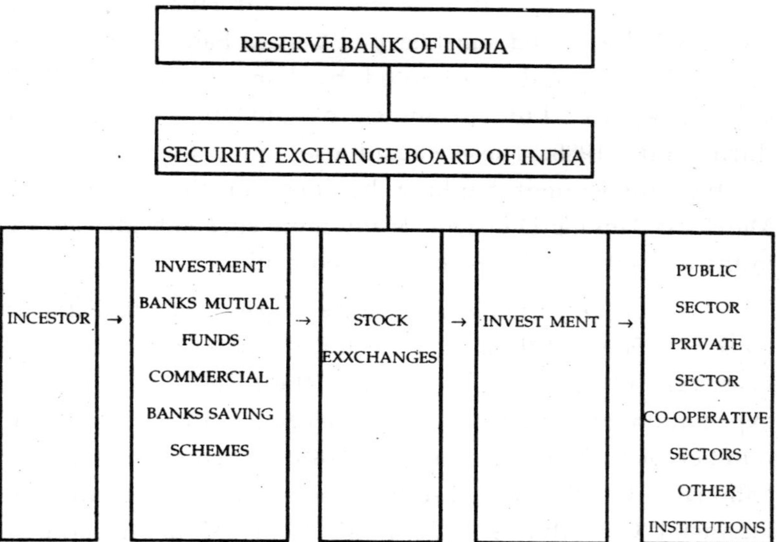

Figure 2. Indian Investment Banking System

Recent Developments

Bank's Subsidiaries— With a view to strengthening the organisational and managerial capabilities, broad-base the resources position, enlarge the scope of operations and activities and to offer more specialised services with professional expertise and skills, the erstwhile Investment Banking Divisions of the nationalised banks have started forming independent subsidiary companies. The first of such subsidiary company was formed by State Bank of India known as SBI Capital Markets Ltd. incorporated on the 2nd July, 1986 and commenced its operations on the 1st August, 1986. The company is wholly owned subsidiary of SBI and took over the investment banking business previously carried on by SBI's investment banking division. The main reason adduced by SBI in the formation of the above subsidiary has been "to meet adequately and effectively the emerging demand for broad based financial services from the corporate sector".[5]

Followed by this came the Canbank Financial Services Ltd., a wholly owned subsidiary of Canara Bank in 1987, BOB Fiscal Services Ltd., promoted by Bank of Baroda, PNB Capital Services Ltd., promoted by Punjab National Bank during mid 1988. These subsidiaries have taken over the existing investment banking business of their respective Merchant Banking Divisions. Many more such subsidiaries are in the offing by the other nationalised banks.

Reorganisation of Private Firms of Investment Bankers— Some of the private sector investment bankers have also taken steps to reorganise their activities in the expectation of facing tough competition with the growing number of investment banking subsidiary companies of the nationalised banks. Amongst these the prominent ones are DSP Financial Consultants Ltd., J. M. financial & Investment Consultancy Ltd., Champaklal Investment & Financial Consultancy Ltd. (CIFCO), the 20th Century Finance

Corporation Ltd., V.B. Desai Financial services Ltd., Credit Capital finance Corporation Ltd. and LKP merchant Finance Ltd.

Stock Broker Underwriters Association— To Professionalise the underwriting activity for promoting new issues market, the 'Stock broker Underwriters Association' (SUA) with its registered office at Bombay and the membership of 95 leading underwriters has also been established during 1984 with broad objectives being, namely:

(1) educate and protect the interest of the general public on various issues related to the capital markets,

(2) provide information about new issues of capital market to members and public,

(3) evolve a code of conduct for under-writers, and

(4) represent grievances to the concerned authorities and companies and render legal and other services to members and public.

The Association envisages effective participation of various stock exchange members by opening chapters at other places. At Calcutta and Bangalore the SUA has already opened the chapters and efforts are being made to establish chapters at other places also.

SUA co-ordinates its activities with the investment bankers and takes steps for promoting the activities of capital market, in particular, by attending to the following tasks:

(i) hold discussions amongst members on issues like appraisal of issues, mailing facilities in new issues, development cases, etc. and make recommendations to appropriate authorities, the problems relating to promotion and development of capital market,

(ii) hold discussion with eminent persons on subjects pertaining to investment banking areas like capital issues, capital markets, etc.,

(iii) hold discussions, relating particularly to the new issues,

(iv) analyse the problems of the investing public and devise solutions thereof. SUA members contemplate to make efforts to professionalise the underwriting activity to strengthen the capital market.

Securities & Exchange Board of India— The Central Government has constituted on April 4, 1988 the Securities and Exchange Board of India (SEBI) as apex Board to promote orderly and healthy growth of the securities market and for investor protection. The Board shall ;

(a) deal with all matters relating to development and regulation of securities market and investor protection and advise Government on these matters,

(b) prepare a comprehensive legislation for the regulation and development of the securities market, and

(c) carry out such functions as may be delegated to the Board/Chairman by the Central Government for the development and regulation of securities market.

Government of India proposes to bring out a comprehensive legislation to rationalise existing legislation relating to securities markets contained in the companies Act, the Capital Issues (Control) Act, and the Securities Contract (Regulation) Act, so as to ensure fairness, efficiency, confidence and flexibility in the capital market. Persons dealing in investment business like merchant bankers, underwriters, sub-brokers and brokers, dealers, investment advisors, portfolio managers, mutual funds, agents for new issues and company deposits, etc. will have to seek authorisation from the Board.

Discount and Finance House of India (DFHI)— DFHI has been incorporated as a company under the Companies Act. 1956 jointly by the Reserve Bank of India, financial institutions and commercial banks with respective shares in its authorised and paid up capital of Rs. 100 crores being RBI Rs. 51 crores, FIs. Rs. 16 crores and Public Sector Banks Rs. 33 crores. DFHI will deal in money market instruments like commercial bills in order to provide liquidity in the money market. Besides, its own share capital, DFHI would have a line of credit from the public sector banks and refinance lines from RBI so as to augment its working funds. The development of short-term money market would definitely lend support to the country's capital market.

Credit Rating Information Services of India Ltd. (CRISIL)— CRISIL has been set up as a joint effort of ICICI and UTI as an independent professional agency to help the investors, investment bankers, underwriters, brokers, banks and financial institutions etc. for taking decisions in making investment in various types of instruments as debt equity and other fixed return securities *viz.* debentures, preference shares etc. The CRISIL has become operational in 1987. CRISIL would rate various types of financial instrument offered to the investing public. CRISIL will establish market standards and thereby improve the efficiency of the capital market and widen the investor base.

Stock-Holding Corporation of India Ltd. (SHC)— SHC set up in 1986 by the All-India Financial Institutions has started its operations in 1987. SHC takes care of safe custody, delivery of shares and collection of sale proceeds of the securities held by the all-India financial institutions to cope with the increase in volume of holding of securities and resultant increase in the transactions and the business in the stock market in recent years. Establishment of SHC is bound to affect in the due course of time, the capital market as the all India financial institutions would operate in the market regularly.[6]

Life Insurance Corporation of India

Life insurance organisations occupy a notable position among the saving institutions of all the countries of the world. This is mainly because they are able to collect small savings from innumerable individuals. The Life insurance, as a form of saving, appeals to the savers due to a number of notable features. It has already been argued that savings being institution-elastic, appropriate savings institutions have positive effect on the volume of personal savings. In this context, life insurance companies are eminently suited in terms of their ability to create the desire among the people to save. The desire to save, an important element in the saving process, is affected by a variety of motives. Life insurance, as a form of personal savings, centres;

(i) to assist the individual in the creation of emergency saving fund to guard his family against any financial misforture

(ii) to build up a potential family estate should the sources of the current earning power of the head of the family be removed by death; and

(iii) to assist in the accumulation and conservation of a fund by the time of retirement from active work.

Secondly, the contractual nature of life insurance also contributes to the mobilisation of savings. The contractual nature of life insurance tends to cause the policy-holders, particularly after the first few years, to continue more firmly in their resolution to save than do most of the other agencies designed for the inculcation of thrift. The significance of this feature should be clear from the fact that to save each year persistently the required amount without the pressure accompanying a contractual obligation and personal solicitation would involve greater self-discipline and systematic management of affairs than they are capable of.

The life insurance, through contractual payment of premium, controls individual impulses and fosters saving habit in them. The principal virtue of life insurance, as promoter of thrift, lies in the peculiar combination of saving and family protection. When once started the desire to continue the protection offered, insurance acts as a powerful spur to continue the saving feature. Moreover, successful thrift is largely the result of force of habit. Regular premium payments tend to strengthen individual's ability to save in a systematic manner. When the necessity of life insurance is once recognised as an important and integral part of the family budget both from the point of protection and saving, household personal expenses are soon adjusted to the necessity of paying the premium. The insured avoids the needless extravagance and makes provision for future contingencies of life.

In brief, besides income, the persuasive efforts of the thrift institutions are important factors in determining the volume and form of savings in an economy. The saving services offered by these institutions are differentiated by the individuals on the basis of their income, motive and future needs. In this connection the distinctive features of life insurance savings are its contractual nature and combination of protection and savings. Due to its ability to create the desire among the people to save and to bind the individual to stick to his decision and pay premium in spite of fluctuation in income, it has a positive influence on the volume and form of personal savings. The statistical data relating to savings passing through the LIC unmistakable support this generalisation. The growing stream of life insurance savings has placed a steadily increasing amount of funds at the LIC's disposal. The insurance saving each year is represented by additions to the Life Fund as shown in table 1[7] Its investment operations and policies can exercise a significant influence on the course of economic development as a very influential factor in the Indian financial system.

Table 1
L.I.C. Growth in Prespective

(Rs. in Crores)

Years	*Total Business*	*Premium Income*	*Inestments*
1957	1,473	88.65	329.75
1960	2,285	97.55	457.43
1966	3,878	112.16	527.45
1969	5,725	151.41	678.81
1974	10,849	260.41	1,528.66
1975	11,852	511.24	2,803.20
1976	13,372	588.25	3,134.64
1977	17,942	653.30	3,552.11
1980	19,243	875.37	5,747.51
1981	21,067	964.88	6,534.32
1982	24,133	1,092.90	7,473.01
1983	26,402	1,217.96	8,498.51
1984	30,426	1,335.10	9,613.74
1985	33,951	1,559.33	10,804.03
1986	40,617	1,782.98	12,264.15
1987	48,151	2,097.21	13,936.00
1988	59,067	2,671.88	16,631.84
1989	74,429	3,432.72	18,702.30
1990	94,823	4,489.39	21,958.80
1991	1,19,179	5,600.80	26,472.76
1992	1,46,667	6,959.92	32,261.73
1993	1,78,120	7,987.24	38,406.62
1994	2,08,619	9,735.32	46,560.63
1995	2,54,572	11,527.80	56,182.44
1996	3,02,425	12,472.80	67,385.16

Source: Annual Report of L.I.C. of India.

Statutory Framework— In every country investment of life insurance fund has been subject to Government control although the nature and dimension of such control have differed from country to country and from time to time according to circumstances. The main objective underlying such control is to safeguard the interest of the policy-holders against embezzlement or misuse of funds by unscrupulous insurers for their own benefits. The Government, therefore, much maintain strict vigilance upon the manner in which these funds are utilised. This is expected to create a sense of confidence in the minds of the people regarding the safety of their funds and thereby encourage the growth of insurance. Another object of control is to direct investment of funds into desirable channels, specially, in Government, and semi-government securities. Such investment regulation by government may be motivated more by its self-interest than the desire to safeguard the interest of the policy-holders.

It was observed that investment in securities by the LIC is only incidental to its main function of providing protection. The basic postulate of its investment policy derived from this feature is the ability of the LIC to discharge its obligation to its policy-holders.[8] The interests of the policy-holders as well as the cannons of sound investment postulate that investment of the LIC should be made so as to yield the highest return consistent with safety of the funds. The investment of LIC's funds are, accordingly, regulated with reference to the types of investment in which funds can be invested. Due to above mentioned reasons Life Insurance business was nationalised in the year 1956. The Life Insurance Corporation of India came into existence on the 1st September, 1956 and since then the Corporation has been enjoying an exclusive monopoly of life insurance business in India. The Corporation has achieved tremendous progress during the last four and half decades of its existence. At the time of nationalisation there were only 32 Divisional Offices and 209 Branch Offices throughout the country which has now been increased to 1000 and 2031 respectively.

Investment Pattern of LIC's Funds— The discussion of the general pattern of investment of the LIC is intended to serve as a background to its capital market activity.

Table 2

Percentage Distribution of L.I.C. Investments in Different Sectors

(Rs. in Crores)

Period	*Public Sector*	*Co-operative Sector*	*Private Sector*
1957	77.3	NIL	22.7
1960	78.7	NIL	21.3
1969	76.8	3.3	19.4
1970	73.6	9.5	16.5
1975	75.4	12.0	12.6
1976	76.3	11.8	11.9
1977	76.6	11.8	11.6
1980	63.4	9.7	13.5
1983	79.0	10.5	10.5
1984	79.3	10.2	10.5
1985	79.6	8.4	10.6
1986	80.3	9.2	10.5
1987	80.1	8.3	11.6
1988	80.3	8.0	11.6
1989	80.9	4.0	11.9
1990	79.8	6.5	13.7
1991	80.2	5.8	14.0
1992	80.4	5.1	14.5
1993	79.8	4.6	15.6
1994	82.1	3.9	14.0
1995	82.8	3.3	13.7
1996	82.2	3.3	14.5

Source: Annual Report of L.I.C. of India.

The LIC is basically an investment institution and not a development institutions. Its primary aim is to spread the message of life insurance and while pursuing this objective, the premia from policy-holders are received which are in the nature of trust funds and are invested and administered in the best interests of the policy-holders as per the guidelines of the government in the matter. The general pattern of investment of life insurance funds in India has undergone marked change particularly in recent years. It may be mentioned in passing that before nationalisation investment in corporate securities accounted for about 16.1 per cent of total assets of the insurers which represented a consistent improvement from 1.8 per cent in 1914 to 6.7 per cent in 1939 and further, to 13.9 per cent in 1949.

The changes in the general pattern of investment of the LIC can be shown in two way. In the first place, the sector-wise investment of the LIC reveals that the share of private sector including the joint sector has steeply declined from 22.6 per cent in 1956-57 to 13.5 per cent in 1998.

Sector -wise Investments

As at end-March 1998, book value of investments/loan outstanding (excluding loans on insurers' policies, house property and land, investments in foreign countries and application money for securities and shares) increased by 20.1% to Rs. 93,600 crore. Private sector accounted for the largest increase (23.4%), followed by public sector (20.2%), co-operative sector (4.6%) and joint sector (2%). Public sector claimed bulk of the investment (84.7%), followed by private sector (12.6%), co-operative sector (2.2%) and joint sector (0.5%)

The second aspect of the General pattern of investment of the LIC relates to its investments in various types of assets. The available data eloquently bear out the statement that the pattern has markedly changed in recent years. The sharp rise in the proportion of resources flowing into housing and other welfare schemes of state governments and into electricity boards are noteworthy. The share of such investments has further increased during the period following the recent amendments in Section 27-A of the Insurance Act which has introduced a new category of socially-oriented sector. With higher proportion of resources going into the welfare schemes of the state governments.

Table -3

Sector-wise Investments

(Rs. crore)

Sector	*Book value of investments and loans outstanding as at end-March.*				
	1991	*1995*	*1996*	*1997*	*1998*
Public	19980	44319	54246	65917	79236
Joint	165	350	380	490	500
Co-operative	1444	1793	1858	1942	2030
Private	3310	7017	7616	9588	11834
Total	**24899**	**53479**	**64099**	**77938**	**93600**

To a small extent the decline in the relative share of the corporate investment in the private sector can be attributed to the nationalisation of major banks, general insurance companies and coal mines. The modification in the relevant provisions governing the investments of its funds in 1975, is, however, the main contributory factor to the much smaller proportion of LIC's resources now being used for financing the expansion of private industry. There is no doubt that they have been mainly responsible for the curtailment of flow of LIC's funds into the capital market.

Capital Market Activity— It is against the background of the proceeding discussion of the general pattern of investment that the subsequent discussion outline the capital market activity of the LIC. The LIC supplies funds to the financing of corporate enterprises in three forms:

(i) subscription to shares and bonds of special industrial financing institutions;

(ii) direct lending to industry; and

(iii) purchase of securities of joint stock companies from the industrial securities market.

Resources Support to Financial Institutions

The LIC finance industry partly indirectly by investing in the shares and bonds of various financial institutions, both state-level as well as all-India. It started subscribing such securities initially to the State Financial Corporations and the Industrial Finance Corporation of India, since its very inception. The LIC provides indirect funds for the financing of private industry through three all-India/National Finance Institutions, namely, the Industrial Finance Corporation of India, the Unit Trust of India and the Industrial Development Bank of India and one state-level institution, that is, the State Financial Corporations.

Besides providing term loans, underwriting/direct subscription, etc., to the corporate sector directly, LIC also assists the industrial sector indirectly by extending resource support to various financial institutions by way of term loans as also subscribing to their shares and bonds. During 1997-98, LIC's resource support to FIs amounted to Rs. 1858 crore as against Rs. 725 crore in 1996-97.

Table -4
Subscription to Bonds of AIFIs

(Rs. Crore)

Institution	*1990-91*	*1994-95*	*1995-96*	*1996-97*	*1997-98*
IDBI	175	-	319	376	589
IFCI*	51	-	29	100	250
ICICI	50	-	49	100	574
IIBI	-	45	55	-	10
Exim Bank	2	3	14	-	-
NHB	-	-	5	-	-
SIDBI	-	25	40	50	-
Others	-	-	5	99	134
Total	**284**	**73**	**512**	**725**	**1858**

Assistance to Corporate Sector

Assistance sanctioned by LIC to the corporate sector in 1997-98 recorded a rise of 20.83% to reach Rs. 3563 crore. Disbursements during the year went up by 25.45% to Rs. 3971.4 crore. Cumulatively up to the end of March 1998, while sanctions aggregated Rs. 21363.4 crore , disbursements amounted to Rs. 19267.9 crore.

Table -5

Assistance Sanctioned Sanctioned And Disbursed to Corporate Sector

(Rs. crore)

Year	*Sanctions*	*Growth rate %*	*Disbursements*	*Growth rate %*
1970-71	17.8		8.1	
1971-72	23.1	29.8	5.3	(-)34.6
1972-73	20.1	(-)13.0	14.-	164.2
1973-74	25.9	28.9	20.0	42.9
1974-75	43.8	69.1	54.1	170.5
1975-76	61.0	39.3	27.5	(-) 49.2
1976-77	57.1	(-)6.4	38.9	41.5
1977-78	52.7	(-)17.7	42.8	10.0
1978-79	65.5	24.3	31.7	(-)25.9
1979-80	80.0	22.1	70.9	123.7
1980-81	70.0	(-) 12.5	65.6	(-)7.5
1981-82	165.5	136.4	135.9	107.2
1982-83	136.5	(-)17.5	86.6	(-)36.3
1983-84	166.8	22.2	140.9	62.7
1984-85	219.9	31.8	161.5	14.6
1985-86	383.6	74.4	261.9	62.2
1986-87	363.8	(-)5.2	389.8	48.8
1987-88	362.7	(-)0.3	342.3	(-)12.2
1988-89	660.2	82.0	442.0	29.1
1989-90	578.2	(-)12.4	455.2	3.0
1990-91	688.1	19.0	427.4	(-)6.1
1991-92	1515.3	120.2	1022.5	139.2
1992-93	1739.8	14.8	1395.4	36.5
1993-94	1664.0	(-)4.4	794.0	(-)43.1
1994-95	1790.0	7.6	1343.3	69.2
1995-96	2341.9	30.8	2529.7	88.3
1996-97	2820.8	20.4	2960.6	17.0
1997-98	3563.1	26.3	3971.4	34.1
Cumulative up to end-March 1998	21363.4		19267.9	

Direct Assistance to Corporate Sector

During 1997-98, direct assistance sanctioned by LIC to industry by way of underwriting/direct subscription to shares/debentures rose by 25.8% to Rs. 3472 crore constituting 97% of total sanctions (Rs. 3,563 crore) as against 46.3% in 1991-92. Sanctions of term loans to corporate sector declined by 29.1% to Rs. 293.7 crore and accounted for a lower share of 16.9% in total sanctions as compared to 27.3% in 1991-92. LIC sanctioned term loans of Rs. 650 crore to other financial institutions during 1992-93 as compared to Rs. 400 crore in the previous year. Assistance disbursed during the year by way of underwriting/direct subscription went up by 14.6% to Rs. 756.8 crore. Disbursements of term loans to corporate sector decreased by 39.5%. Term loans disbursed to other financial institutioins during 1992-93 amounted to Rs. 450 crore as against Rs. 50 crore in 1991-92.

On a cumulative basis, up to the end of March 1998, assistance sanctioned by LIC aggregated Rs. 25363 crore with term loans to corporate sector accounting for 32.4% underwriting/direct subscription 53.8% and term loans to other financial institutions 13.8%. The corresponding shares in disbursements stood at 32.6% , 58.7% and 8.7%. Total assistance outstanding as on March 31, 1993 was Rs. 6585.5 crore.

Table -6

Scheme -wise Assistance Sanctioned to Corporate Sector

(Rs. crore)

Scheme	*1994 -95*	*1995 -96*	*1996 -97*	*1997 -98*	*Cumulative up to end-March 1998*
Loans	443	865	765	677	5335
Underwriting, direct subscriptions, firm allotments and rights issues					
(i) Equity/perference	257	79	156	78	1341
(ii) Debentures/bonds	721	972	1680	2718	10697
Sub-Total	**1421**	**1916**	**2601**	**3472**	**17373**
Short-term Loans/ Unsecured term deposits	119	326	199	90	1346
Term loans to FIs	250	100	20	-	2644
Total	**1790**	**2342**	**2821**	**3563**	**21363**

Industry-wise Assistance to Corporate Sector

Industry-wise, services (manifold), electrical machinery (525%), electricity generation (150.6%), textiles (88.9%) and transport equipment (38.9%) recorded considerable increases in sanctions by LIC for the 1997-98. Industries which claimed a substantial portion of LIC's sanctions during 1997-98 include basic metals (20.6%), services (18.3%), electricity generation (14.7%), refineries & oil exploration (7.8%), textiles (7.2%) and transport equipment (7%).

Table -7

Industry-wise Assistance Sanctioned to Corporate Sector

(Rs. crore)

Industry	*1990-91*	*1994-95*	*1995-96*	*1996-97*	*1997-98*	*Cumulative up to end March 1998*
Chemicals and chemical products	249	32	270	293	-	-
Basic Metals	22	245	254	557	716	3004
Electrical and electronic equipment	78					
Electricity generation	-	130	180	203	509	2021
Textile	60	-	247	133		251
Refineries & oil exploration	-	-	150	343	270	1958
Total (including others)	**688**	**1421**	**1916**	**2601**	**3473**	**17373**

State Wise Assistance to Corporate Sector

During 1997-98, Punjab (420%), Madhya Pradesh (274%), National Capital Territory of Delhi (131.7%), Orissa (116.3%) and Rajasthan (70.9%) recorded substantial increases in sanctions. National Capital Territory of Delhi (34%), Maharashtra (30.2%), Gujarat (11.9%), Madhya Pradesh (5.9%) and West Bengal(4.6) accounted for substantial share of sanctions.

Table -8

State-wise Assistance Sanctioned to Corporate Sector

(Rs. crore)

State	*1990-91*	*1994-95*	*1995-96*	*1996-97*	*1997-98*	*Cumulative up to end March 1998*
Gujarat	190	419	239	545	414	2890
Madhya Pradesh	22	-	56	55	206	648
Maharashtra	254	216	509	722	1049	4541
Tamil Nadu	56	5	116	129	120	949
West Bengal	13	31	250	137	159	1223
National Capital Territory of Delhi	-	395	304	509	1180	3353
Total (Including others)	**688**	**1421**	**1916**	**2601**	**3472**	**17373**

Sector -wise Assistance to Corporate Sector

Sanctions to joint sector increased manifold, while public sector recorded and increase of 75.3% during 1997-98 . Private sector accounted for the maximum share (50.6%) of the sanctions, while public sector (30.4%) and joint sector (19%) claimed the balance .

Table -9

Secter -Wise Assistance Sanctioned to Corporate Sector

(Rs. crore)

Sector	*1990-91*	*1994-95*	*1995-96*	*1996-97*	*1997-98*	*Cumulative up to end March 1998*
Public	157	484	300	602	1056	4400
Joint	27	3	-	4	660	664
Co-operative	9.9	113	-	-	-	254
Private	495	821	1616	1995	1756	12055
Total	**688**	**1421**	**1916**	**2601**	**3472**	**17373**

Purpose -wise Assistance to Corporate Sector

Sanctions by LIC for new projects recorded the maximum increase (106.3%), followed by modernisation (20.6%) and other purposes (mainly for relieving constraints of cash resources (69%). Major portion of the sanctions was for other purpose (55.7%), followed by new projects (26.9%), expansion/diversification (10.2%) and modernisation (7.2%).

Table -10

Purpose-wise Assistance Sanctioned to Corporate Sector

(Rs. crore)

Sector	*1990-91*	*1994-95*	*1995-96*	*1996-97*	*1997-98*
New	220	530	368	453	934
Expansion/Diversification	209	443	599	796	352
Modernisation/ Balancing equipment/Rehabilitation	108	176	328	208	251
Others	152	272	620	1145	1936
Total	**688**	**1421**	**1916**	**2601**	**3472**

LIC's direct financing of industry includes loans to companies in the private corporate sector. It, however, started granting loans to joint stock companies in the private sector only in 1963-64. It is probable that the project cost has increased substantially during recent years and entrepreneurs finding themselvs unable to raise by themselves such large finance are increasingly depending on loans from financial institutions including the LIC. Apart from granting loans to companies; the LIC also finances industrial projects by directly subscribing to their shares and debentures. The purchase and under-writing of industrial securities constitute by far the most important contribution of the LIC to the financing of industry.

The purchases of securities by the LIC are made both in the 'new issue' market and the 'secondary' market. The purchases of 'secondhand" securities do not contribute directly to the financing of new real investment in industry. They do, however, contribute to such financing in indirect ways and have important bearing on the supply of finance for industrial development. The usual course in the development of industrial enterprises seems to be that those who bear the initial burden of financing a new enterprise pass on a large part of its to other after the enterprise has become well-established. The existence of institutions willing to take over from the promoters at some stage later a part of the original securities enables the promoters to initiate a number of new enterprises in successioin. Institutional purchases of industrial securities by the LIC play an important part in this process.

New Issues Market Activity— A part of the LIC's purchases of industrial securities consist of new issues. The purchases of new issues by the LIC largely take the form of underwriting. The participation of LIC in underwriting issues of capital on a fairly massive scale marks an important development in the Indian capital market. Life insurance companies in India, before nationalisation in 1956, did not play any significant role in underwriting of industrial Issues. Most of them were, individually, small companies. The Committee on Finances for the Private Sector (popularly known as Shroff Committee), 1954, had recommended the active participation of insurance companies in underwriting by forming an underwriting consortium together with the commercial banks. No action was, however, taken on this particular recommendation but the amalgamation of all the companies into a single State-owned Corporation/institution brought about nearly the same result. As a result of massive participation the LIC emerged as a dominant factor in the underwriting system in India.

Progress of LIC Business— We shall now analyse the progress of the life insurance corporation of India with regard to total business, premium collected and investments made in different sectors from its establishment year 1956-57 to financial year 1995-96. The table -1 reveals that the total business of the corporation has continuously increasing from 1957 to 1998. The total business was Rs. 1,473 crores in the year of 1956-57 has increased to Rs. 11,852 crores in the year of 1956-57 has increased to Rs.26, crores in the year of 1983 and has touched to Rs. 3,02,425 crores in the financial year 1995-96.

Though there is a continuous increase in the amount of premium year after year but the percentage increase over the previous year is fluctuating. The premium income which was Rs. 88.65 crores in the year of 1956-57 rose to Rs. 511.24 crores in the year of 1975, Rs. 1,217.96 crores in 1983, Rs. 3,432.72 crores in 1989, Rs. 7,987.24 crores in 1993 and has touched the figure of Rs. 12,472.20 crores in the financial year of 1995-96.

The Life Insurance Corporation of India (LIC) was established under the LIC Act in 1956 after taking over life insurance busines from private companies to carry on the business of life insurance and deploy the funds in accordance with the Plan priorities. LIC operates a variety of schemes so as to benefit individuals and groups from both the urban and rural areas.

As dictated by its investment policy, LIC has to invest not less than 75% of the accretions to its Controlled Fund in Central and State Government securities including Government guaranteed marketable securities and i n the socially oriented sectors. Besides investngin Government and other approved securities. LIC provides loans for housing rural electrification, water supply, sewerage and other socially oriented purposes. It also provides direct assistance to the corporate sector in the form of term loans and underwriting/direct subscription to shares and debentures. Besides, it extends resources support to other term lending institutions by way of subscription to their shares and bonds and also by way of term loans.

Investible Funds

As at end-March 1998, the investible funds of LIC at Rs. 1,09,954 crore registered a growth of 20% over the previous year. Life Insurance Business accounted for almost the entire investible funds.

Table-11

Investible Funds

(Rs. crore)

Investible Fund	*As at end-March*				
	1991	*1995*	*1996*	*1997*	*1998*
Life Insurance Business	29480	62505	75887	91279	109672
Capital Redemption (including Annuity Certain) Insurance Business	39	58	63	68	73
Jeevan Suraksha Business	-	-	-	101	209
Total	**29519**	**62563**	**75951**	**91448**	**109954**

There is a significant increase in L.I.C.'s invested funds. It was merely Rs. 329.25 crores in the year of 1956-57 which increased to Rs. 2,803.20 crores in the year of 1975 and again to Rs. 8,498.51 crores in 1983, Rs. 18,702.30 crores in 1989, Rs. 38,406.62 crores in 1993 and Rs. 109954 crores in the financial year 1998 More fund means more investment in nation's build up. The LIC has to invest at least 50 per cent of its available fund in gilt-edged securities, *i.e.* central government and state Governments Securities. More than 60 per cent of the total available fund is invested at present in this field. Next comes the private sector.

The investment in public sector was 77.3 per cent and in private sector it was only 22.7 per cent. This ratio has changed in the year of 1975, and the investment in public sector was 75.4 per cent and 12.6 in private sector. The remaining investment 12.0 per cent was made in the co-operative sector. Further, the investment in public sector was 79.0 per cent, 9.7 per cent in co-operative sector and remaining 12.5 per cent was in private sector in the year of 1983. This ratio has changed to 80.90 per cent in public sector, 7.2 per cent in co-operative sector and 11.9 per cent to private sector in the year of 1989. Again this distribution has changed to 79.8 per cent in public sector, 4.6 per cent in co-operative sector and 15.6 per cent in private sector. The sector wise investment distribution is 82.2 per cent in public sector, 3.3 in co-operative sector and 14.5 per cent in the private sector in the current financial year of 1995-96.

Investment Pattern

Outstanding investment as at end March 1998 by LIC stood at Rs. 98,948 crore, recording a growth of 19.7% over the previous year. Assistance to industry comprising loans to sugar co-operatives, loans to and investments in shares and debentures of companies recorded the maximum increase (24%), followed by investment in Government and other approved securities (21.5%) and infrastructural facilities (13.2%). Major portion of LIC's outstnading investment continued to be in Government and other approved securities (57.7%) followed by assistance to industry (19.4%), infrastructural facilities (9.8%) and loans for housing development (8.6%)

Sector-wise Investments

As at end-March 1998 book value of investment loan outstanding (excluding loans on insurers' policies, house property and land, investments in foreign countries and application money for securities and shares) increased by 20.1% to Rs. 93,600 crore. Private sector accounted for the largest increase (23.4%), followed by public sector (20.2%), co-operative sector (4.6%) and joint sector (2%). Public sector claimed builk of the investment (84.7), followed by private sector (12.6%), co-operative sector (2.2%) and joint sector (0.5%).

Table-12

Sector-wise Investments

(Rs. crore)

Sector	*Book value of investment and loans outstanding as at end-March*		
	1996	*1997*	*1998*
Public	54245.6	65917.4	79235.7
Joint	380.3	490.3	500.0
Co-operative	1857.6	1941.8	2030.3
Private	7616.3	9588.5	11834.3
Total	**64099.8**	**77938.0**	**93600.3**

Unit Trust of India.

The Unit Trust of India was established in February 1964 is both relatively new and relatively intriguing-perhaps because it is the only institution of its kind of India. Even in the

United Kingdom and the United States of America it was there not until ten years after the second world war that unit trusts became instruments par excellence for mobilising savings from the small and medium income groups. The Unit Trust of India, though modelled broadly on the Unit Trust of India, though modelled broadly on the Unit Trust operating in the United Kingdom, has certain distinctive features tailored to suit local conditions. It is a public sector entity, having been established under an Act of Parliament, namely the Unit Trust of India Act 1963, and had completed 47 years of active operations. It might be useful to review the Trust's Progress against the background of savings and investment in the economy.

In consideration of the role of institutions in the mobilisation of savings, it is desirable to bear in mind one or two important features. *First*, it is the household sector which accounts for the major share in the aggregate savings of the economy; the share of other sectors, *viz*, the government and the domestic corporate sectors are relatively small. Therefore, effort must necessarily be directed towards the household sector. Another important consideration is the growing institutionalisation of the savings of the household sector. Thus, increasingly larger volume of individual savings are governed and channelled by institution into various types of investment.

In the case of savers in the relatively small and medium income groups, one of the basic characteristics underlying their motivations is the desire for study and growing income, consistent with the safety of capital invested. It is precisely to meet the investment objectives of these classes of people that the Unit Trust of India was established. The basic objective of the trust is to provide a facility whereby relatively small investors can enjoy the benefit of equity investment with the inherent risk in such investments considerably reduced, if not eliminated. The trust seeks to provide safety of capital through diversification of investments over a large number of securities of various types. It offers liquidity of investment in that it always stands ready to repurchase units from unit holders who may want to sell these back to the Trust. Besides, there is the automatic access to the investment expertise of the Board of Directors and management of the Trust. In addition, as a special incentive to savers, substantial tax concessions operate with regard to the income received from units.

Every year millions of Indians entrust their savings to Unit Trust of India (UTI) in anticipation of a financially secure future. Thus, faith and confidence of investors stem from UTI's commitment, as reflected in its long track record, to ensure its investors safety, liquidity, and an attractive yield on their investments. As a result, within three decades since it was set up in 1964 through an Act of Parliament, UTI has grown into one of the biggest players in the Indian capital market with a portfolio of Rs. 570 billion (US $ 17 billion) under management. An array of 66 saving schemes catering to a broad cross section of investors. An investor base of 48 million unit holding accounts. a distribution network of agents, numbering nearly 96,000, along with 310 District Representatives spread all over the country. A network of 49 UTI branch offices; and 25 franchise offices. A low cost of service, with gross (annual) cost of less than 0.8 per cent of investible funds as against 3 per cent permissible under SEBI regulation.

Over the years, UTI has evolved into a distinctive financial institution, combining elements of fund management with other activities like project financing, underwriting, and setting up associate institutions towards creating a diversified financial conglomerate. All this reflects UTI's dedication to developing and marketing financial products and services to meet the needs of investors. U.T.I. associates are the UTI Bank Ltd. (1994); the first private sector bank to be set up under RBI guidelines. UTI securities exchange Ltd. (1994): the first institutionally sponsored corporate stock-broking firm. UTI Investor Services Ltd. (1993): the first institutionally sponsored Registrar and Transfer agency. UTI Institute of Capital Markets (1989): the first such institute in Asia, excluding Japan and UTI Investment Advisory Services Ltd. (1988): the first Indian Investment Advisor registered with SEC (US).

Variety of Funds

UTI has adapted to changing financial conditions and new investor needs by expanding its product range and services to suit a broad spectrum of investment goals. Between 1990 and 1996 the number of schemes managed by UTI doubled from 30 to 66, while the number of unit holding accounts jumped sevenfold, from 65 lakhs to 480 lakhs. These schemes managed by UTI include savings plan for income and growth. UTI has also introduced schemes backed by a strong social perspective. Examples of such schemes include the Unit-linked Insurance Plan for insurance cover at a minimal cost. Monthly income schemes to meet regular and recurring income needs of retired persons, women, and persons looking for much income. Scheme to manage funds of religious and charitable institutions and trust. These schemes specially designed to meet the rising cost of education and career plans for children. Schemes that pay special attention to girl child and women's needs. Schemes for providing medical insurance for the aged and Pension Plan for senior citizens. Foreign portfolio investment has become a major source of foreign exchange. The Trust has pioneered such investment with the India Fund-the first mutual fund floated abroad to give foreign investors an opportunity to buy Indian shares. The India Fund was launched as a closed-ended fund in 1986. In 1994, it became a multi class open-end fund. It has outperformed the Bombay Stock Indices since inception. In 1988 UTI floated the India Growth Fund. Its share has been generally quoting at a premium at the New York Stock Exchange.

Reaching Investors

To mobilize the savings of the community, particularly from the small and middle income group, UTI has depended upon a marketing force of 96,000 commission-based canvassing agents who are trained to provide service to investors and support investors education. UTI's Chief Representatives (CRs) guide the investors, organize, train and motivate the agents in their respective areas of operation (specified districts). Today, the agents are supervised by 310 Chief Representatives. As a result of its marketing strategy and strong distribution network, UTI has been able to reach out to unit holders from much wider geographical areas and, in particular, to those who remain outside the bounds of the share market. Investors have also responded with great confidence to our recent schemes. Unit Scheme 64 mobilised more than Rs. 2000 crores in 1995-96 and the three schemes in the Children's segment (CGGF, CCCF and RUP) collectively mobilised more than Rs. 300 crores during 1995-96. Our assessment of the future of mutual funds, the market, and the economy in general, leads us to believe that the industry has great potential for the future and the Trust will continue to account for a dominant share f this market during the years to come.

Services to Investors

UTI's investors are now serviced through a country-wide network of 49 UTI branches, 190 collection centres and 6 Registrar and Transfer Agents. To ensure better service, UTI has introduced the concept of franchisee collection centres, which accept applications and distribute certificates to unit holders. UTI is aware of the servicing problems and continuous efforts are made to address investors' concerns and worries. UTI has set up an associate R&T company-UTI-Investor Services Limited (UTISL) and is implementing a technology upgradation program, involving networking of on-line computer systems at UTI's offices.

Equity Market

Fifty percent of UTI's total investible funds has been invested in equity. It has been the largest operator in the Indian equity market with total investments worth over Rs. 28,000 crores at book value (about $ 8 billion). Its various funds collectively hold stocks in more than 1500 Indian companies and account for over 8 percent of the market capitalization of all listed scrips on the Bombay Stock Exchange.

Corporate Credit/Debt

The Trust continues to remain one of the main provider of debt finance to the corporate sector, with investment in debut instruments accounting for 35 percent of the total invisible funds. Credit market operations cover a range of instruments including publicity issued and privately placed debenture, bonds and medium term notes. Credit decisions are backed by strong in-house research on individual sectors and companies.

Table -13
Growth Perspective of U.T.I.

(Rs. in crores)

Year	Sales under all Schemes	Out-standing Unit Capital	Out-standing Unit Holding Accounts (in lakhs)	Investi-ble Funds	Reserves & Pro-visions	Gross Income	Gross Expendit ure	Income Distri-bution
1964-65	19.14	18.73	1.32	24.67	0.07	1.53	0.23	1.29
1965-66	2.15	19.80	1.25	25.94	0.11	1.83	0.22	1.60
1966-67	9.24	27.05	1.70	33.86	0.22	2.52	0.31	2.08
1967-68	15.34	41.16	2.19	48.70	0.38	3.67	0.51	3.03
1968-69	17.16	56.65	2.69	65.40	0.69	4.83	0.58	4.20
1969-70	22.83	77.45	3.35	88.30	1.03	6.29	0.67	5.78
1970-71	18.00	92.25	3.84	101.14	1.77	8.41	0.80	7.64
1971-72	15.11	104.75	4.35	119.26	2.43	9.68	0.81	8.92
1972-73	23.17	124.95	5.08	141.96	3.17	11.80	0.99	10.91
1973-74	30.64	151.92	5.97	172.09	4.25	14.53	1.33	13.19
1974-75	17.24	148.81	6.01	169.95	3.59	13.05	1.82	12.78
1975-76	28.97	166.80	6.37	176.66	3.99	16.02	1077	14.01
1976-77	34.59	193.34	6.81	206.84	4.54	20.34	1.89	17.22
1977-78	73.27	255.39	7.70	279.91	8.48	26.49	2.52	22.81
1978-79	101.53	347.47	9.04	393.70	26.09	39.04	2.65	31.05
1979-80	57.85	390.89	9.86	456.30	37.88	47.55	2.44	38.74
1980-81	52.10	425.35	10.47	513.97	52.03	60.12	3.03	47.98
1981-82	157.37	55.46	12.23	679.24	76.14	78.50	4.14	59.34
1982-83	166.90	706.91	13.66	870.24	98.20	101.69	5.05	86.44
1983-84	330.16	1021.33	14.92	1261.33	150.46	142.64	6.61	126.29
1984-85	756.19	1757.30	17.01	2209.61	299.87	257.05	11.77	214.92
1985-86	891.75	2586.3	20.38	3218.34	445.08	389.97	15.39	316.79
1986-87	1261.06	3726.11	29.79	4563.68	567.18	524.58	22.21	427.86
1987-88	2059.42	5449.58	38.56	6738.81	940.72	840.90	41.36	682.68
1988-89	3855.01	8905.11	48.58	11834.65	2075.10	1687.02	64.03	1246.46
1989-90	5583.59	13391.73	65.12	17650.92	3155.19	2142.84	98.26	1895.15
1990-91	4550.95	16409.33	102.73	21376.48	3695.28	2821.59	119.35	2354.98
1991-92	12182.35	24815.41	235.73	31805.69	5133.29	5035.95	289.64	3011.99
1992-93	6492.00	30649.46	300.32	38976.81	7008.24	5532.76	265.96	3491.64
1993-94	10982.25	39297.95	378.15	51708.88	9873.38	7907.98	318.81	5179.47
1994-95	12852.61	45432.86	497.74	59618.64	11094.52	7994.79	469.07	6233.05
1995-96	4942.00	43257.00	480.00	56841.00	-	-	-	-

Money Market

UTI is also one of the largest investors, among non banking financial institutions, in the money market. About 15 percent of the total investible funds of UTI is accounted for by government paper and call deposits. Consistent with UTI Act, UTI's investment decisions are made giving due considerations to investors' interests. UTI's operations are guided by UTI Act, 1963, UTI General Regulations and SEBI guidelines. The regulations provide prudential exposure norms and limits as directed by the Board of trustees. UTI's investments are subject to these norms and limits. UTI cannot invest more than 5 per cent of a particular schemes corpus in the equity of any one company. All stock investment decisions are backed by research which evaluates long-term growth potential. UTI invests in rated debt instruments. Where rating by external agencies is not available, the instruments are rated by an internal independent credit rating cell. More than 98% of debt portfolio is performing assets.

Research Support

UTI has its own research support for investment and marketing. The areas of research cover macro-economic trends, capital markets, financial sector, industry, corporate performance and mutual funds, as well as an analysis of credit rating to support financing decisions. UTI Investment Advisory Services Ltd. act as an investment advisor to the India Growth Fund, UTI Institute of Capital Markets trains the financial community, help to develop modern and scientific approach towards investment management as also serves as a forum to discuss ideas and issues relevant to the capital market besides publishing research papers relating to capital market. UTI publishes weekly NAVs for all its listed schemes, offers a prospectus for every scheme, publishes half yearly results for all schemes and releases information on largest shareholding for growth schemes and Unit Scheme 1964.

Institution Building

UTI has played a significant role in institution building. It has helped promote/co-promote many institutions that would aid the healthy development of the financial sector, and the economy in general. These institutions include

Infrastructure Leasing & Financial Services (ILFS), Credit Rating and Information Services Ltd. (CRISIL), Stock Holding Corporation of India (SHCIL),Technology Development & Information Company Ltd. (TDICI), and Over-the Counter Exchange of India Limited (OTCEI), National Securities Depository Ltd. (NSDL), North Eastern Development Finance Corporation Ltd. (NEDFCL) etc. UTI's support has even been extended across the border. Trust has provided technical/advisory services for the development of Unit Trusts in countries like Sri Lanka and Egypt.

Operatioin

UTI during 1997-98 added 19 lakh new accounts in its various schemes. It has launched 16 new schemes -10 income-oriented debt schemes and six equity schemes-to mobilise Rs. 6750 crore. Three new offshore funds were launched by the Trust during the year viz. The India Debt Fund, The India PSU Fund and India IT Fund. The Trust has made special arrangment with the National Securities Depository Ltd. (NSDL) to enable dematerialisation of unit certificate under the US 64 scheme. Branch offices of UTI and the offices of the registrars have been connected through VSAT. UTI has extended Electronic Clearing Service (ECS) of cheques to 16 centres. The number of franchise offices in the country has been increased to 43 and an exclusive NRI service branch has been opened at Mumbai.

As per the announcement made in the Union Budget 1998-99, UTI proposes to launch 'India Millennium Scheme' to channlise the savings of NRIs. The money collected under the Scheme would be invested in shares of Indian companies with high potential for growth and in high quality Indian debt. UTI is setting up systems to begin stock lending and use of derivatives and has already been active in dematerialising a large part of its holding in stocks.

Table-14

Assistance Sanctioned And Disbursed

(Rs. crore)

Year	*Sanctions*	*Growth rate %*	*Disbursement*	*Growth rate %*
1971-72	15.0		1.6	
1972-73	9.9	(-) 34.0	5.6	250
1973-74	7.7	(-)22.2	7.7	37.5
1974-75	7.0	(-)9.1	7.6	(-)1.3
1975-76	7.8	11.4	4.9	(-)35.5
1976-77	9.0	15.4	6.1	24.5
1977-78	26.5	194.4	15.8	159.0
1978-79	50.7	91.3	20.1	27.2
1979-80	74.8	47.5	63.9	217.9
1980-81	40.4	(-)46.0	51.0	(-)20.2
1981-82	85.5	111.6	62.7	22.9
1982-83	127.5	49.1	71.7	14.4
1983-84	165.8	30.0	139.3	94.3
1984-85	357.3	115.5	236.2	69.6
1985-86	696.6	95.0	528.9	123.9
1986-87	465.0	(-)33.2	417.6	(-)21.0
1987-88	966.0	107.7	707.2	(-)69.3
1988-89	1878.1	94.4	1054.6	49.1
1989-90	1202.8	(-)36.0	1017.5	(-)3.5
1990-91	2809.6	133.6	2241.0	120.3
1991-92	3814.1	35.8	2906.4	29.7
1992-93	10302.5	170.1	7469.4	157.0
1993-94	8332.6	(-)19.1	6612.4	(-)11.5
1994-95	7522.8	(-)9.7	4791.2	(-)27.5
1995-96	3685.7	(-)51.0	3006.5	(-)37.2
1996-97	3633.1	(-)1.4	3237.3	7.7
1997-98	4585.8	26.2	3499.0	8.1
Cumulative up to end-March 1998	51554.5		39009.6	

Sales and Repurchase of Units

Total sale of units under various schemes during 1997-98 amounted to Rs. 13,479 crore. The US 64 scheme accounted for the largest share in sales (28.6%), followed by Monthly Income Plan - 98 (7.2%), Institutional Investors Special Fund Unit Scheme-98 (IISFUS) (6.8%), Monthly Income Plan -97IV (6.7%), Monthly Income Plan -98 II (6.2%) and Monthly Income Plan -97 III (5.9%). Total repurchase during 1997-98 amounted to Rs. 7950 crore. As at end-June 1998, units outstanding under various schemes stood at Rs. 50,493 crore.

Table -15

Sale, Repurchase and Outstanding of Units

(July-June)

(Rs. crore)

Scheme	*1996-97*		
	Sale	*Repurchase*	*Outstanding*
Unit Scheme 1964	2654	2141	14028
Monthly income scheme (MISG 90 pool)	328	1382	2765
Unit Scheme 1971 (ULIP)	745	248	3171
Mastergain 1992 (CGUS 1992)	15	277	2176
Children's Gift Growth Fund Unit Scheme, 1986 (C.G.G.F.)	431	33	2414
Monthly Income Plan 1996	1209	-	1209
Monthly Income Plan 1997	2647	-	2647
Deferred Income Plan 1991 (DIP 1991)	209	-	209
UGS 200	197	51	467
Master Equity Plan 1997 (MEP 1997)	73	-	73
Institutional Investors Special Fund Unit Scheme (L.I.S.F. U. S. 1997)	675	-	675
India Access Fund	176	-	176
Ohter Schemes	534	2861	17280
Total	**9896**	**6992**	**47292**

Pattern of Investment

As at end-June 1998, total investible funds of UTI stood at Rs. 61,110 crore, registering a growth of 7% over last year. Of this , investments in corporate sector accounted for 88.8% (Rs. 54,268 crore). Equity shares accounted for 52.3% of total investments, followed by debentures (31.5%) and term loans (4.7%). Other investments included deposits and other investments with banks (7.1%) and Government securities (4.1%)

Direct Assistance to Corporate Sector

Assistance sanctioned and disbursed by UTI to the corporate sector more than doubled to Rs. 7546.3 crore and Rs. 5734.6 crore resectively. Sanctions by way of underwriting/direct subscription to shares/bonds/debentures increased by over one and a half times to Rs. 4108 crore and accounted for bulk (54.4%) of UTI's sanctions. Sanctions by way of privately placed debentures/term loans more than doubled to Rs. 2245.6 crore acconting for a share of 29.8% in total sanctions. Assistance sanctioned by way of special deposits increased by 52% to Rs. 1192.7 crore, their share in total sanctions being 15.8% as compared to 21.4% in 1991-92.

Cumulative assistance sanctioned and disbursed by UTI up to end March 1998, amounted to Rs. 51554 crore and Rs. 39009crore respectively. Sanctions by way of underwriting /direc subscription constituted the bulk (52%), followed by privately placed debentures/term loans (30.8%).

Table -16

Component-wise Assistance Sanctioned

(Rs. crore)

Form of Assistance	*1994-95*	*1995-96*	*1996-97*	*1997-98*	*Cumulative up to end March 1998*
Asset Creation					
(a) Rupee Loans	1109	-	-	-	11254
(b) Direct subscriptions					
(i) Equity/ Preference	2616	798	376	226	1399
(ii) Debentures	2469	2274	2925	4233	9432
(c) Special deposits	432	65	-	-	8577
(d) Underwriting					
(i) Equity/preference	44	163	45	5	5418
(ii) Debentures	305	56	-	5	15473
Total	**6976**	**3686**	**3633**	**4585**	**51554**

Industry-wise Assistance

Industries such as textiles (11.5%), basic metals (7.7%), chemicals & chemical products (3.8%), cement 2.9%), fertilisers (2.3%) and services (50%) accounted for bulk of UTI's sanctions. Significant increases in sanctions were recorded by such industries as electricity generation (122.7%), textiles (51.7%), transport equipment (5.6%) and services (96.9%)during 1997-98 .

Table -17
Industry-wise Assistance Sanctioed

(Rs. crore)

Industry	*1990-91*	*1994-95*	*1995-96*	*1996-97*	*1997-98*	*Cumulative up to end March 1998*
Textile	123	360	242	339	515	4167
Chemicals & chemical products	356	217	322	371	168	5256
Fertilisers	-	73	21	152	102	1263
Basic Metals	124	845	211	632	346	5442
Services	21	1056	1052	1136	2236	8094
Total (including others)	**1413**	**6659**	**3291**	**3347**	**4469**	**42969**

State-wise Assistance

Major portion of UTI's assistance during recent years was in respect of units located in more than one state and non-specific areas and as such state-wise shares have been worked out excludeding such assistance. Maharashtra claimed the maximum share in sanctions (35.7%), followed by Gujarat (21.6%), Karnataka (12.1%), Andhra Pradesh (11.4%) and Rajasthan (6.9%). The states which recorded significant increase in sanctions by UTI were Gujarat and West Bengal (manifold) and Maharashtra (more than doubled).

Table -18

State -wise Assistance Sanctioned

(Rs. crore)

States	*1990-91*	*1994-95*	*1995-96*	*1996-97*	*1997-98*	*Cumulative up to end March 1998*
Andhra Pradesh	42	-	-	-	66	671
Gujarat	320	375	120	3	125	3194
Maharashtra	616	826	235	100	206	7788
Karnataka	31	-	100	0	70	926
Rajasthan	-	-	-	-	40	235
West Bengal	-	-	125	0.9	-	-
Total (including others)	**1413**	**6659**	**3291**	**3347**	**4468**	**42969**

Sector-wise Assistance

Sanctions to public sector during 1997-98 increased by 180-8%, while all other sectors recorded declines. Private sector accounted for the largest share (50.8%) of sanctions, followed by public (48.9%) and joint sectors (0.3%).

Table -19

Sector-wise Assistance Sanctioned

(Rs. crore)

Sector	*1990-91*	*1994-95*	*1995-96*	*1996-97*	*1997-98*	*Cumulative up to end March 1998*
Public	406	719	951	777	2182	11070
Joint	71	-	-	30	15	555
Co-operative	10	-	-	-	-	179
Private	927	5941	2340	2539	2271	31165
Total	**1413**	**6659**	**3291**	**3347**	**4468**	**42969**

Purpose -wise Assistance

Sanctions for other purposes comprising mainly working capital loans claimed almost the entire assistance sanctioned (97.8%), followed by new projects (1.7%) , while expansioin/diversification and modernisation/balancing equipment/rehabilitation accounted for the balance. Sanctions for other purposes recorded an increase of 44.5%, followed by new projects (22.3%), while others registered declines.

Table -20

Purpose -wise Assistance Sanctioned

(Rs. crore)

Purpose	*1990-91*	*1994-95*	*1995-96*	*1996-97*	*1997-98*
New	348	3391	851	63	77
Expansion/ Diversification	297	861	576	258	8
Modernisation/Rehabilitation / Balancing equipment	306	113	-	-	11
Others	462	2293	1865	3026	4373
Total	**1313**	**6659**	**3291**	**3347**	**4468**

REFERENCES

1. Wills, H. Parker., *Investment Banking*, Harper & Brothers New York, 1946. PP 5-10.

2. Knifen, William H., *Commercial Banking*, New York, 1953, Vol. I, Chapt. 2.

3 Scott William A., *Investment Vs. Commercial Banking*, IBAA, proceedings, 1913, Vol. I, PP. 76-80.

4. Wills, H. P., & Chapman, J. M., *The Banking Situation*, New York, 1943, Chapt. X.

5. Report of Fiscal Commission of India, 1945-50, P. 200.

6 Industrial Finance Corporation of India, Second Annual Report, 1950.

7. Mehta, R.C., *Capital Market in India for Planned Growth*, Kitabl Ghar, Gwalior, 1965. P. 70.

8 Stock Exchange Division, Ministry of Finance, Govt. of India.

9. Report of Banking Commission, Got. of India, PP. 164-66.

10. R.B.I. Bulletin, Reserve Bank of India, March, 1968 P. 239.

11. Rao, B. S., *Function of L.I.C.* 1976, Chapt. I & II.

12. Singh, P., *Life Insurance Corporation and Indian Capital Market*, 1979, Chapt. V & VIII.

13 Mohsin, M., *Investment of Life Insurance Corporation's funds*, 1966, Chapt. II & VII.

14. Annual Reports, Life Insurance Corporation of India, 1985-96.

15. Annual Reports, Unit Trust of India, 1985-86.

❑